Henry Cowell, Bohemian

Music in American Life

*A list of books in the series appears
at the end of this book.*

Henry Cowell, Bohemian

Michael Hicks

University of Illinois Press

Urbana and Chicago

Library of Congress Cataloging-in-Publication Data
Hicks, Michael, 1956–
Henry Cowell, bohemian / Michael Hicks.
p.   cm. — (Music in American life)
Includes bibliographical references (p.) and index.
ISBN 0-252-02751-5 (cloth : alk. paper)
1. Cowell, Henry, 1897–1965.
2. Composers—United States—Biography.
I. Title. II. Series.
ML410.C859H53   2002
780'.92—dc21   2001007064

Contents

Acknowledgments

I had a great deal of help with this book, most of it from Steven Johnson. Although I eventually wrote this book myself, Steven and I had originally envisioned it as a collaboration, sharing research, outlining and discussing the book's potential contents over a period of almost a decade. The collaboration dissipated as other topics drew us away from this. But after speaking at the Cowell centennial conference in 1997, I realized that all the piecemeal work I had done in previous years—spading through archives, packing file drawers full of photocopies, jotting sheaves of notes, and writing conference papers and journal articles—had left me with a larger view of Cowell's bohemianism and something to say about it.

Along the way I have been encouraged by a handful of other scholars and kindred spirits. David Nicholls was unfailingly gracious with his attention, knowledge, and counsel over the years. H. Wiley Hitchcock and Wayne Shirley helped me get documents and permissions related to Cowell's music. Countless other scholars and "Cowell people," many cited in footnotes, led me via mail and telephone calls to sources I would not have known otherwise or, better still, shared their own reminiscences from years of Cowell research—I think most readily of Joscelyn Godwin and William Lichtenwanger. Others read (or heard me read) and commented on portions of what became this book: Charles Hamm, for example, and John Cage. Still others, although they may not know it, gave priceless encouragement at critical moments, men and women such as Richard Taruskin and Vivian Perlis.

George Boziwick, Peter Hirsch, and others connected with the Henry Cowell Collection at the New York Public Library were supremely gracious and helpful, both via e-mail and in person. Many other university librarians also eagerly helped, most notably those of Stanford, Yale, Juilliard, Johns Hopkins, the Institute for Studies in American Music (at Brooklyn College of the City University of New York), the University of Wisconsin at Madison, and the University of California at Berkeley. Local historical societies also gave avid assistance, especially the Menlo Park Historical Society, the Lehigh County Historical Society, and the Carmel Historical Society. Especially warm and valuable was the help given by the archivists at the Temple of the People, Halcyon, California. And the Palo Alto Public Library proved a goldmine of information in its old newspaper microfilms and clippings files. Several newspaper corporations opened up their archives—the Palo Alto Times, the San Francisco Chronicle, the San Francisco Examiner, and the White Plains Gazette. Many government offices helped as well: the FBI, the Library of Congress (and Copyright Office), the National Archives, the National Personnel Records Center, the California State Archives, the California State Board of Pardons, and several other California state and local offices, most conspicuously the San Mateo County Clerk-Recorder.

Many thanks go to the Cowell Estate (as supervised by Richard Teitelbaum and James Kendrick) for kindly granting permission to use quotations, musical examples, and photographs. Thanks also go to the many living descendants of Cowell's friends (Jaime de Angulo, Russell Varian, et al.), who granted permission for me to cite the correspondence of their progenitors.

Obviously I would have been sunk without the aid of a first-rate library such as the Harold B. Lee Library at Brigham Young University, with its excellent interlibrary loan office to fill in gaps. Likewise, I counted heavily on the encouraging words of colleagues in the theory, composition, and history areas of the BYU School of Music, not to mention the generous funding of the College of Fine Arts and Communications.

I have lost track of many other individuals who helped during what proved to be a fourteen-year period—like the dozen or so Davidsons in the Des Moines area who used the self-addressed stamped envelopes I sent them to say they weren't related to Cowell's half-brother, Clarence. I have not lost track of other behind-the-scenes friends, like the steel mill CEO who used his frequent flier credit to get me a great hotel room in Washington so I could read Percy Grainger letters in the Library of Congress. To anyone who helped in any way, thank you for the little details that make or break a work like this.

Two final words of thanks. The first is to my mother, Marilyn Thompson, the semi-bohemian who raised me in Cowell country (near Menlo Park) and who was the first patron of this book, generous with time, advice, lodging, food, and more, all the way through. The second goes to my wife, Pamela, daughters, Rachel and Julia, and sons, Caleb and John, for always liking (or saying they like) their husband and dad to be a writer.

Henry Cowell, Bohemian

Introduction

In 1955 Henry Cowell and his wife, Sidney, published the first book-length biography of the American composer Charles Ives. In it they laid the foundation for what has become the enduring mythology of Ives's life and works. Only somewhat educated in music, the mythology goes, Ives trampled his teachers' instruction and reinvented the art of composition according to his own bent for speculation and experimentation—out-thinking those who were better educated by intuiting the genuinely fresh ideas that would prove most potent in the modern age. Possessed of "a rugged masculinity and all the heroic pioneer virtues," the Cowells wrote, Ives "continued to plow virgin soil and to open up one new area after another to the imagination." He had, in fact, "prophetically" augured "a whole new world of music."[1]

In depicting Ives as an aesthetic frontiersman, they showed what it meant to be a truly "American" composer, playing into the cherished self-image of the "New World," a world that saw itself as free, independent, revolutionary, defiant amidst convention, transcendent amidst adversity. Ives was the re-sourceful individualist, the self-reliant hero, and that made him emblematic of their whole culture. By drawing Ives in this way, the Cowells had also drawn the blueprint for how they wanted Henry Cowell himself to be remembered.

Music historians tend to depict Cowell in the same terms as Ives—a pioneer, a rebel, a genius. Cowell is remembered as the creator of "tone clusters," playing with fists and forearms on the piano keys; the originator of playing inside the piano, directly on the strings; the codifier and evangelist of various radical musical techniques, and the coiner of many terms that have become standard in music theory: not only "tone clusters," but "polychords," "polymeter," "polyrhythm," and so forth. He proposed new compositional technologies that others picked up (writing odd rhythmic ratios directly onto player piano rolls, for example, a method whose principal exponent would be Conlon Nancarrow).[2] He founded and led international organizations devoted to performing, publishing, and recording new music. And he is regarded as a fountainhead of musical multiculturalism. Small wonder that scholars dote on him. Charles Hamm, for example, calls Cowell "the 'godfather' of the avant-garde"; Eric Salzman dubs Cowell "one of the most prolific innovators of the [twentieth] century."[3]

In all of these respects, Cowell deserves his reputation as an innovator, and indeed as the initiator of the extraordinary regard in which modern musical innovation is now held. Cowell, perhaps more than any other man in the twentieth century, helped shift the criteria for a composer's worth from the elegance of his achievements to the novelty of his techniques. He left to his students the task of developing the ideas and techniques that he proposed (which they have done in astonishing ways). Books, articles, symposia, and lectures all rightly celebrate his influence on the generation that included Cage and Harrison, not to mention younger generations that are still being wooed by Cowell's *New Musical Resources* and pieces like *The Tides of Manaunaun* or *The Banshee.*

What has been missing from most of the celebrations is a sense of how Cowell himself was influenced. Clearly, he was not only an oracle of ideas but also a disciple of ideas. One would not recognize that in much of the Cowell literature. Few scholars, for example, have even alluded to the effect of Cowell's parents on his musical aesthetics. Scholars of Charles Ives—including Cowell—emphasize Ives's dependence on the ideas of his father, George. And Ives himself *wanted* his ideas to be seen as an extension of his father's. Henry Cowell, on the other hand, and those who have written about him have always seemed averse to crediting his parents for his artistic outlook or, in any case, seemed content to circumvent their influence by adopting surrogate "parents"—including Ives, of whom Cowell once remarked, "I regard Ives the same as a father."[4]

Cowell's reluctance to dwell on the ideological influence of his parents is symptomatic of his frequent failure to acknowledge to any degree how others shaped his techniques and opinions. That failure probably stems from a deep-seated need to be deemed a genuine *American* artist, with all that that implied. Like many artists of the twentieth century, he acted on the well-understood (but seldom overtly expressed) premise that artists must compete for historical priority in order to stake their claims on the landscape of art's future. Thus, he did what some of his musical forebears (such as Stravinsky) or descendants (such as Cage) did: magnify one's innovations, isolate oneself from progenitors, and tinge one's self-portrait with uniqueness.

Behind such behavior is the truth that Cowell was always utterly dependent on artistic communities, either ones he inherited (like Carmel) or ones he constructed (like the New Music Society). At the heart of almost all of these communities was a vague but palpable reality: California bohemianism, an eclectic and often elitist subculture that tried to mix leftist politics, mysticism, scientific experimentation, and multiculturalism. One cannot begin to understand Henry Cowell's achievements unless one is prepared to savor this cultural stew.

One trauma in Cowell's life has blocked scholars from doing so. That trauma was his exile from California following his notorious arrest and incarceration in 1936. For years historians tiptoed around (or threw a blanket over) the facts of Cowell's imprisonment—understandably, given the troublesome behavior that placed him in San Quentin. Nevertheless, Cowell's encounter with the American judicial system in the 1930s showed just how remarkably resilient a human being he could be.

His incarceration not only destroyed his reputation, it forever changed how he wanted his earlier life to be regarded. Before going to San Quentin (for a homosexual liaison with a seventeen-year-old), Cowell reveled in the eccentricities of his bohemian upbringing. Paroled after four years, he fled California, tempered his artistic radicalism, and disowned his bohemian past. He claimed to have been "rehabilitated," but he was in equal measure artistically damaged. His friend Peter Yates discerned the damage when Cowell visited him a year after being paroled. Yates remarked that "the old forwardness he must have had to drive himself and his purposes before unfriendly and amused audiences has been replaced by a fearfulness and suspicion. He is unlikely ever to lose the prison mark, the expression of something said or felt behind his back, the uncertain secrecy."[5]

That "uncertain secrecy" is where Cowell's biography has run aground. A friend of Cowell's summed up Henry's attitude: "it was obvious to all of [us] that the less said and even thought [about the prison years] the better."[6] That attitude not only warded the more polite scholars away from inquiries into those years, it also seemed to block their passage into Cowell's life before prison. After considering the awkwardness of the prison years in Cowell's biography, some would avoid the fray altogether and choose another topic.

Even so, some scholars could not resist at least the attempt. Wanting to write her son's life story, Cowell's mother herself produced a document about him as early as 1915 entitled "Material for Biography." Cowell's widow also planned a biography but later delegated it to others, first Hugo Weisgall, who later backed out, and then Joel Sachs, who has, as of this writing, produced nothing publishable after more than eleven years at the job. More than thirty years ago Joscelyn Godwin completed his dissertation, "The Music of Henry Cowell" (1969), still far and away the best one-volume introduction to Cowell's compositional opus.[7] Sidney Cowell, just four years after her husband's death, and alarmed by Godwin's treatment of him, suppressed the dissertation. "Godwin was a mistake," she would later say.[8] In 1981 Rita Mead, with Sidney's help, published what will remain the definitive history of Cowell's New Music Society. Regrettably, Mead died before she could delve further into Cowell's life and work. Since then, several catalogs, articles, and books have meticulously investigated Cowell's music, writings, and the assessments of his contemporaries, notably, William Lichtenwanger's *The Music of Henry Cowell*, Bruce Saylor's *The Writings of Henry Cowell*, and Martha Manion's *Writings about Henry Cowell*.[9] But these later, post-Godwin writers neither attempted or provided a holistic vision of Cowell's life and music. Nor did they always challenge Sidney by looking for second opinions.

Into so occasionally turbulent a sea of scholarship I launch this book, essentially a study of Cowell's life and work through the mid-1920s, with a look at his later years through the lens of the earlier. The earlier years are the most important of Cowell's career, the formative years, the years that produced virtually all of the novelties for which he became known, the years in which he doggedly chased the artistic vision that his California upbringing had given him, and the years in which he built a dynasty of "ultra-modern" music that has shaped the spirit of many younger composers around the world.

These are the "bohemian" years simply because in Cowell's youth all of the pursuits in which he engaged were understood to be a part of California bohemianism. It was the poet laureate of San Francisco and one of the founders of the Carmel community of arts, George Sterling, who defined what was understood by the term "bohemianism" amid the Bay Area culture that shaped Henry Cowell: "There are two elements . . . essential to Bohemianism. The first is devotion or addiction to one or more of the Seven Arts; the other is poverty. Other factors suggest themselves: for instance, I like to think of my Bohemians as young, as radical in their outlook on art and life, as unconventional, and, though this is debatable, as dwellers in a city large enough to have the somewhat cruel atmosphere of all great cities."[10] The Henry Cowell I wanted to explore in this book is not the venerable, professorial, textbook-celebrated patron saint of modern music, but the young, Bay Area–based, lower-class, obsessively wayward composer, radical not only in his music but in his appearance, politics, and private life.

Cowell's earlier, more bohemian years are not only the most interesting, they comprise the only part of his life for which one could reasonably attempt to do the kind of work that I have tried to do here. Throughout almost all of the writing of this book none of Cowell's personal papers, housed for decades in the New York Public Library, were open to me. Those papers are absolutely indispensable to a historiography of his later, post-prison period, especially because Cowell was a compulsive saver of paper (to the point of saving for decades heavy bundles of bus ticket stubs from his early European tours).[11] But those papers were less needful for his younger period. I have long believed (and tried to demonstrate) that the records Cowell did not keep of himself have much to say about him in his formative years.

Without access to his papers, I was both cursed and blessed in having to live by my scholarly wits. Cursed in that I had to work harder to determine the occasional fact, blessed in that I had to follow paths of evidence that authorized scholars have sometimes neglected: obscure public records, useful secondary sources, and the views of Cowell held by others, not just those he held (or presented) of himself. I was disadvantaged by being barred from Cowell's own materials, yet advantaged by not having to rely so heavily on his own self-assessment. Writing against the closed door of Cowell's personal archive, I tried to stay true to the spirit of my subject, a spirit that savored the denial of barriers. As Slonimsky remarked in 1933, "Henry Cowell would not be himself if he did not follow the path of most resistance."[12]

Besides, I had no desire to write Cowell's posthumous autobiography. Writers about Cowell, I believe, have often been tempted merely to paraphrase his reminiscences (or Sidney's), even though—as we have seen in the cases of Stravinsky, Ives, and Cage—that sort of deference can mislead us, blurring our vision of the music's connection to other musics.[13] Like those composers, Cowell has often been allowed to be the undisputed oracle of his role in history. And like them, he ultimately deserves a critical investigation of the best published and unpublished sources concerning his life and work.[14] I probably would not have done such an investigation had I begun this work awash in the thousands of (often self-serving) documents and reminiscences carefully sifted and preserved by Sidney Cowell for the use of her select biographer. For better or worse, I tried to avoid the "widow syndrome," a situation in which, as Robert Gittings puts it, "biographers often had their eye on the great man's widow—or even worse, were the widow."[15] Instead, I tried to bring as many lenses onto each event or composition as were available to me, in the belief that diverse angles of vision would bring the truest and most humane image.

Nevertheless, after my book manuscript was finished and the book contract was signed, the door of Henry's archive suddenly swung open—a full fifteen years earlier than I had expected. Sidney Cowell, the New York Public Library, and a handful of East Coast–based scholars had forecast various dates for the opening of Cowell's papers, the most common being the year 2015. But when Sidney died in 1995, attorneys considered her various wills and other documents, then fixed the official date at 20 June 2000.[16] When I arrived at the New York Public Library that June, I had the advantage of knowing well the sources outside the collection and, consequently, the kinds of things I still needed to see. What I found there usually confirmed, sometimes contradicted, and always deepened my understanding of Cowell's bohemian upbringing and experimentalist career. Now, having brought hundreds of sources from Cowell's own collection into the picture, I hope that what one sees and feels in this book will be a reliable topography of the shape of Cowell's early life. Not everyone will agree with all the conclusions I have drawn. But those conclusions are decidedly hard won and, if for no other reason, worth the reader's indulgence.

As I reread and reflect on the chapters of this book, I am struck by several things. First, it is sometimes hard to believe that these chapters are all about the same man. Even in the 1930s, Nicolas Slonimsky displayed a kind of lip-chewing amazement over the "many adventurous chapters" in Cowell's youth, a boyhood so remarkable that, as a psychologist of the time put it, it resembled "a fairy story."[17] For Cowell, the fantastic adventure only grew more elaborate and sometimes bizarre as life went on. He set so many tasks for himself, achieved so much, and overcame so many obstacles, all the while displaying a dizzying ability to leap from one enterprise to another, then back again, as easily as if he had been turning the knob on a radio.

Likewise, one finds in Henry Cowell's music an extraordinary breadth of style. A thoroughly abstract, dissonant piece may follow a simple diatonic one. The same piano piece may harbor modernist noise in one hand and a modal folk tune in the other. Or an ensemble piece built with traditional harmonic materials may exhibit radically new formal concepts. Late works based on American vernacular, baroque concerto grosso, and Japanese gagaku traditions may appear in close proximity; and Javanese gamelan and Latin American dance styles may appear in the same work at the same time.

Although Cowell's polystylistic, pan-ethnic sensibility became most conspicuous in his later years, the impulse behind it came early: "I had [in my youth] an idea which I've never given up and which is, curiously enough, to me a very informal one, and that is that instead of studying one brand of harmony and counterpoint and applying this to every thought in music, that I should have a different kind of musical material for each different idea that I have. So even from the very start, I was sometimes extremely modernistic and sometimes quite old-fashioned, and very often in between."[18]

Yet, despite that superficial diversity, one also finds a great deal of uniformity. Weisgall observed this in a celebratory article in 1959: "Despite what may seem at first a great diversity of musical impulses, it becomes clear that [Cowell's] music is of a piece. . . . There is a perceptible consistency in the choice of musical materials, and . . . there is an equal consistency in the handling of these materials."[19] This dichotomy is something that commentators on Cowell's music seem always to have noticed. As one wrote in 1923, "Cowell's technic is ahead of his time, . . . while his inspiration—which one can't deny—is old-fashioned."[20]

In this book I try to treat Cowell as the stylistic chameleon he was, not only in the music he wrote but in the roles he played as a musical guru of the age. Yet I also treat him as quite consistent in the rhetoric of his music and the single-mindedness of his cultural vision. To walk the line of paradox is the task of anyone who would interpret another's life. I hope that in what follows I have done so fairly and gracefully.

1

Easily Explained by Heredity

Amid the eucalyptus groves and wildflower meadows in the foothills above the San Francisco peninsula, far from a hospital but close to a university, a forty-six-year-old woman sat in a cabin made of scrapwood, holding her newborn son. The woman, a popular lecturer and author, would henceforth refuse to have sex with her husband, renouncing mortal passions, but not motherhood. "Among women," she would later write, "the world has found no Raphael, no Beethoven, no Shakespeare, no Kant, no Darwin; no one pre-eminent in art . . . in discovery or invention." But, she added, "It is much to be mothers of such men; they are not commonly born of mediocre women."[1] Determined to be the mother of such a man, she would spend her remaining nineteen years teaching her son to be a discoverer, an inventor, and an artist as free spirited as the seaborne breezes that whistled through the cracks in the walls.

§ § §

In 1878 Father Hugh Quigley of San Francisco published some "candid advice" to his countrymen who remained in Ireland: "Settle *anywhere* in California."[2] But by then his advice went without saying. Since the famines of the 1840s millions of Irish had fled their impoverished homeland in search of prosperity in America. While most settled on the eastern seaboard, thousands continued westward to the Pacific Coast, a region with certain irresistible attractions to poor emigrants: cheap housing, fertile soil, a booming gold economy, and no established social order to exclude them. With its boundless promise, its natural beauty, and nothing but the future to contemplate, California became a haven for Ireland's dispossessed.

Most of these California Irish lived in close-knit families, many of whom were barely literate. Although they looked forward to building a new life, many Irish folk tried to maintain their ethnic identity by preserving their traditions, folklore, art, and music. At the core of all these was a Celtic mythology that taught of a cosmos populated by gods, fairies, sprites, and other preternatural creatures whose deeds were celebrated in poems and songs. Overlaying this mythology was Roman Catholicism, its transcendent view of the world, its miracles and its pageantry.

That quirky mix of pagan and Christian myth found a congenial home in San Francisco, a booming metropolis that by 1880 was one-third Irish.[3] The eclectic free-spiritedness of San Francisco was rooted in the very physique of the city—its erratic architecture and incessant hills, doused every morning with seaborne fog. The physical turbulence was mirrored in the aesthetics of Bay Area artists, who prized rhapsody and sensuality above symmetry and form. Nevertheless, the evenness of the seasons and the tranquility of the region's vast unsettled landscape fostered contemplation and spirituality. A poet of the early twentieth-century West described California's effect on people like himself: "there was healing in her protective hands, and consolation in her beauty. . . . For artists and souls awakened to the spiritual and romantic influences of fair, stately, or historic places, the mystical emanation of California's personality is ineluctable." That personality was traceable, he wrote, not only to the fair climate and landscape, but also to the "haunting, occult bewitchment" of the place and "the strange spirit which, blowing where it lists, has elected to place a special seal of romantic beauty upon this lonely, lovely land."[4]

Such a "strange spirit" was the breath of life to San Francisco's bohemian community: the loose affiliation of visionary poets, playwrights, painters, and musicians who mingled with the nouveaux riches of the post–Gold Rush era in order to practice, in one scholar's words, an "explicitly aesthetic life style"[5]— a life style that, given a booming economy and mild weather, seemed more feasible here than perhaps anywhere. Led by such literary notables as Ambrose Bierce, Jack London, and George Sterling, San Francisco bohemians expressed their devotion to art in everything from public readings in local hotels to outings among the redwoods north of the bay.

San Francisco was also the scene of constant musical activity. The Bohemian Club—an upper-class group devoted to new art—had its musicals; the Symphonic Society played occasional concerts; churches, theaters, and the YMCA sponsored recitals by local talent and by visiting artists ranging from Lillian Nordica to Edward MacDowell. Because the city saw itself as progressive, it craved the latest fashions; because it saw itself as free spirited, it craved novelty. An 1899 review of the pianist Teresa Carreño expressed the values of the city: "She is the best woman pianist who ever lived . . . eminently a progressive artist, having an instinctive horror of the rut, of the conventional, or main traveled thoroughfares."[6] The bohemians in the city prized any sort of devotion to music in the face of an increasingly materialistic age. As one of San Francisco's music critics wrote in 1903: "A man who could give his life to music in a country and a day like this [is] nothing short of a hero."[7]

Sometime around 1890, Henry Clayton Blackwood Cowell arrived in San Francisco. Born in 1866 in a small village in Carlow County, Ireland, Henry was one of the well-pedigreed Cowells of Logadowden, Dublin County. (His name bespoke his own pedigree: "Henry" and "Clayton" were favorite names of the Cowell clan; "Blackwood" was his mother's maiden name.) His Trinity College–trained father, George, had risen through the ecclesiastical ranks of the Church of Ireland from priest at the lowly parish of Clonmore to the esteemed position of Bishop of Kildare. But what in George was a deeply rooted Protestantism emerged in Henry as a spirit of separatism. A loner and a transient, Henry shunned the family-centered life of his kinsmen and more or less rejected the faith of his parents—though not the lore of religion. He hoped to penetrate the exotic circles of the San Francisco bohemians. Along the way, Henry discarded his regal Christian name in favor of the diminutive "Harry,"[8] probably to avoid being confused with the well-known proprietor of Henry Cowell and Company, local manufacturer of brick, cement, and lime.

A true bohemian, Harry attempted to shroud his own past in myth, describing his upbringing and subsequent life in America only in vaguely poetic terms. He told of a "miraculous escape from a liberal education" at two universities and likened his schooling in Ireland to the ordeal of the Israelites in the fiery furnace. From these he had escaped "without a scar or a whiff of smoke being left to tell the tale." After arriving in North America, he said, he began a life of assorted vocations; he had "broken bronchos, ridden the range in Canada, cooked in cow-camps, felled timber in the backwoods, set type, taught fancy skating and tennis."[9] He seems to have been vague about when and how he actually made his way to San Francisco. His daughter-in-law reported that he was sent to the United States for studies at the age of sixteen in the company of two sisters and a tutor; the tutor abandoned them in New York, the sisters sailed home, but Harry decided to stay.[10] His third wife, however, writes that he originally left Trinity College with his brother after a year of study to go to western Canada and work for a "pioneer society" selling books, which he did for two years before he had saved enough to go to California.[11] Both accounts agree on one thing: Harry wanted to land in San Francisco—"the most modern city in the world," as he called it[12]—in order to become a writer.

Hoping to join the corps of San Francisco's bohemian authors, Harry aspired to certain traits, especially a romance with nature coupled with cynicism toward orthodoxies of form or genre. He fraternized with the local writers and boasted throughout his life of friendships with celebrities. Whether he was as friendly with them as he later claimed is questionable. George Sterling once referred to Harry as "a winged ape," and Harry's penchant for boasting—combined with what one well-known photographer called Harry's constant "babble and cackle"—seems to have repulsed many.[13] With an ego fed by his personal motto that "self-love is a lesser sin . . . than self-neglect," Harry Cowell seems to have alienated many of the San Francisco literati.[14] His third wife later claimed that "he was not one of them in a sense," mainly because Harry was "never out for a good time carousing with men and drinking."[15] Sidney Cowell characterized him differently: "Harry was incapable of being anybody but himself, but it was not a very attractive self."[16] Nevertheless, Harry did manage to establish himself in the shadow of the better-known bohemian literati of San Francisco, becoming a jack-of-all-trades writer who published often, in genres ranging from political essays to sentimental short stories, from newspaper columns to high-flown poetry.

His poetry suggests the full range of his craft. Many of the poems celebrate nature in a way typical of writers in California, not to mention those in Ireland.[17] In particular, Harry liked to use his verse to herald the changing seasons (ironically, since their changing was less detectable in California than in most places).[18] He also ruminates at length on marriage and the relations between the sexes.[19] Many of his more philosophical poems deal with death[20] or expound a general skepticism—with religion, on the one hand ("Rondeau of Disbelief"),[21] and with science, on the other ("The Despair of Science").[22] A few are blatantly Christian in their outlook:

> O Thou, adored of heaven, abhorred of hell,
> Lord Jesus, mild just Jew whom Gentiles own!
> Hear how the murderous Muscovite makes moan
> Thy Brethren who in Darkest Russia dwell.[23]

In some of his longer poems Harry celebrates California as a place of unlimited possibilities, a haven for dreamers. In such poems as "The Winds of the West," "To California," and "Ode to California," he trumpets his discovery of the promised land with a latent religiosity that probably derived both from his clerical upbringing and his reading of Romantic poets.[24] The "Ode," for example, begins:

Hail, California, land of dreams come true,
Where life is wonder still and Earth yet young,
Retaining much of its first morning's dew
And that primordial melody God sung
For very gladness, self-moved to create!

He continues, describing California as "An undefiled Eden that has stood / Remote from Evil" and a "Hope-land of the human race, / Thou cradle-place / Of a great rebeginning for man," a place where "No Angel guards thy gate / Against the eternal dreamer: big of breast, / Thou[, California,] mak'st him feel at home."

Harry's essays published during his early years in San Francisco manifest his flight from orthodoxy. In "An Alleged State Duty," appearing in the *American Journal of Politics* in 1893, he critiques the church and the state, both of which present themselves as "all-powerful, all-wise, all-just, all-loving, preserve their sway and dignity by awe-inspiring titles, ceremonies, language, dress. Both . . . act in ways mysterious, arbitrary." Equally arbitrary is the Christian God himself, who "creates life which feeds on life, and is called 'good'; destroys by famine, pestilence, flood, storm, and is said to 'visit'; boasts himself a man of war, jealous, vengeful, and is not reprobated; afflicts children for their parents' sins, and is named 'The Just'; 'to eternal tortures' consigns his opponents, and is accounted 'merciful.'"[25]

Harry is confident, however, that the new age will transform the state into "an association for the preservation of equal freedom" and the church into "a school of scientific ethics, which shall teach, not a conventional approval or disapproval of actions determined by myths, majorities, customs, fashions, and manners, but a philosophical approval or disapproval of actions determined by the laws of social life"—that is, the principles of Social Darwinism. In time, with the triumph of these principles, "the good gardener Competition, with free and ungloved hands, shall have weeded out the socially unfit," that is, the lazy and the incompetent. Those that survive this weeding, of course, would include men who, like himself, were physically robust and socially self-sufficient. But as it turned out, the good gardener History spared Harry's memory for only one deed: he fathered one of America's most radical composers.

Somewhere around the time that Harry moved to San Francisco, a midwestern divorcée named Clarissa Dixon did the same. A full sixteen years older than Harry, she was the fourth child and eldest daughter of a cabinetmaker in the Illinois River logging town of Hennepin.[26] She had been a political activist while still young; at sixteen, according to one source, "she boldly wrote and spoke in defense of a miner's strike."[27] Like Harry, she had renounced her orthodox upbringing, having "publicly dissolved her connection with the church . . . and with all doctrinal religion" while still a teenager. At twenty, while working as a schoolteacher in Iowa, Clarissa (or "Clara," as she was then more commonly known) married a lawyer, George Davidson; in about 1872 she bore him a son, whom she named more or less after herself—Clarence. In time she was publishing essays in progressive, aesthetically oriented journals such as Philip Goepp's short-lived *Fortnightly*. By the 1890s she had left George and Clarence, returned to her maiden name, and moved to the San Francisco Bay area, apparently in search of fresh inspiration and like-minded thinkers. At that time, as one friend described her, Clarissa was "lovely, unforgettable, impressive [with] wavy, short almost white hair . . . very red cheeks, somewhat plump form and large wide-set dark eyes."[28]

How she met Harry is not known, although they did travel in the same circles of avant-garde poets, philosophers, and artists. Both he and she espoused Spencerian ideals and libertarianism. And both were cheerfully oblivious to the impracticality of making a living from writing. As one observer put it, "the two of them [tried] to write for a living, because the two of them had something they wanted to give the world that the world needed, and undoubtedly it did need it, but it wasn't taking it, for any price."[29] Nevertheless, like Harry, Clara was able to sell some of the prose she wrote after her move to San Francisco. That prose consisted of scientific and philosophical essays, short fiction, and children's stories (usually published under another name).[30]

Her short story "A Fatal Doubt," published in San Francisco's *Overland Monthly* in 1893, is typical of Clarissa's work. It is a tract on individual liberty in the guise of a fictional family drama. It tells of an elderly, fastidious woman who lives with her unmarried middle-aged son. She seems obsessed with domestic pursuits, while the son finds spiritual sustenance in nature: he "felt interest in sunrises and sunsets, the structure of plants, the habits of insects, the formation of hailstones, and a hundred sights, sounds, and subjects without practical bearing on the actual affairs of life."[31] The mother fears that his devotion to nature will one day make him leave her; she berates him whenever he comes home late. One evening, when he returns from town unusually late, he finds she has killed herself, apparently despondent that he has abandoned her. The moral is clear: live for yourself and let your children do likewise.

At about the time "A Fatal Doubt" appeared in print, Harry and Clara are said to have married.[32] Soon they moved down the peninsula in order to be close to the new university just outside of Palo Alto. Not long before, Palo Alto had been little more than a "pioneer settlement," one settler recalled. Its "downtown" area consisted of "Parkinson's lumber yard, with a tiny shanty for a postoffice at one corner, Mrs. Yale's little thread-and-needle shop and Simpkin's little store. The Sunday-school assembled on benches under the big oaks by the station, and for week-days the dozen or less children went bumping over to Mayfield, driven by Theodore Zscokke in his old express wagon."[33] But this rustic life style was about to end. In 1891, on the advice of a spiritualist, the Nob Hill railroad baron Leland Stanford built a university in Palo Alto as a tribute to his dead son. Within its first two years Stanford University became a mecca for progressive intellectuals who, like Harry and Clara, hoped to usher in the new century with new ideas, to create a foundation of progress for the dawning of the second millennium. Blending the poetics of California and the intellectual rigor of the European university tradition, Stanford University more or less institutionalized bohemianism.[34]

Seated just to the north of Stanford, the village of Menlo Park had been founded by two Irish emigrants who found its spacious groves and rolling foothills reminiscent of their home at Menlo Park, Ireland.[35] Fellow Irish settlers bought small tracts of land in this community at the same time that monied landowners discovered the area and began erecting splendid mansions there. To the mixture of middle-class immigrants and the wealthy native-born was added another breed—the intellectuals who were drawn to Stanford University in the early 1890s. Professors and students began buying up the local real estate. Soon the town became a whistle stop on the railroad line that ran from San Francisco down the coast.

Irresistibly drawn to Menlo Park's blend of Irish and bohemian cultures, Harry and Clara chose a lot among the patchwork of homesteads on "the hill," the slope that rises to the west not far from El Camino Real, the main road that had been trodden by Junipero Serra on his mission journeys up and down California's coastline. On a heavily shaded spot on "the hill," a lot surrounded by wide fields and a few dirt roads, Harry built a cottage for two beside a small pond. Although he could not finish the cottage as he envisioned it—all of the lumber came to him as payment for typesetting at the *Palo Alto Times*[36]—the isolation and natural beauty of the spot provided an agreeable working place. One of the earliest visitors to this house recalls that the Cowells had a few small tables with books and manuscripts lying about and, on the otherwise bare walls, a large portrait of Shelley.[37]

Shortly after moving in, the forty-five-year-old Clara discovered she was pregnant with her second child. The precise date of the birth was not recorded by the state; family records place it on 11 March 1897, at 8:30 A.M.[38] Although the parents were an unconventional couple even by the standards of California bohemians, they named their son in the most conventional of ways: the father's Christian name first, then the mother's maiden name, then the father's family name—Henry Dixon Cowell.

What these parents would want for their boy was clear: he should be free, independent, progressive, literate, versatile, devoted to nature in both its scientific and poetic aspects, versed in religious tradition but skeptical, and perhaps above all, devoted to art. As if to confirm their aspirations for little Henry, a friend of Clarissa's prepared a detailed astrological chart on the boy. He would have many friends, it said, and would be very smart. "Business of an Emotional nature will engross his whole Being," the chart went on. But the boy would also grow up to be "eccentric."[39]

Clarissa tried to raise the boy scientifically. Having read in books that it was unwise to hold a young child too closely, she refused to cuddle him at all and left him, in her words, "in the middle of a big bed, like a rose in the desert."[40] When the baby suffered chronic chills she placed hot irons around him to keep him warm. In time a neighbor persuaded Clarissa to throw out her scientific pretensions and follow her intuition. From then on she cuddled Henry eagerly.

Consumed as she was with words, Clarissa kept careful notes on her new son's verbal skills. When twenty months old, she recorded, he mastered three words. Within two months his vocabulary was 180 words. By his second birthday "I had written down all 272 of his words," she noted, adding that "I am not sure that I heard them all."[41] Within the year he could recognize all capital letters at sight and could read about twenty-five words.

Clarissa attempted to teach him not only words but ideas of freedom and responsibility. She first constructed experiments in "choice" for him, laying out a series of colored objects, for example, to see which color he favored. Because Henry chose pink again and again, his mother lavished the color on him from then on, surrounding him in it and even dressing him in it—to Harry's chagrin, no doubt. She also taught Henry "property rights" by having him identify which things belonged to him and which to others. And, to set an example in equality between genders, she divided the domestic responsibilities with Harry, each parent taking an alternate week of housekeeping. Their experiment was less than successful, however, at least when it came to feeding the family. A friend recalls that "in Clara's week it was quite all right, far from luxurious, but there was enough; in Harry's—there was tea and soda crackers."[42]

While Henry was still an infant his family moved to San Francisco and his father began taking occasional jobs in Sacramento. They also maintained the Menlo Park cottage, returning there from time to time. The chronology of their transience is difficult to make out: in true bohemian fashion, the family managed to avoid such people as census takers and city directory compilers. But the reasons behind their transience are clear. Stanford and San Francisco represented two great poles for people such as themselves, the former with its contemplative intellectualism, the latter with its eccentric inhabitants and cosmopolitanism.

In either environ, Clarissa became increasingly domestic in her outlook, having been given a second chance at motherhood by a very precocious child. Her renewed domesticity is evident in this poem written about Henry when he was not yet four years old, which she sold to a magazine for the tidy sum of three dollars:

> All the good wives in the neighborhood say
> Dear little Dimplekins rings every day.
> Smiling, he greets them with, "How do you do?
> I'm pretty well, and my mama's well, too."
> Laughing and whistling, he's off with a bound;
> So they have named him their "merry-go-round."[43]

To record such precocity, Clarissa began a notebook of his sayings, presumably for posterity. She expected, or more precisely, planned that her son would become one of the new age's great men.

"The outstanding fact about Henry from birth," a friend recalls, "is that he was loved—not only with a parental love as infinite as the skies but with a love of parents who respected the rights of Men in the life of an individual [even] one day old. There was never a deviation, never any momentary temptation on the part of Clara or Harry to bear down on the child . . . in any way." They believed that "all influence is bad influence." On one occasion, this friend, Anna Strunsky Walling, recalls, she saved Henry's life by extracting a handful of pebbles from his mouth as he was choking on them. When she heard of it, Clarissa anxiously questioned Walling about whether she had used "violence" in removing the pebbles. Walling answered heatedly, "I certainly did [and] you certainly would not have had the baby if I had not."[44] But for the rest of her life Clarissa insisted that children should always remain on equal terms with adults. She later would boast that her relationship with Henry "had always been that of comradeship. No arbitrary power and authority had ever been felt by him. He stood on equal footing."[45] As it turned out, that doctrine would disrupt Henry's education in what appeared to be his greatest gift, music.

In later life Henry claimed that his parents never "embraced music" and never introduced him to any of their musician friends (hard to believe, given how Clarissa doted on him).[46] But they did sing and hum to Henry songs from their own youth—Clarissa, Ozark mountain tunes, and Harry, Irish airs.[47] It is clear from others' reminiscences that he assimilated at least some of these. Anna Walling recalls that before Henry was eighteen months old, he could be heard humming such tunes in his highchair.[48] Clarissa dutifully kept a list of the many tunes he learned and preferred. When he was only two he would sing these for admiring friends. But when he was about two and a half, Clarissa noted, he completely stopped singing the tunes he had learned and sang only new ones. None of these was familiar and none was repeated.[49] Impressed by his talent, a neighbor gave Henry a mandolin-harp for his fourth birthday. Soon thereafter Clarissa found him in the backyard sitting on a large stone and improvising "variations" on "Home, Sweet Home."[50] Although not musicians themselves, his parents could not have been more pleased with his early improvisations, for they showed that their son had two of the qualities they valued most—artistry and independence. Another neighbor, impressed with Henry's tune-spinning talent, gave him a quarter-sized violin.

On 16 November 1902, the five-year-old boy took his first music lesson with Sylvia Holmes, a San Francisco violinist who had been trained by her father, Henry Holmes.[51] Within a few weeks Sylvia injured her finger and her father took over the lessons, assigning the boy a steady diet of Spohr exercises (as edited by Holmes himself). Meanwhile the short pieces Henry learned were conservatively classical—Haydn, Mozart, and early Beethoven—because Holmes would brook no "modernism" (e.g., the music of Schubert and Schumann). Nevertheless, Cowell spent much of his time improvising little melodies of his own. Photographs from these months suggest the musical confidence and determination the young Henry was acquiring: he stone-facedly plays his violin, his face both haloed and obscured by a fluffy mane of wavy blonde hair.

But his journey toward musical proficiency jerked to a stop when Henry offended his teacher. During one lesson, while trying to correct mistakes the boy was making, Holmes continued to talk while Cowell was playing. When Henry complained about this, Holmes told him to put the violin in its case and never come back for another lesson.[52] Clarissa was shocked—but pleased that her son had not let an adult condescend to him. Henry, however, was disinclined to practice without the discipline of lesson-going. He stopped playing the violin and resumed singing, sometimes attracting neighbors to his yard when he sang outside. A few of them left him small change as tips, something he reviled as undignified.[53]

Meanwhile, Harry and Clarissa's reputation prospered in the bohemian circles of San Francisco, partly via a chance meeting on the street, as Henry recalls.

I remember being with my parents when I was about 5 years old, and we stopped and waited for a street car in Berkeley, California. There was a man digging a ditch, and he overheard my father and mother talking something about writing, and he chipped in, and proved to be a person [who] obviously had astounding ideas and great clarity of speech and had read a great deal. And this was Jack London.

So my father invited him and he came to see us. I think it was my father who persuaded Jack London that he should really write his experiences. In any case, he was a great friend of the family, and I remember very well playing with his children while the parents talked, and thinking of [him] as being most kindly toward children, being very benign, liking children and being well understood by them, his own children. I was immediately drawn and attracted to him.[54]

Anna Walling, a onetime collaborator with London, recalls that Harry frequently took Henry to London's house. "Clara did not approve of his being taken across the bay at night and brought back late, and felt it was hard on the child. But again the idea of never invading the rights of others held her back." Harry, as the father, "felt it was all right and Clara did not feel that she had the right to interfere."[55] Nevertheless, despite her misgivings about Henry's trips across the bay, London remained fond of Clarissa as a writer and intellectual and spoke to Anna glowingly about lectures Mrs. Cowell delivered in San Francisco.[56]

But while the Cowells aspired to be counted among San Francisco's literary celebrities, their apartment sat on the fringe of San Francisco's chief refuge of exoticism, Chinatown. The "oriental district," as it was more politely known, consisted of a dozen or so crowded blocks of the city that were, in one author's words, "at once a living community and a ghetto prison."[57] Although the Chinese had been indispensable in building the empires of the railroad barons (who were among the city's most exalted citizens), they were now a "yellow peril," isolated from the society built on their backs. Many people thought the Chinese something less than human, fit only for furnishing opium, prostitutes, and cuisine for "slummers," the wealthy but idle whites who visited the district. The stagnant routine of daily life was punctuated by an occasional noisy, brightly colored holiday parade. Nestled among the laundries, butcher shops, and opium dens, were the "joss houses"—small temples erected to the gods who presided over religions that were devoted, not surprisingly, to transcending the hardships of material being.

Henry probably found friends easily in Chinatown: children were few there and they would have relished companions of any race. Among his Asian playmates Henry learned musical sounds he had never known before. He was disposed to value such sounds: they were exotic, and his parents had taught him to prize exoticism. In place of the traditional repertoire in which he had been immersed, Henry began to appreciate the strange scales of Asian melodies, the boom of ceremonial drums, and the resonance of gongs. By the time he was nine years old, he later recalled, he had learned to hum oriental melodies as naturally as he had those of his parents.[58]

During the Cowells' stay in San Francisco the progressivism that had once united Harry and Clarissa began now to erode their marriage. Perhaps troubled by her continuing fertility, Clarissa had insisted in the name of progress that she should no longer have sexual relations. Henry later explained that "she emphasized the absolute wickedness of having sex-relations" and insisted that intercourse had been "only tolerated" in former ages for the purpose of producing children. Now, she taught, medical science allowed for the man's seed to be carried sanitarily to the woman for implantation through injection. Thus all legitimate needs for sexual relations had passed away.[59]

Her sudden quasi-Victorianism seems to have intensified Harry's doubts about the finality of the marriage contract. He wrote in a news article that marriage was something of a "trial,"[60] born of a morality that was perhaps unnatural. Passion was as likely to take hold of him now, a married man, as at any earlier time in his life. This was because "the forces . . . we call natural, are morally indifferent. Nature is neither just nor unjust; it neither hates nor loves; it is neither kind nor unkind; it is indifferent."[61] There were also hints that Harry could seem indifferent to his son, as suggested in a touching passage recorded by Clarissa: the young Henry chides Harry, saying, "don't look at the book, look at me. I love you, the book doesn't love you."[62] Amid the relentless obligations of fatherhood and the conjugal denials of his wife, Harry's passions drew him to a local music teacher named Henrietta Grothwell, who would become his second wife. Soon Harry was a distant yet intermittently intrusive figure in Henry's life, one whose influence Henry never lost and whose absence he never overcame.

Harry and Clarissa divorced and she moved back to Menlo Park with Henry now old enough to attend school. Whatever their differences, however, both parents despised the public educational system. In a just society, Clarissa had written, "a power which forcibly deprives an individual of his property . . . is anti-social, violating the elementary law of society." A free school system, then, is unjust because it "derives its support from compulsory taxation." More important, she contended against public education in the name of progress, which she defines as society's evolution from homogeneity to heterogeneity. "An institution which tends to reverse this order," she wrote, "is not only unprogressive, it is retrogressive."[63] Later in life she would grow even more severe in her critique, insisting that public schools were "crushing all children into a shapeless, pulpous mass and then pouring them into molds, like hot tallow, from which it was the delight of educators to see them issue all alike, the tallow become hard, cold, flawless candles, each with exactly the same light-producing capacity for the lighting of the world."[64]

Although Harry may have held similar views, he seemed more concerned about the lack of social training in all schools, whether public or private. Even the best-bred children are savages at heart, he wrote in his most widely circulated essay on schooling. If schoolmasters do not vigorously curb this savagery, it may become fixed and irreversible. A place to begin curbing, he said, was in the brutal hazings given to new students. In virtually all schools "newcomers are expected to bear with good humor at the hands of strangers assaults upon their persons and destruction of their property." Such injustices must be banished "before we may expect to see fair play in the game of life."[65]

Forced by poverty either to teach her son at home or send him to a public school, Clarissa chose the latter, possibly concerned that her need to write for a living would leave little time to train Henry properly. Besides, she later argued, Henry needed the fellowship of children his own age. Though public schooling might harm him slightly, she believed he would "survive."[66] The decision was sweetened by the proximity of the local school, which was only a short walk from the Cowells' cottage. The school, Las Lomitas, was reminiscent of the schools Clara knew in the Midwest: it was one room only, wood-framed, with a large stove in the center of the room around which less than twenty students would gather for their studies.[67] But Harry's views on the brutality of schoolchildren would soon prove prophetic.

Henry recalled the hazing he got at Las Lomitas: "During the first day or so that I was at this school . . . a group of other children lassoed me about the neck, and dragged me about the school yard, resulting in enough strangulation to cause me a high fever, and some weeks in bed."[68] Clarissa reported that the two instigators of this attack, both teenage Hispanic boys, actually threw Henry's head against the school steps. When Henry finally returned to school the boys then swarmed around him and took turns slugging his face. While there seemed to be no particular reason for the attacks, Clarissa thought that Harry's absence made Henry an easy target—he had no father at home to avenge him.[69] Whatever the reason for these events, Henry was sure that they "caused my mother to fear public schools," which she had previously opposed only in principle.[70]

Keeping him at home, Clarissa launched Henry on a rigorous, if haphazard, course of study. The subjects consisted of ancient history, astronomy, classical literature, geology, and botany. There was little conventional instruction. In one informant's words, Clara "talked with [Henry] endlessly, read to him occasionally, and sometimes he read to her. They discussed religion, politics, and matters of literature and art."[71] Not surprisingly, Clarissa kept a running list of the books that Henry read. But while there was no time for arithmetic and spelling in his home curriculum, there was time for music.

Somewhere during this period of his life, Henry later claimed, "I was compelled to make my mind into a musical instrument."[72] He tried to spend one hour each day (4:00 to 5:00 P.M.) engaged in a series of exercises of remembering, imagining, and notating music. Regarding these exercises, Cowell later remarked that "it wasn't to write compositions so much as it was to hear sounds in my mind in order to prepare myself to write compositions. For instance, I'd think of a melody. I'd think of it as though sung by a soprano, then by a contralto, then as played by a violin, as played by an oboe, and so on and so on."[73]

But the great earthquake and fire of April 1906 put an end to Henry's exotic education. When the disaster struck, Harry was living in the old Chinatown apartment. He heatedly described the joss houses in flames:

> In the luminous clouds of smoke ever forming and reforming began forthwith to appear and disappear majestic figures clothed in resplendent purple and gold; and palaces of unearthly pomp, fit dwelling-places for the princes of the powers of the air; and the forms of fleeing women, with a splendor of flowing garments and a glory of loosened hair wind-blown behind them; and finally, when the flames reached their temples, the faces, if such they may be called, of the incredible deities of the Orient—gorgeous grotesques, now refined, transfigured, wooden images on their way, as it were, to immaterial, immeasurable divinity.[74]

In the wake of this catastrophe, Harry's religious training suddenly resurfaced, at least for literary purposes. The earthquake, he wrote, was a chastening from God of the city named for St. Francis, a divine punishment akin to God's wrath on Babylon, Nineveh, and Tyre.[75]

The devastation reached down the peninsula, even to Clarissa's cottage in Menlo Park. The gates of Stanford University toppled; walls cracked, fixtures fell, and some homes even slid from their foundations. One survivor in Menlo Park recalled her neighbors living in tents and sheds or at best in the undamaged parts of their houses. From the foothills they could see the waves of people who had abandoned their homes in San Francisco and begun walking south down El Camino Real in search of new lives far from the site of the disaster.[76] Clara resolved to leave too, fleeing toward her ancestral home in the Midwest. Henry hastily wrote a postcard to his father: "Dear papa we are going to start tomorrow so good by."[77]

§ § §

They went first to the farm near Collyer, Kansas, where her sister Jennie lived with her husband, James Guilbert, and their bachelor son, Walter. There, in the cool country air, Henry took delight in the strange sounds of the seventy pigs on the farm: "it is fun to hear them squeal," he wrote to Harry.[78] After two months Clarissa took Henry for a month to her parents' house, then moved on to the home of her son Clarence, who was working as a typesetter in Des Moines.

There Henry made a brief, final attempt at public schooling, although his third-grade teacher was unsure how to deal with him: Henry was, she said, below his grade in drawing and penmanship, at the fifth grade level in math, the sixth in geography, and at a fully adult level in reading.[79] Despite this confusing academic profile, Henry attended for four months. But a series of illnesses ended his schooling in Des Moines: he caught, in succession, scarlet fever, measles, the flu, and, worst of all, juvenile chorea ("St. Vitus' Dance"). This last disease was characterized by persistent tics and spasms in the extremities, especially the so-called "milkmaid's grip"—the uncontrollable drawing of the hands into fists. When, in the first month of fourth grade, Henry had to crawl home because of St. Vitus convulsions, Clarissa decided to end his schooling once and for all. Everything valuable he had learned was learned outside of school, she argued; and everything he had suffered came from within it.[80]

Henry's home schooling continued, though now more in the form of self-education. He exhausted the juvenile section of the Des Moines public library at the age of ten and a half, moving thence to adult books.[81] Upon seeing an opera for the first time—*Il Trovatore*—he immediately began to learn the stories of over twenty different operas, as well as the names of their composers and librettists.[82] When his mother got her own place, Clarence's wife gave Henry one of her two pianos—a very old one, Clarissa recalled, but "usable through the middle range of the keyboard."[83] He continued his daily exercises; in Des Moines, Henry recalls, he "went through what really is a crucial step for a composer, and that is to think chor[d]ally, to think of several tones at once."[84] He began to try to write down the tunes he heard in his head and to set texts he had learned from his reading. The earliest surviving attempt from Des Moines is a brief solo melody, a setting of some California-inspired lines:

"Oh the waves with dashing spray / Come with roaring every day." He mailed the tune to his father.[85]

While they were in Des Moines, Clarissa finally saw the *Westminster Review* publish the protofeminist manifesto that it had accepted from her a full seven years earlier. "No avenue of growth ought to be artificially closed against any human being," especially because of gender, Clarissa had written in her essay, "Woman and Nature."[86] The world was now destined to see the production of a "new" woman, or, if not new, at least "different from the woman of a hundred years ago." (The difference, she adds, probably will be "greatly increased in another hundred years.") Nevertheless, she conceded, present circumstances still required a more sacrificial role for women, a role she eagerly embraced with Henry, upon whom she continually doted.

Nevertheless, that role was not enough for Clarissa, who still longed to be a famous author. In order to enhance her chances, she decided shortly after Henry's eleventh birthday to move with him to New York City. Perhaps through her connection to the Strunsky family, one of whom had become a chief developer of Greenwich Village, she started her new metropolitan life as the caretaker of the home of General Winfield Scott, which was being renovated. For sweeping the walk, answering the doorbell, and protecting the house, she and Henry lived there rent free and earned fifteen dollars a month.[87]

For decades the Village, like San Francisco, had enticed bohemians from around the country by, in one writer's words, "its promise of artistic gypsydom together with Left Bank atmosphere and minuscule rents."[88] Those who congregated in the Village understood their status to be as New Yorker Ada Clare had defined it: "The Bohemian is by nature, if not by habit, a cosmopolite, with a general sympathy for the fine arts, and for all things above and beyond convention. The Bohemian is not, like the creature of society, a victim of rules and customs; he steps over them with an easy, graceful unconsciousness. . . . Above all others, essentially, the Bohemian must not be narrowminded; if he be, he is degraded back to the position of mere worldling."[89] Poets, sculptors, mimes, painters, singers, and all other sorts of artists mingled in the circuitous alleyways, in the abundant cafes, and in the broad plaza of Washington Square. West Twelfth Street, the Cowells' new neighborhood, was dotted with small but neatly kept gable-roofed houses with ivy-covered walls and slanted skylights. Among some of the more rundown houses, one could rent a room for two or three dollars a week.

The Cowells' house, however, was lavish. The expensive furnishings intimidated Henry: "I look at my shabby clothes in a $500.00 mirror," he wrote to his father. But the renovations kept the Cowells humble. Clarissa wrote that the house had been "a gale of lime-dust all summer" and Henry noted that "we have plenty of mosquitoes, indeed all night they fly like fishermen, trying to get a bite. They're wonderful things, they turn boys into hamburg steak."[90] All day Henry had to amuse himself by playing on the scaffolding, reading library books, and cataloging the size of Broadway buildings—"the lowest building is 1-stories," he wrote to his father, "and the highest is 42." He also collected stamps from his neighbors.[91] His stamp collection became not only his pride and joy but a source for the study of geography, history, and politics. Clarissa wrote glowingly but wearily of the prodigiously growing collection, likening it to yet another childhood illness for the boy: "He really does learn a surprising lot" from stamp collecting, she observed, but "I am growing rather tired of the subject. I suppose it is a sort of measles that he has to go through."[92]

Despite Henry's isolation, Clarissa knew that this time would be good for his artistic future. "He belongs where life is stirring and full, though he is capable of filling it himself with small resources," she wrote, and proclaimed to Harry that her boy "loves a land of art galleries and libraries, and big grand opera advertisements—even if he can't go in and pay for a seat."[93] But Henry did go to children's operas when Harry sent money, and Clarissa took him to free musical events: symphony concerts in Central Park, chamber music in Cooper Union, and organ recitals in churches.[94]

It is from this period of his life that Henry began his first composition (now lost)—a setting of Longfellow's "Golden Legend"—and that he resumed his mental musical exercises, about which he would later write fulsomely:

> I formed the habit . . . of deliberately rehearsing the compositions I heard [in concert] and liked, in order that I might play them over mentally whenever I chose. At first the rehearsal was very imperfect. I could only hear the melody and a mere snatch of the harmony, and had to make great effort to hear the right tone-quality. I would try, for instance, to hear a violin tone, but unless I worked hard to keep a grip on it, it would shade off into something indeterminate.
>
> No sooner did I begin this self-training than I had at times curious experiences of having glorious sounds leap unexpectedly into my mind—original melodies and complete harmonies such as I could not conjure forth at will, and exalted qualities of tone such as I had never heard nor before imagined. I had at first not the slightest control over what was being played in my mind at these times; I could not bring the music about at will, nor could I capture the material sufficiently to write it down. Perhaps these experiences constituted what is known as an "inspiration."
>
> I believe, had I let well enough alone and remained passive, that the state of being subject to these occasional musical visitations would have remained, and

that I would now be one of those who have to "wait for an inspiration." But I was intensely curious concerning the experiences and strove constantly to gain some sort of control over them, and finally found that by an almost super-human effort I could bring one of them about. I practiced doing this until I became able to produce them with ease. It was not until then that I began to develop some slight control over the musical materials. At first able to control only a note or two during a musical flow lasting perhaps half an hour, I be-came able, by constant attempt, to produce more and more readily whatever melodies and harmonies and tone-qualities I desired, without altering the nature of the flow of sounds. I practiced directing the flow into the channels of the sounds of a few instruments at a time, until I could conjure their sounds perfectly at will.[95]

At the same time that Henry experienced these early musical visitations, Clarissa achieved her greatest success as a writer. In mid-1908, she was able to secure a contract and a hundred-dollar advance from the Frederick Stokes Company for the publication of a novel, which was inspired, she said, by "her little son, together with certain vivid recollections of her own early life."[96] When it came out, early in 1909, Stokes advertised *Janet and Her Dear Phebe* as "a revelation of love between children." It is a brief, episodic tale of two girls from "Amity," Iowa. Phebe is slightly older than Janet—like Clarissa and her sister Jennie—and they are kindred spirits. Yet, because of her greater maturity and breadth of education, Phebe acts as something of a tutor toward Janet: "Janet wondered at everything and Phebe explained everything."[97] The two girls meet day after day at a spring in a nearby meadow and spend hours mythologizing the world around them. People who walk off the edge of the earth, Phebe ex-plains, become flowers; in these flowers, she adds, fairies dwell. But what is important about each flower is its rarity, for that is the true source of beauty. And it isn't the smell of weeds that makes them undesirable, says Phebe, "it's the *plentiness*. . . . If there was only one dog-fennel and only one blossom on it, people'd call it a flower and walk a mile to look at it."[98]

The girls' mutual affection is threatened by their fathers' mutual hatred. Janet's father is devout, Phebe's is intellectual, and their differences turn into hostility when a new college is built in the town. Janet's father publicly attacks Phebe's and, in turn, Phebe's father vows to keep the girls apart. Their sepa-ration prompts the girls to begin leaving letters to each other at the spring where they used to meet. At first the letters are rather formal, until Phebe writes what amounts to a bohemian literary manifesto: "Let's write as we would talk if we were sitting on the grass near the spring with our feet bare and our dresses patched."[99] In the letters that follow they offer their "childish philosophy" on such matters as the nature of maturity, lamenting how age diminishes the purity of the self: "Everybody used to be little, and the big is just grown on the outside of the little, like bark round a tree."[100] When Phebe's father discovers the girls' exchange of such sentiments he puts a stop to their letter writing.

Soon thereafter, the girls meet at the local Independence Day celebration and steal away to their old meadow. Phebe, who has always proclaimed her devotion to reading—"any book is better than none," she says[101]—now confesses that she has abandoned nonfiction in favor of fables, legends, and fairy tales. She and Janet again muse together about nature, telling stories of the sun, clouds, wind, rain, bees, and flowers. After some hours the girls are discovered and returned to their homes, but not before vowing henceforth to write to each other in poems instead of letters.

Their poems fill the next five chapters of the book, with a naive mixture of nature-love, philosophy, and, above all, pledges of love toward each other. Some of the poems express the spirit of Clara's bohemianism, as in these lines from "My Aunt":

> My Auntie has a garden
> Laid out in rings and rows
> All pruned and kept in order
> With walks that you'd suppose
> Were made with wax and rollers,
> and yet my Aunt declares:
> "Ide rather have a forest
> where things don't grow in Squares!"[102]

The poetic exchange abruptly ceases when Phebe decides that she and Janet must stop acting surreptitiously: "It is not bad to love each other; it is not bad to write verses and stories; but it is bad to be sly and secret, hiding things, afraid of being found out. It'll make cowards and sneaks of us, Janet, and perhaps liars, too."[103] The remainder of the book discusses the relocation of Phebe's family, the death of Janet's father, and, eventually, the bittersweet reunion of the two girls, now grown, near their old haunt by the river. Recounting to each other their separate pasts—Phebe has become a teacher—they pledge eternal love and walk off into the sunset.

The book aroused little critical attention, although the *New York Times* did print a paragraph praising what it called "a very intense sort of a love story in which the lovers are two little girls who are devoted to each other with that fervency known only to feminine childhood. . . . In the talk and the letters and verse of the children the author has kept very close to the child heart and the child mind. They are credited with neither that overwise thought nor that maturity of feeling with which too many authors endeavor to interpret childhood and succeed only in falsifying it. A sweeter, truer picture of childish philosophy and childish feeling has not been made in a long time."[104]

But even such praise does not amount to large sales, Clarissa discovered. In the space of four years fewer than six hundred copies were sold, despite Stokes's valiant efforts to promote the book. And because the first thousand copies were, by contract, exempt from royalties, Clarissa made nothing beyond her advance. She held out hope that Stokes would pick up one of the subsequent novels she sent the publisher, since it had claimed first right of refusal on her next five books. But Stokes rejected all three that she eventually sent.[105]

Her other attempts to make a living as a writer also failed. In her first year and a half in New York she earned less than a hundred dollars more than she had gotten for her novel. She and Henry became, in his words, "shockingly poor."[106] He tried to help by working as a delivery boy for a card manufacturer, but to little avail. He later recalled that "for some months we had only bread and cocoa to sustain us, and little enough of that." Both of them spent part of each day in bed, weakened by malnutrition.[107] Their sorry condition persisted until, according to one early account, an old friend met Henry on the street and followed the boy home. There he found Clarissa "lying on the bed an emaciated, broken woman, too weak to rise."[108]

In May 1909, after two years in the city, the twelve-year-old Henry wrote stoically to his father:

> I . . . long to go to California. New York is a wonderful city but I would rather be in the country.
>
> I like to go on the roof, but all I see is an endless mass of skyscrapers. To see you is not the l[e]ast part of my wanting to go to California.
>
> I have learned much by coming here. I know what it feels like to live in the largest literary centre of the U.S. I have the history of the ancient world on the tip of my tongue. . . . but no[w] I wish to go back, I have had enough of New York.[109]

Apprised of Clarissa and Henry's poverty, a local charitable society provided the two with food and train tickets to return to Jennie Guilbert's farm in Kansas.[110] As they left New York, Clarissa recalled, Henry vowed never to live in a city again.[111]

Henry recalls his stay with the Guilberts as a time of exhausting labor, long days of farm chores for himself and his mother—he being just twelve and his mother now nearly sixty. When not doing farm work, Henry explored the countryside on horseback, collected rocks, and gardened. He also imbibed the conservative values of Kansas's "simple people."[112] The Guilberts apparently had little interest in progressive culture and even less in Clarissa's literary pursuits, which had failed to provide her a living. Clarissa soon realized that Kansas represented the old heritage from which she hoped to deliver her son. Although secure, the Guilbert farm was the past; and, for all its catastrophes, California was the future. When Henry proudly wrote Harry about all of the plants he was growing on the Guilbert farm, he was quick to add that "I am not so much interested in any of these things as I am how to get to California. The prairies are not good company."[113]

Within weeks of that letter, Henry and his mother fled Kansas as eagerly as they once had fled California. When they arrived at their deserted cabin in Menlo Park, they found all of the windows and the skylight broken, the front door blocked by overgrown rosebushes, the backyard thick with wild mustard plants, and the inside filled with spider webs and wasp nests. The neighbors pitched in, mending the windows, hosing out the rooms, cutting back plants, and helping Clarissa buy stoves, chairs, groceries, and a table, across which an unused door was laid for Henry to sleep on, his mattress a big muslin bag he stitched together and stuffed with wild oatstraw. Clarissa later recalled that the two of them lived from September 1910 through the following February on just a hundred dollars.[114]

Since, clearly, Clarissa could not support the two of them with her writing, Henry used his self-taught knowledge of botany to create his own business. Tramping fourteen miles into the hills behind Redwood City three days a week, he dug up enormous ferns, with fronds as much as eight feet in length, then tried to sell them for a few dollars apiece to Stanford professors and other monied residents of Menlo Park and Palo Alto. At first he was discouraged, writing to his father in words that seemed to echo his mother's novel: the "plentyfullness" of the ferns in that area dissuaded people from buying them.[115] But gradually he picked up customers, added orchids and other rarer flowers to his inventory, and, if he couldn't get paid, traded for bulbs that he then sold or grew for their marketable blossoms. When Clarissa learned that there were cougars in the mountains, she convinced Henry not to go hunting for plants there so much. To compensate, he took a twelve-dollar-a-month job as a janitor at Las Lomitas—the school where he had been beaten seven years earlier.[116]

Having survived four years of transience and isolation, Henry Cowell had returned to the land for which he had yearned and to the house in which he was born and would live until he was almost forty years old. But while his sojourns had kept him free spirited and intellectually lithe, his daily regimen, whether farm chores or mental exercises, had given him discipline. At the same time, he had assimilated both classical repertoire and vernacular music, absorbed both local and exotic musical traits. He came back to California steeped in bohemianism with all its paradoxes: a love of learning but mistrust of schooling; a love of the progressive but mistrust for the unnatural; and a love of myth and religion but mistrust of both. He was, in short, a pure product of the "strange spirit" of his native state, especially as it had been embodied by his parents. In 1922 the *Palo Alto Times* would say that Henry Cowell's success was "easily explained by heredity."[117] But that was only part of the explanation. Henry would also be nourished by whole communities of like-minded souls that welcomed him as one of their own.

2

The Pulse of Chords
Tremendous and Remote

Most people who knew Henry Cowell in his early teens considered him bright, knowledgeable, and hard-working enough to succeed in any number of occupations. But the only occupation that came naturally and inevitably to him—if, as he said, music flooded continually into his mind—was that of composer. That occupation well suited a bohemian teenager: a life's work just close enough to his parents' ideals to please them but far enough from their own careers to show independence. After his return to California in 1910, he began to forge his destiny in a decidedly workmanlike way. By his midteens the essential aspects of his compositional style would be largely fixed—a piquant style born of ego and imitativeness, picturesque imagery, and sheer love of sonority. At the same time he would take his first steps in the slow passage from recluseness to celebrity, from private to public life. Both the musical style and the public persona blossomed not only in the shadow of Stanford University, where Cowell was earning a reputation as an intellectual *Wunderkind,* but also in some of the wildest domains of bohemian California, the bizarre artist colonies that sprung up on the coastline south of San Francisco Bay.

Cowell's gateway to academia was opened by one man: Lewis Terman, a Stanford psychologist who considered Cowell one of the greatest geniuses he had encountered. Terman was among the first psychologists who tried to document the phenomenon of "genius" itself, an exceptional gift of intellectual or intuitive insight, the idea of which had a long history in Western culture. Renaissance writers applied the term "genius" to men fitted by nature to acquire superior knowledge or create sublime art. Successive generations embellished this notion of genius, characterizing a "genius" as a person naturally set apart from his or her peers and unaccountable to common rules of thought and behavior. Such a person needed no schooling, as Edward Young wrote in one of the first books on the subject: "To the neglect of learning, genius sometimes owes its greatest glory" (1759).[1] Rather than needing to study, the genius himself should be studied, and in the early twentieth century some scholars undertook to do so in a scientific way.

In 1906 at Clark University, Terman completed his doctoral thesis, "Genius and Stupidity: A Study of the Intellectual Processes of Seven 'Bright' and Seven 'Stupid' Boys." In this work Terman used methods of intelligence testing resembling those developed by Alfred Binet in France. At the conclusion of the thesis, Terman wrote that his work had "strengthened my impression of the relatively greater importance of *endowment* over *training*, as a determinant of an individual's intellectual rank among his fellows."[2] But during the next four years, Terman virtually retired from such matters. He was weakened from tuberculosis and fit for academic work only in a salubrious climate—like California's. When a former classmate of Terman's was offered an assistant professorship at Stanford in 1910, he declined it but recommended Terman. Upon being hired, Terman immediately began a new research project, a study designed to measure the intelligence of hundreds of children.

When Terman asked his colleagues to help him find suitable children, education professor Percy Davidson recommended a neighborhood boy who was a janitor, one who had little parental guidance and was "a very free child."[3] Terman found the boy, Henry, herding pigs in a field next to Terman's garden.[4] He later described Cowell as he came to know him in 1910:

> As a boy of a dozen years, Henry's appearance was odd and interesting in the extreme. His speech was quaint, and rather drawled and stilted; his face was childish, but he looked at you with eyes that seemed utterly void of self-consciousness; his clothes were often ragged and always ill-fitting; his hair hid his ears and straggled down to his shoulders; his face and shoulders twitched occasionally with choreic spasms.
>
>   Everybody considered Henry as queer, not to say freakish. If employed to weed a lawn he was likely to forget what he was doing while trying to compose and whistle a tune. His janitor work was hardly more successful.[5]

For almost two years Terman and a graduate assistant kept Cowell "under our observation" while they worked on a revision of the Binet-Simon intelligence test scales.

In the fall of 1911, Terman tested Cowell's intelligence. The young man had to demonstrate his vocabulary—which Terman measured at an extraordinary 15,500 words—his ability to make sense of an incomplete story by filling in the missing words, and his skill at interpreting Aesop's fables. He also had to draw in a circle the path he would take to find a missing ball among tall weeds.[6] All of these tasks suited Henry well. His knowledge of literature was vast for a boy his age: in interviews with Terman he listed over three hundred books he had read before the age of fourteen. And Clarissa, as Terman recalled, "talked with [Henry] endlessly, read to him occasionally [and] they discussed religion, politics, and matters of literature and art." In interviews with the boy, Terman made "bulky notes of extensive conversations which we had with him on such questions as socialism, atheism, scientific problems, etc." At the age of fourteen, Terman recalled, Henry "discussed these matters with greater breadth of knowledge and much deeper understanding than the average university senior." Meanwhile, Henry was skilled in the art of finding things among weeds.

Nevertheless, Henry's ignorance of some subjects was "striking." He could do arithmetic only meagerly and his spelling Terman considered "wretched." Perhaps ill training in such rote matters led to Henry's somewhat disappointing test results: at fourteen years and ten months of age Cowell possessed the "mental age" of just over nineteen. This was disappointing, at least, to Terman, who thought that Henry should have scored higher; he remarked that "the limit of the [test] scale was inadequate to measure [Henry's] ability."[7] In 1916 Terman devised the concept of "intelligence quotient," or "IQ," a number equal to the mental age of the child divided by the chronological age then multiplied by 100. Cowell's IQ was 132. "Although [that] IQ is satisfactory," Terman would write, "it is matched by scores of others among our records; but there is only one Henry." When Terman published his first book on the subject, he included his description of the young Cowell under this heading: "*Henry*. Illustrating the relative independence of IQ and schooling. Scientific ability overshadowed by musical genius. Extreme poverty."[8]

If Terman was Henry's intellectual champion, his artistic champion was Ellen Veblen. For twenty-four years the wife of the legendary economist Thorstein Veblen, Ellen was a wealthy and well-bred woman with a quirky sense of humor, a strong sense of intuition, a love of the outdoors, and, as a friend later recalled, "no particular care for personal appearance, unless it was a whimsical delight in suiting her own taste and mood, without regard to prevailing styles."[9] She was also a gifted scholar and writer, who devoured the works of Herbert Spencer and claimed that her reading of Edward Bellamy's socialist utopian novel *Looking Backward* was the "turning point" in her life.[10] Physically incapable of bearing a child, she loved telling stories to neighbor children. In 1902 she published some of her stories as a children's book entitled *The Goosenbury Pilgrims,* a personal revision of the Mother Goose tales.

Among the eccentricities of that book was the "Earth Song," a textless ten-measure atonal tune that contained all twelve pitches and a verbal direction that the tune should be harmonized with "easy chords in C" (example 1).[11]

Through all of their marriage, Ellen and Thorstein frequently broke up, usually because of his very public love affairs with female students. In 1909, after only three years as a Stanford professor, Thorstein Veblen was dismissed for unseemly behavior. He moved to Missouri without Ellen, who preferred life alone in a rented Menlo Park bungalow to life with him. In 1912 she divorced him, received a sizable settlement, and built a small cabin in a remote meadow near a grove of fir and pine trees, about a mile from the Cowell cabin. It was a makeshift home with a typically Californian novelty, a movable roof: by cranking its pulleys she could open the house to the moon and stars at night.

Within months of her return to Menlo Park, Clarissa met Ellen at the home of a friend. "As soon as Mrs. Veblen had opened her mouth and spoken a few words," Clarissa recalled, "I knew that I was not too old for another love."[12] Soon Veblen visited the Cowell home and met Henry. She later recalled to Clarissa how strange a meeting that was: "She saw a small, anaemic-looking boy swallowed up in a big chair," Clarissa wrote. After being introduced, Henry "asked some question, not usual to hear from the lips of a child; and in a few minutes she forgot that she was listening to a little boy, because he talked like a philosopher."[13] As they came to know each other in the following months, Veblen found in this bohemian boy a kindred spirit, a surrogate son, and ultimately a cause on which she could lavish her remaining money. Soon she began to leave money outdoors in places where he would find it.

Sometime in early 1912, Clarissa recalls, Henry came into the house and said,

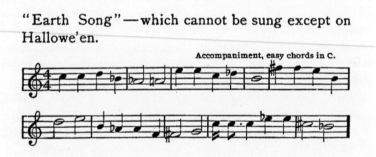

Example 1. Ellen Veblen's "Earth Song," from *The Goosenbury Pilgrims*

desperately, "I can't do without a piano any longer!" Surprised by the outburst, she said that he could spend the sixty dollars they had left in the bank if he could find a piano at that price.[14] He did, and on 17 February 1912 he bought a "battered, chipped relic" from F. M. Ostrander, a local music shop three blocks from the massive stone-gated entrance to Stanford University.[15] Clarissa commented that the instrument, previously owned by a boys' school, was "so badly worn that it could not be kept in tune without paying sums to a tuner almost equal to the rent of an instrument."[16] The piano had to be hauled by horse-cart to the Cowells' cabin on roads that one resident described as "one dreary stretch of dust in the summer, and an unending chain of black mud holes in winter."[17] The last two miles up the hill to the cabin were especially treacherous, the rains having made the road almost impassable with mud ruts and cracks. It appears to have been this first piano that Cowell described to his friend Clarence Weaver in 1916: "Henry told us that when they delivered [it] the piano fell off the [horsedrawn] truck because one of the wheels of the truck slipped in one of those ruts and the piano fell on the ground, and as Henry said, 'It broke in a million pieces.' But, he said, 'A piano man came out and put it all back together again and it worked just fine.'"[18]

A few days before Henry's fifteenth birthday he began taking lessons with a neighbor in exchange for his gardening services (an hour for an hour). But within five weeks the neighbor left town. By then the piano was already unplayably out of tune. After six weeks of not playing, Henry got the piano tuned and began with a new teacher. After six lessons she quit and the cycle continued, Henry stopped playing, the piano went out of tune, got retuned, and Henry began with a new teacher. All the while, however, he played ahead in his lesson books, bought an occasional extra piece (or, more often, had music given to him by neighbors), and began writing his own pieces. A Stanford student who also composed showed Henry how to notate properly, creating what Clarissa called a "revolution" in her son's methods and ability.[19]

In October of that year, Henry and Clarissa traded their piano for fifty dollars toward a better instrument, one costing $235. The Cowells promised— "with some misgivings," Clarissa later wrote—to pay off the rest at six dollars a month. After four months of this arrangement, Ellen Veblen paid off the balance.[20]

By January 1913 Henry had decided on who was the "greatest composer" of all time: Bach. But a few weeks earlier, he had taken a step toward entering the pantheon in which Bach dwelt—his first bona fide opus number. "I have finished Opus I by Henry Cowell," he wrote proudly to his father, "and bound it, as a Christmas present to myself."[21] Opus I was actually a collection of twelve short pieces he had written since acquiring a piano. Half of them had generic names (such as "Etude," "Scherzo," "Lullaby"), and half, picturesque names (for example, "The Cloudlet," "The Frisk," "The Lotus"). Henry dedicated one of the twelve pieces to his father and eight others to female neighbors, including Ellen Veblen. With Opus I, Cowell began a logbook of compositions, a list in which he would enter the names and dates of the pieces he composed until 1924.[22] Unfortunately, of the twelve pieces that formed Opus I, only two survive.

Perhaps the more evocative of those two is *Flashes of Hell Fire: A Dance of Devils*, written as a Christmas present to Veblen (see example 2). This piece is a forty-six-measure *presto con brio* in D major (with frequent D minor borrowings). It consists almost entirely of two- or four-beat quasi-cadential figurations, insistently repeated, with the left hand hammering out triads and seventh chords while the right hand plays tiny motives and chromatic runs. Although there is some irregularity of harmonic rhythm, the harmony is nearly all made from primary triads. Yet there are no real chord *progressions,* only oscillations between pairs of chords or, in two brief sequential passages, triads that slide down by half steps.

Flashes of Hell Fire clearly aspires to a kind of flashy nineteenth-century virtuosity, although its score contains many notational flaws of juvenilia: measures split across systems, moments where Cowell obviously forgets which clef he is in, moments where he less obviously forgets an accidental, and so forth. But its perpetual nondescript harmony and seemingly purposeless motion foreshadows much of Cowell's writing over a lifetime. Although many of its predilections would be trained out of him, this early piece harbors traits that would characterize much of his later and more celebrated music: the musical restlessness of youth in the form of velocity without direction and activity without structure.

As Ellen Veblen grew in her affection for Henry, she introduced him to friends who, along with her, had bought property down the coast. Since the Great Earthquake, painters, poets, photographers, and playwrights had fled San Francisco Bohemia and built little artists' colonies along the Monterey peninsula. Some lived there year-round, others only visited, all of them drawn to the beaches and coastal forests, whose limitless beauty and freedom was both bewitching and healing. In early 1913, Veblen insisted to Clarissa that Henry belonged in such a place, where he could develop his knack for composing among freethinkers and collaborate with some of her literary friends. Since many of Clarissa's writer friends from San Francisco now lived down the coast, and since she herself had no job or strong ties to Menlo Park, she accepted Veblen's invitation. Clarissa and Henry moved into Ellen's cabin in Carmel.

Example 2. *Flashes of Hell Fire*, opening (Reprinted by permission of the David and Sylvia Teitelbaum Fund, as successors to Henry and Sidney Cowell)

Situated near one of the old missions, the valley of Carmel was named for the Carmelite friars who had landed there in 1602. In recent decades, the lonely seaside brushland of that valley, with its oak thickets and twisted cypress trees, had been home to a few reclusive artists and writers such as Robert Louis Stevenson, who had based many of the picturesque descriptions in *Treasure Island* on the land around Carmel. In 1903 real estate developers founded a colony there that they hoped to populate exclusively with intellectuals and aesthetes. The developers sought out and invited some of the Bay Area's best-known literati, such as the naturalist Mary Austin, who later described the place as "a virgin thicket of buckthorn sage and sea-blue lilac spread between the beach and the high road. . . . bearded men from Tassajara with bear meat and wild-honey to sell; great teams from [Big] Sur, going by on the highroad with a sound of bells; . . . shadowy recesses within the wood, white with the dropping of night-haunting birds. . . . drift-wood fires on the opal tinted beaches, the sound of a Japanese flute issuing out of the fog . . . great spray heads bursting in the violet-tinted air over [Point] Lobos."[23] By 1910 Carmel had become a place for dozens like Austin to congregate: the Kiplingesque fiction writer James Hopper, the "poet of the Sierras" Joaquin Miller, the celebrated photographer Arnold Genthe, and many more, including, at one time or another, Ambrose Bierce, Upton Sinclair, William Rose Benét, Sinclair Lewis, and Jack London. A common aesthetic united such artists, an aesthetic that orbited around nature and spirit, Indian religion, Celtic mythology, and oriental mysticism. The artists had a common life style, as well: simple bungalows under the pines, no electricity, spare furnishings, and a devotion to sunshine and exotic health food.[24] To outsiders, the artists of Carmel appeared as pretentious, trivial artisans. But to insiders, Carmel held the keys to California's cultural future.

The variety of bohemian personalities in Carmel may be seen in two men to whom Cowell dedicated some early piano pieces. One was Jaime de Angulo, who had lived for a time in Menlo Park before settling in Carmel. A geneticist by profession, de Angulo was better known in Carmel as a ragged Hispanic caballero who reveled in bizarre, sometimes terrifying behavior, a vivid storyteller who could dance and chant like an Indian and in the same breath give a lecture on physics or anthropology. When he spoke, one friend recalls, it was "with extraordinary lucidity—rather like a pure gem in whose center existed a deep, still, quiet pool, rather like a crystal. The feeling one got at such moments was of pure beauty."[25] Yet, he was also, as his daughter recalls, "an awful liar" who, when drinking heavily—most of the time—displayed a perversity that led the author Henry Miller to say that there was "something satanic" about the man.[26] Perhaps it was the mystique surrounding de Angulo, the volatile mix of scientific mind and surreal behavior, that fascinated Cowell. In any case, Cowell inscribed one of his first Carmel pieces to de Angulo: the *Freak de Concert,* opus 4.

Very different from de Angulo, at least superficially, was the writer who essentially presided over Carmel, George Sterling.[27] Once known as San Francisco's foremost bohemian poet, Sterling had quit his job as an office worker in 1905 and moved to the Monterey peninsula, hoping to live off the land. He was characteristically Californian, an offbeat mixture of hedonism and puritanism: although more or less addicted to wine, women, and song, he shunned tobacco, coffee, and profanity. He was also renowned as a latter-day pagan who had a kind of altar on his property, consisting of a circle of trees with the skulls of horses and cattle hung on their trunks.

Whereas Jaime de Angulo was eclectic and charismatic, strikingly handsome and garish, Sterling was single-minded, plain, homely, and rather homespun. Dedicated to the craft of poetry, Sterling had been a literary hero to bohemians in San Francisco and Carmel, who hoped that he would validate and dignify their regional art. But his poetry, although competent, was perhaps overly grandiose and too controlled by its stiff rhyme schemes and sentimentality toward nature. Whereas de Angulo was given to colorful and somewhat raw vernacular idioms and palpable imagery, Sterling preferred an elevated, loquacious style with philosophical underpinnings. One of his "Sonnets on the Sea's Voice"—which Cowell set to music in spring 1914—was typical. It spoke of the Pacific's "voice" as

> Unchanging, immemorial, profound,
> A sorrowing the caverned cliffs prolong,
> Where foam is choral and where thunders throng,
> Or where the sands uncharted or renowned,
> Tremble forever to its elder sound,
> The ground-note of the planet's undersong.

Perhaps the lines that most attracted Cowell came in the next stanza, in which Sterling calls the sea's voice "that dirge of life, that music not of man . . . the pulse of chords tremendous and remote."[28] It was the very sort of imagery that would find its expression in some of Cowell's best-known works of the decade.

At about the same time that he wrote his *Freak de Concert* for de Angulo, Cowell wrote a suite of pieces dedicated to George Sterling. Corresponding to Sterling's "pagan" leanings, the new piece was entitled *Savage Suite*—a set of ten short pieces with evocative titles. Three of the titles included the adjective "savage" (applied respectively to "dance," "music," and "rhythm"), and four of the pieces had "dance" in their titles (respectively prefixed by the modifiers "savage," "war," "fire," and "joy"). Both words, "savage" and "dance," enabled Cowell to indulge in his characteristically repetitive, nondevelopmental music with the air of a studied primitivism. Like Opus I and the dozen pieces he wrote between it and the *Savage Suite,* these pieces were tonal, sometimes fragmentary in character, and often had conventional A-B-A designs. They also represented two recurring traits of Cowell's compositional style. The first was what Godwin calls "a youthful enthusiasm for the fast and loud," which Cowell now learned could be legitimized by attaching a picturesque, primitivist title (or, in later years, a *futurist* title).[29] Second was his method of amassing a group of terse, disconnected pieces into one superficially "major" work. This allowed Cowell, like most young composers, to accrue compositional girth before grappling with the deeper issues of development that would arise in longer, more labored compositions.

Cowell noted in his logbook that the *Savage Suite,* his opus 14, was "usually said [to be his] best" work thus far. In what was apparently his first attempt at getting published, he sent the suite to the G. Schirmer publishing house on 1 June 1913. But the work, he sadly noted in his logbook, was "regected."[30] That rejection hardly seems to have daunted him. According to his logbook, he wrote about sixty other pieces in Carmel during 1913–14.

The majority of these pieces were short, elementary compositions dedicated to the children (most of them about eight years old) of prominent families in Carmel—the Murphys, the Herons, the Places, and others.[31] The pieces were probably intended for use in piano lessons. Most of the dedicatees were students of Mrs. Carrington, a piano teacher in Carmel, to whom Cowell also dedicated two pieces. Cowell seems to have churned out dozens of these little pieces without revision or fussing of any kind, scrawling them out on page after page of manuscript paper, finishing one piece, skipping a couple of staves, then beginning the next piece.

To understand the character of these pieces, consider a group of three of them, written in succession (op. 16–18): the Etude (to Bernice Place), the Lullaby, and the *Hunting Song* (to Frank [Murphy?]). All three bear common traits—a tune in the right hand, accompanied by simple block chords, often reiterated, in the left hand. The thirteen-measure E minor Etude is chiefly a study in playing octaves in the right hand. It features a galloping melody, virtually no harmonic progression, and an abundance of figuration. The Lullaby in C major is only slightly more substantial. It consists of twenty-five mostly diatonic measures arranged into an A-B-A form. In the first eight measures, Cowell presents a simple, charming contrasting period. Four measures of a wandering tune follow, whereupon a false reprise of the opening period ensues. After three measures it gives way to a real reprise, which is extended by the addition of two closing, cadential measures. The last piece, *Hunting Song*, epitomizes most of Cowell's early ephemera: it is a mere eleven measures, most of which are simply rapid reiterations of a naive two-chord pattern or of a single broken octave, played solo in the right hand (see example 3).

Such pieces were far from the experimental works for which Cowell would become known. Still, on occasion, Cowell began in Carmel to dabble in some biting "wrong-note" harmony. The oddest example is probably *Sounds from the Conservatory*, a six-measure polytonal fragment written in late spring 1913 for two pianos (example 4). The first piano plays in B♭ major in a high treble register, with the right hand playing a disjunct hornlike melody while the left hand plays an Alberti bass texture with changing chords over a B♭ pedal tone. The second piano plays a narrow conjunct tune in D major in the right hand and a chordal accompaniment pattern in B major in the left hand. The left hand also plays this pattern in what amounts to 3/4 time, while the other voices play in the given 4/4 meter—thus anticipating what Cowell would later call "cross meter."

Although clearly one of the vast collection of children's pieces written in Carmel, *Sounds from the Conservatory* is one of Cowell's first tentative steps toward radical modernism—tentative, that is, because of its conceptual nature and its brevity. Cowell seems able to justify such harmonic juxtapositions only by pretending to evoke the sounds one might hear in a wing full of practice rooms (although at this time he probably never had been in such a place). Apparently not knowing where to go within this conceptual framework, he ends it almost as quickly as he began it.

What is perhaps as interesting as the music in this and Cowell's other Carmel children's pieces is the motivation behind them. Beyond the evident desire to multiply opus numbers, why did Cowell write so many of these tiny juvenile pieces during his two years in Carmel? To begin with, they demonstrated Cowell's strong instinct for self-promotion. Each piece dedicated to a child not only won Cowell a lifelong fan and perhaps patron, but it also ingratiated the child's parents. Each piece allowed Cowell to build an audience one admirer, or one family, at a time. And to Cowell, admirers may have had to compensate for a lack of real friends, a lack that was exacerbated by his mother's determination to have him be a famous man and the determination of others (like Ellen Veblen) to dote on him. In Carmel and for many years thereafter, Cowell exchanged the companionship of people his own age for that of much younger people, or much older. Cowell would later complain that he had to spend most of his time as a child in the company of his mother's adult

Example 3. *Hunting Song* (complete) (Reprinted by permission of the David and Sylvia Teitelbaum Fund, as successors to Henry and Sidney Cowell)

Example 4. *Sounds from the Conservatory* (complete) (Reprinted by permission of the
David and Sylvia Teitelbaum Fund, as successors to Henry and Sidney Cowell)

friends.[32] Nevertheless, it was the company of these older literati that gave Cowell some of his best compositional inspiration.

There may have been one other attraction to the children of Carmel: their teacher at Carmel's Garden School. Edna Smith had been born in Aurora, Illinois, the same year as Henry. Her father was the millionaire Captain C. H. Smith, the owner of the Western Wheeled Scraper Works, then the largest such company in the world. Pretty, well-educated, and precocious, she was uncommonly charitable, establishing schools for less fortunate children in Aurora, New York City, and Carmel. Almost nothing is known about her early relationship with Henry. He might well have been fascinated not only by her independence of mind but also by the company she kept—she was a close friend of Jaime de Angulo. As it turned out, within a few years she would become the most important woman in Henry Cowell's life.[33]

During the spring and summer of 1913, Cowell gave many short recitals in Carmel, Pacific Grove, Salinas, and other small communities in the region— probably in any place that had a decent piano. One of these pianos sat in the Arts and Crafts Hall in Carmel, where, in June 1913, he premiered his largest work yet, *Adventures in Harmony*. Dedicated to Ellen Veblen and subtitled "a Novelette," *Adventures in Harmony* was divided into six movements called "chapters." Those names suggest that Cowell wanted his music to connect with the literary ambitions of his adult mentors. But this piece was also a series of true "adventures" in harmonic thinking for a young, unschooled pianist and composer. Some of the adventures were simply matters of writing for difficult keys, while others involved more salient matters of chord structure and syntax.

The first chapter opens with a display of what Joscelyn Godwin has called "the Grand Manner."[34] In a long series of chords pounded out in multiple octaves and transpositions, Cowell's introduction to Chapter I seems to echo and embellish music such as the opening of Tchaikovsky's First Piano Concerto (example 5).[35] The second chapter opens with the left hand playing a thunking F♯ minor chord, while the right hand plays against it with repeated "wrong-note" dyads that rhythmically echo the first chapter, and then with a compulsive, one-measure rhythmic figure that becomes a winding stream of parallel thirds—epitomizing what Godwin calls the "anonymous" style of Cowell's early music (and much of the later music).[36] Subsequent chapters explore similar ideas and methods, as Godwin suggests. But it is the third chapter, the shortest of them all, that is easily the most important of the chapters in *Adventures in Harmony*. It provides the first appearance in Cowell's music of what he would later call "tone clusters."

Example 5. *Adventures in Harmony,* chapter I, opening (Reprinted by permission of the David and Sylvia Teitelbaum Fund, as successors to Henry and Sidney Cowell)

At the opening of Chapter III (example 6), in a *grave expressivo* tempo, Cowell calls for slow metric pulsations produced by repeatedly pressing down the entire bottom octave of the piano "with the whole hand," as the manuscript indicates. (Actually, all of the notes of the octave are not given—G, G♯, and B are omitted—inadvertently, no doubt, since as written it is impossible to play.) The resultant gonglike effect accompanies a meandering, arioso bass melody in the right hand. (The effect reversed the layout of Veblen's "Earth Song": there an atonal melody was to be harmonized with diatonic chords; here a tonal melody is harmonized with dense, atonal chords.) At measure 11 he introduces a new figure—two-octave clusters as "backbeats" (i.e., strong pulsations on beats 2 and 4) amid two-handed chordal fanfares (example 7). These are denoted in the score as "arm chords." This particular harmonic "adventure" appears to be an attempt to portray something like the "sea's voice," as described by Sterling: "that dirge of life, that music not of man . . . the pulse of chords tremendous and remote." The slow gonging of thick tone-clusters perhaps seemed the only way to represent such a voice.

♮   ♮   ♮

The most plausible explanation for how and why Cowell had begun writing these "hand" and "arm" chords appears in one of the first encyclopedia articles on Cowell. In 1936 David Ewen reported: "He tells us that when, as a boy,

Example 6. *Adventures in Harmony,* chapter III, opening (Reprinted by permission of the David and Sylvia Teitelbaum Fund, as successors to Henry and Sidney Cowell)

Example 7. *Adventures in Harmony,* chapter III, mm. 12–13 (Reprinted by permission of the David and Sylvia Teitelbaum Fund, as successors to Henry and Sidney Cowell)

he first stumbled across an old, decrepit piano, he began at once to experiment with new possibilities on it—not far different from the experiments which were later to make him one of the most original forces in music."[37] In other words, when Cowell first approached the keyboard, he instinctively behaved as most children do, playing groups of adjacent pitches *ad libitum,* with whatever physical means were available. Sidney Cowell gave the same explanation: "The first time he saw a piano he must have sat down and played as a child will play with the palms and the fists and so on to see what it would do. . . . I don't think that was an idea that he worked at developing at all—a lot of children have it."[38]

But there is another reason why Cowell may have been prone to playing the piano with fists and forearms: his earlier bout with St. Vitus' Dance and the so-called "milkmaid's grip." Although Cowell's disease subsided with time, he retained these spasms for many years. In the observation of Lewis Terman, Cowell still exhibited choreic symptoms when he was fourteen, the year he bought his first piano.[39] However obliquely, his pathology must have affected his technique.

Cowell, however, shunned such mundane explanations of tone clusters, insisting rather that he created clusters purposefully to capture the sounds he had imagined. In 1932 Homer Henley summed up what Cowell explained to him was the origin of his clusters: "the sounds which [he] produced were heard first in his own brain and . . . the effects he produced on the piano were but the necessitous inventions which he had to create to produce those sounds. . . . First he heard the clusters of sounds; then he invented the medium for their expression."[40]

Although this seems less plausible than the idea that he simply played at the piano "as a child will play," the resonant percussive sounds of his earliest musical experiences probably did affect his aural aesthetic. His first instrument was a kind of zither, a band of strings from which a single stroke could produce a huge band of adjacent pitches—a thick tone cluster. And after Henry and Clarissa had moved to Chinatown, he often heard the sound of gongs and ceremonial drums. He would later write: "The Chinese found out many centuries ago that . . . banging noises have musical value and enjoyment-giving possibilities."[41] His frequent exposure to those "banging noises" must have saturated his musical imagination.

An early biographical treatment of Cowell suggests that his imagined clusters were tied to specific images. Marion Todd wrote in 1925 that Cowell experienced his musical visitations while acting out the mythic tales his mother told him, "stories of battles between gods and giants, of stars and flaming comets rushing through black space, and of a splendid world springing out of chaos. Then all day out on the hills [of Menlo Park] he re-lived the tales he had heard at night and in his imagination heard powerful, magnificent music accompanying them. He longed to express this music but he had no instrument."[42]

If there is no "true" origin to Cowell's clusters, no single mental or physical habit that spawned them, this much, at least, is clear: when Paul Rosenfeld credited Cowell in 1924 with "the discovery of a method" in his cluster music (see appendix 1), he surely was mistaken: that "discovery" was something akin to Columbus's "discovery" of a land already long since populated. Countless children had used the method before Cowell. The difference was that none of them before had called it a "method." Whatever else clusters may have expressed, they bespoke the divine infantilism to which modern art routinely surrenders, a return to childlike principles in the hopes of rejuvenating technique.

§ § §

Clarissa could not attend the premiere of *Adventures in Harmony*. She had grown deathly sick from chest pain, which she thought was consumption. It turned out to be breast cancer and at the end of June 1913 she had a mastectomy. A friend in San Francisco nursed her while Henry continued performing his music around the Monterey Bay area and, for the first time, made money doing so. He wrote to his mother from Pacific Grove: "The recital went successfully, I was well received and made 18 Dollars. Dear Mama, I am happier than I have ever been since you were sick. It is such wonderful news that you have not consumption. And the operation was successful I hear. Can you use your arm? How long will you be there?" After talking more about his experiences in Pacific Grove, he adds, "I had about 5 clippings from papers about the recital[,] very flattering."[43] But he didn't know that he was about to reach yet another artistic milestone: the composition and premiere of his first major theatrical collaboration at the Forest Theater in Carmel.

One of many such outdoor theaters that opened in the early twentieth century, the Forest Theater had been founded on a local hillside by Herbert Heron, who was inspired and spiritually energized to do so by Mary Austin and George Sterling. Like most such outdoor theaters of this generation, the Forest Theater was an amphitheater, a bare patch of ground lit up by torches, with moths flickering in the light, the occasional animal roaming across the stage, and thick woods for a backdrop. Situated at Carmel, this theater also had a peculiar aura of mystery, because of the resonant ocean waves sounding in the distance and the sea fog rolling into the woods.[44] The Forest Theater mounted its first play in 1910, a visionary rumination on the biblical King David, written by Constance Skinner. The reviewer for the *San Francisco Chronicle* claimed that at the performance he saw, about a thousand people were in attendance, making the play a great success for a community that numbered probably half that number.[45] During the following two years seven more productions were mounted, four of them Shakespeare plays, and the others ranging from Yeats's *Land of Heart's Desire* to an adaptation of Lewis Carroll's *Alice in Wonderland*. The theater's biggest year would be 1913, during which eight plays were produced, most of them by local authors.[46]

In July of that year Cowell wrote his first bit of incidental music for the Forest Theater, a brief, now lost piece for Mary Austin's *Fire*. Austin's drama was a so-called Indian play in broken verse and folk rhythm, called by one critic in 1933 "probably the best Indian drama produced during the last eighty years."[47] When Austin herself reminisced about the Forest Theater, however, she did not mention Cowell's music for *Fire*. Yet she did mention the music Cowell wrote for the theater's next and probably strangest production, Takeshi Kanno's *Creation Dawn*.[48]

Kanno had been raised in a Samurai household in Japan, fluent since he was a toddler in the classic oriental traditions of literature and chant. During college in Kyoto, he studied Hebrew, Christian, and Asian religions, as well as Hellenic literature. For some time after college he led a nomadic life, rhapsodically described by his wife in prose evocative of Kanno's verbiage and indeed the whole tenor of Carmel literary life: "He journeyed forth into the far distant parts of his country, from village to hamlet strolling by running brook;

wandering like free wind through time-ruined castle or along sylvan shore; teaching, lecturing anon, singing his song alway, his scroll of sonnets . . . lengthening with each step of the journey."[49] Kanno, she wrote, then sailed to California and found near San Francisco Bay "a spot in harmony with the meditative spirit so strong within him." His mysticism deepened as he plunged "deep into the great sea of philosophy, seeking some hidden jewel in its gloom-cavern; rising to hover like cloud of doubt over the waters of feeling; soaring to lofty mountain-peak of religion, wrapped in mists of inspiration; on the wings of the wind drifting, floating, sailing o'er purple seas of dawn, over flowery plains of poetry and love." Kanno himself explained that "sublime music guides my soul," and that he wanted to "plunge into the vast bigness of chaos" where one could "hear the deep drone of mingling waves,—the great sounds of eternal tides."

Only fragments of his Forest Theater play, *Creation Dawn*, appear to have survived. They show that this "vision drama," as he called it, is more a recitation than a play, a loquacious lyrical duet between "an unknown poet" named Sagano and his "beauteous" lover Saarashi. It begins with the two outside a castle by the sea, "transported into the sublimest vision of Creation; their souls enraptured with [the] solemn music of love-ocean." The two intone some sprawling ruminations on what they are beholding, on the "waves of life pulsing" through the cosmos, the "billowing tides of life mingling . . . devouring white foams of passion breakers" amid the preexistential chaos. Suddenly, for unexplained reasons, Saarashi dies and the remainder of *Creation Dawn* is an enormous soliloquy by Sagano concerning love, creation, death, and nature, while the astral body of Saarashi mistily emerges and retreats. Only a few directions in the text of the play suggest stage action and musical accompaniment. The first scene of part 3 notes that, at a given moment, the "voice of waves [is] heard." In part 4, scene 1, the sound of gongs is called for; scene 2 contains the subheading "music judgment" and directs that Sagano's head be bowed, "his thought drunken in music."[50]

It is not clear how Henry Cowell came to be the composer for all of these effects. Mary Austin recalls that recently "a number of local musicians had taken an interest in [the] playing" of sixteen-year-old Henry Cowell. When Austin prepared "a dramatic setting of Kanno's poem," as she called it, Cowell was recommended to write the music. Clarissa, however, wrote that Kanno himself had heard Henry perform at Carmel and asked him personally to write the music.[51] Whatever the provocation, Henry was reportedly given about a week to prepare the music—short notice, even by his whirlwind compositional standards. Cowell began by assembling seventeen already composed pieces, the more recent of which contained some exotic dissonances. Consider, for instance, the opening seven measures of *Mist Music No. 2,* the measures that also close the piece (see example 8).

Cowell also wrote ten new pieces for *Creation Dawn,* although, like most of his children's pieces, most of these new ones were little more than fragments. The F minor "Moonlight Music," for example, written for the "music judgment" scene (act 4, scene 2), has in the left hand only nine successive triads, the first six of which are merely root-position minor triads descending by half steps. With each of these left-hand chords the right hand plays a little solo line that ascends chromatically from the root to the third of the chord. Amidst all of the new music he wrote for *Creation Dawn,* only one measure stands out. For act 1 he wrote a picturesque figuration, under the handwritten inscription "hungry ocean in the human soul"—an undulating tone cluster (example 9). This was the first time that he explicitly associated the sonority of a tone cluster with the sound of the ocean.

The play was produced on 11 August 1913 to an audience probably in the hundreds and with an effect that Mary Austin recalled as "strangely weird and macabre." To an audience of musically untrained listeners, pieces like *Mist Music No. 2* and effects like the "hungry ocean" cluster must have been striking indeed. Austin recalled that Cowell played the piano "in a manner so new, so ultra modern, that it seemed another instrument."[52] A photo taken at the

Example 8. "Mist Music No. 2" (from *Creation Dawn*), opening (Reprinted by permission of the David and Sylvia Teitelbaum Fund, as successors to Henry and Sidney Cowell)

Example 9. Undulating Cluster from *Creation Dawn* (Reprinted by permission of the David and Sylvia Teitelbaum Fund, as successors to Henry and Sidney Cowell)

production shows the bohemian Cowell in his element: a handsome, open-faced sixteen-year-old at the keyboard, his face several days unshaven, his thick, brown, uncombed hair nearly covering the ears and the collar at the back of a rumpled denim shirt. Based on the report of someone who was in attendance, Clarissa wrote that, when the play was over, "the woods rang with Henry's name. [It] was shouted over and over and over. Henry was surrounded by boys offering candy, and by men and women offering congratulations."[53] Upon hearing the music a few months later, a music critic wrote admiringly that it was "a total presentation of chaos which is excellent in conception."[54]

Although Cowell's reputation as a composer was finally gaining momentum, he wrote relatively little in the months following the production of *Creation Dawn*—only one piece in August, four in September, and none during October and November. In December he had a burst of creative energy. Apparently as Christmas presents, he wrote sixteen small pieces, mostly for Carmel children; he also wrote a piano sketch for an orchestral piece and a sonata entitled *Sonate Progressive,* with four derivative movements: "Classic," "Romantic," "Modern," and "Humoreske." After Christmas he wrote no more pieces until March.

The pieces he wrote just after *Creation Dawn* continued to crystallize the stylistic traits that would characterize his style for much of his career. The *Anaemic Rag,* composed that September, provides an apt example. It begins with a perfect-fifth ostinato in the left hand, above which Cowell plays a one-measure syncopated idea in parallel thirds (example 10). He repeats and varies the syncopated idea, transposes the ostinato down a half step, then switches the hands' roles (the ostinato in the right hand, and so on). For a climactic contrasting section, Cowell plays a new chordal syncopated figure; each chord consists of a perfect fifth stacked on top of a minor sixth. Following this the left hand takes up the transposed ostinato, while the right hand plays syncopated triads. This contrasting section lasts six measures, after which Cowell calls for a *da capo* reprise of the opening seventeen measures followed by a six-measure coda with the left hand playing an incessant eighth-quarter-eighth figure. Above it the right hand descends in quarter-note dyads—all perfect fifths, each a half step lower than the previous one, until he arrives at the final dyad, a major sixth on E♭-C, members of the left hand's A♭ major chord.

The *Aenemic Rag* contains many traits that seem now distinctly "Cowellesque." It is riff-based music, a music that thrives on the dauntless repetition of a self-contained one-measure idea. The harmony is in perpetual stasis, with chord successions consisting mainly of chromatic sliding and the "adventurous" harmony consisting of either nonharmonic tones in motion or "wrong-note" harmony, in which a simple idea is made to seem complex

Example 10. *Anaemic Rag*, opening (Reprinted by permission of the David and Sylvia Teitelbaum Fund, as successors to Henry and Sidney Cowell)

by turning octaves into minor ninths (or, in his later pieces, into tone clusters). The only development of material is more or less neo-Baroque. It consists either of sequence or of recalibrating the main motive, changing its characteristic intervals or its contour. But whereas in Baroque music such techniques worked only in conjunction with florid counterpoint and strong harmonic progressions, Cowell pressed the techniques into the service of squared-off measures that were essentially noncontrapuntal, harmonically static, and goalless, yet constantly changing in contour.

What Cowell lacked in traditional developmental skill—or, indeed, interest in development itself—he made up for in zeal. His almost obsessive need to be prolific may have led to the sheer *writing* of notes for their own sake, a cache of notes that sometimes overwhelmed the ideas behind them. But not only could he write pieces at a prodigious rate, he practiced them on the piano assiduously and played them everywhere. During his Carmel period he apparently played for anyone who cared to listen, from music critics to novelists, from senior scholars to poor school children. And people responded by giving him (or his mother) money—a dollar here, a dollar there, accumulating into as much as twenty dollars a month. Often the gifts were anonymous, sometimes arriving in the mail without return address. One of these, addressed to Clarissa in December 1913, carried this note: "Now you do not know me or I do not know you but I know Your Son and I think he will make a great Musician some day I only wish I could do more for you and your Son no one knows anything about this but my own Self or ever will so God Bless You and give you Health and Strength [signed] A Friend."[55]

§ § §

Meanwhile, in the Stanford area, tangible plans were well under way to ensure that Henry would get academic training, seemingly rescuing him (in the minds of some) from the lowbrow rhapsodic vernacularism of the Carmel artists. Cowell had often conversed on academic topics with Stanford professors around the neighborhood and at the El Camino train station where he tried to sell his exotic ferns and flowers. One professor who grew quite fond of Cowell was a Columbia-trained English professor in his late thirties named Samuel S. Seward Jr.

Seward had been teaching at Stanford since 1900 and by 1910 had published two books. Taken together, the books show the scope of his pedagogical interests. His first book was a 500-page anthology of narrative and lyric poetry in English. It heavily favored romantic poets—especially Shelley, Browning, and, above all, Wordsworth—and emphasized themes such as "joy in life," "the world of nature," "the problem of life," and "the imagination." The preface revealed not only his personal romance with poetry (and the desire not to become pedantic about it) but also his belief that a student must test a poem's validity "concretely by his own experience." A student should "wander at will" among poems and if one did not "find friends" among them, one should abandon the study of poetry. His second book was a small text entitled *Note-Taking*. It was written partly "from personal knowledge of the insufficient, jumbled, and often misleading material with which the average student's notebooks are filled."[56] It advocated and explained some disciplined methods of taking notes from a lecture or from books.

Seward, then, strove for balance in the craft of writing. He cherished rhapsody yet insisted on orderliness. If he had to choose between genius without mechanics and mechanics without inspiration, however, he would choose the former—that is, just the sort of style possessed by young Henry Cowell. One incident illustrates this. In teaching a seminar to other English teachers, Seward read an essay that consisted of "a school-boy's description of what caught his eye on a morning after a rain—the reflections of sky and trees in the pools of water on the street." The essay was full of mechanical errors, however, and the class "pounced" on it. After their criticism, Seward said, "Is it possible there is no one of you teachers of English who would give that paper an 'A,' for the good and sufficient reason that this boy had the mind to notice those things and the wish to try to write them down? That is the very stuff of which literature is made."[57]

How Seward came to know Henry Cowell is not known. But as he did, he saw in the boy the same kinds of artistic qualities he had commended to his English-teacher friends. These qualities, as expressed in Cowell's music, spurred Seward to start raising money to send Cowell away to a music school—hopefully in Germany, "where he can get the best instruction obtainable."[58] To heighten interest in his prodigious young friend, Seward organized a 15 January 1914 recital at his next-door neighbors' house (they had more room and a better piano than he did).

The cream of Stanford-area musicians—all women and most of them piano teachers—crowded into the house to hear Henry play pieces he had created and refined in Carmel: *Adventures in Harmony,* excerpts from *Creation Dawn,* his etude entitled *The Cauldron* (the name of a vortex on the Carmel coast), the children's piece *Constance,* named for Herbert Heron's daughter, and his sketches for an orchestral piece. Jaime de Angulo's wife, Cary, attended, but doubted that the staid, well-to-do audience would appreciate the sixteen-year-old's deliberately provocative music. To her amazement, she wrote, "the effect on the audience was delightful to watch, one and all were intensely interested, several of them obviously astounded and delighted." She added that they were "no more amazed at his music than at his incisive way of expressing himself," which she thought more "engaging" than she had ever seen in him.[59] When he had finished, the audience called for encores. After playing them, Henry discussed the pieces with his new admirers and asked what were their favorite pieces. One woman said that hers was *Fairy Dance,* because "it has more consecutive thought in it." Henry replied that "that might be true, but that other pieces had much more worthy thought, & that between worthy thoughts not wholly consecutive & less worthy consecutive ones he felt prouder of the former." The discussion wore on into the night, more so than any other post-recital discussion she had seen, Cary de Angulo wrote. But Henry's mother and Ellen Veblen were not there to witness it: Clarissa had never fully recovered, indeed had worsened, and was being cared for by Veblen in Carmel all that winter.

This recital was a kind of turning point. The *Palo Alto Times,* under the headline "Youthful Wonder Has Charm of Genius," wrote that "everyone" at the recital "proclaimed [Cowell] an artist of unusual talent." The ferocity with which he played, the naive bombast of his musical gestures, and the picturesque California imagery of many of his titles all combined to make him a specimen of the free-spirited and high-spirited temperament that Californians saw as their most precious trait. When Cowell played, he played into his audiences' ideas of themselves. And that, of course, persuaded them to open their pocketbooks. Thus the *Palo Alto Times* article carried this notice: "There is now a movement on foot to provide a fund for [Henry Cowell's] further musical education. All those who desire to contribute to this fund will kindly communicate with Professor Seward at 262 Kingsley Avenue. It is hoped that a sufficient sum can be raised to give this lad an opportunity to excel in his chosen musical art."[60]

The Palo Alto recital led to another one that would forever be enshrined as Cowell's formal "debut." Mrs. Bates, one of the piano teachers who had attended the former recital, arranged to have Cowell appear that March on a program of the San Francisco Musical Club, a high-society showcase for amateur performers.[61] Cowell's performance was scheduled for a Thursday morning program, 5 March 1914, a program that he shared with Mrs. Charles L. Barrett, Emelie Gnauck, and Ernst Wilhelmy. Each participant had twenty minutes; Cowell went last.[62] For his twenty minutes, Cowell played an eclectic assortment of showpieces, which largely reprised his Palo Alto program. He began with his most daring work, *Adventures in Harmony,* with its "hand chords" and "arm chords." He then played three small pieces from *Creation Dawn,* each with a colorful title—*Wind Sprites' Music, Sunset Music,* and *Fairies' Dance.* Next he played the pseudo-romantic slow movement from his Sonata in A Major, "op. 26," which he had dedicated "to mama." He closed with one of his etudes, although it is not clear which one.[63]

The critics from San Francisco's two rival newspapers diverged in their assessment of the Cowell debut. Writing for the *Chronicle,* Anna Cora Winchell lovingly acclaimed the young composers' gifts. She praised the *Creation Dawn* pieces and the Etude, which "was filled with delicious originality of tones in their correlation and written in an intricate style." She reserved her highest praise for *Adventures in Harmony.* That work, she wrote, "shows an unusual grasp on the bigness of color and its value as interpretive of deep feeling, the combination of notes being almost symphonic." The various sections of the work (the "chapters") were "unrhythmical," she conceded, and "attempt[ed] to carry little of melody." But that was not their intention, which, in fact, was "only to express a feeling or picture." For that reason, "the meter constantly changed, but without jar to the ear or conveying the impression that the work is out of time." All in all, Winchell considered Cowell gifted but nonetheless modest, "a clever young lad who offered his natural gifts without egotism or frenzy."[64]

The critic for the *Examiner,* however, was more reserved. Redfern Mason— a fellow Irishman who was a frequent enough visitor to Carmel that he may have already heard Cowell there—wrote: "Mr. Cowell has talent. I am convinced of that. But he needs a thorough schooling, and I think he will repay it. . . . [His compositions] are very lawless; they do not show much melodic originality. They are dithyrambic impressionizing without so much as a hint of counterpoint." He faulted Cowell for laying out idea after idea then going nowhere with them: Cowell, he said, "has not the faintest idea of what is meant by development." He recommended that the boy get "several years drill in a conservatory," preferably in Germany, away from "idolizing womenfolk who mistake anarchistic rhapsodizing for inspiration." Nevertheless, Mason admitted, despite Cowell's lack of training, "this boy of sixteen succeeds in getting his effects 'across the footlights'. . . in a way that, to my mind, argues talent."[65]

After the reviews came out Cowell wrote to his mother that the concert was "a success," partly because he was "not so nervous" as at earlier performances. He then urged her to read the *Chronicle* for the "best notice."[66] Clarissa, however, upon reading the *Examiner* review, let loose her own barrage of verbiage on critics such as Mason, who "expecting weaknesses, are determined to find them. So, departures from ancient law are set down as breaches of musical taste instead of efforts to win for musical art a freedom already partly achieved by artists of the brush." Rules, she said, are "indispensable to mediocrity and useful to modest talent." But "they hamper genius, which learns them in order to break them with larger wisdom."[67] Unfortunately, she did not read the *Chronicle*'s glowing review until Harry brought it to her in the hospital, where she had just undergone her second surgery for breast cancer.[68]

Despite the ambivalence of the critics toward Henry's "anarchistic rhapsodizing," the San Francisco Musical Club recital became a milestone and a myth in Cowell's career. He referred to it throughout his life as his threshold into professional musical life—although he routinely rolled back its date to 1912 to make himself seem more precocious and claimed that at this recital he premiered one of his most famous tone cluster pieces, the *Tides of Manaunaun,* which he in fact did not write down until at least 1917.[69] While he had played for bigger and perhaps more like-minded audiences, this was the first time Cowell had gotten big-city newspaper reviews, the first time the estranged bohemian had been welcomed by high society and praised by a professional music critic. But it was also the first time a critic said in print what critics were to say throughout his career: he had ideas but didn't know how to develop them.

When Clarissa Dixon pulled her son out of public school, she both blessed and cursed him. She ensured that he could follow his own interests and learn at his own pace. But she risked cutting him off from the academic culture through which he could someday promulgate his ideas. Although Clarissa wanted her son to exemplify her Spencerian ideals, by his midteens Henry seemed doomed to life as a kind of idiot savant: he could impress people with his quirky and mystifying piano pieces, but might never be taken seriously enough to support himself as a musician. So for now he was only a brilliant janitor working at a high school he was not allowed to attend. All of this changed when a few neighbors rallied to rescue Cowell from his precarious state by sending him to school.

3

Trusting His Muse to a Guiding Intellect

When Henry played his San Francisco debut in March 1914, Clarissa lay in Mary's Help Hospital awaiting another operation (performed free because of her poverty). After her discharge, she went to a friend's home and Henry resumed his visits to Carmel, where he played occasional concerts, basking in the goodwill of the patrons who had come to consider him a prodigy. Not only did he make about fifteen dollars a concert in donations, but some of his audience gave him clothes and a haircut to transform his appearance from an unwashed bohemian into an almost dashing blue-eyed Irish gent.[1] Meanwhile, he reveled in the cultural affairs of the Monterey Bay area, playing music that Veblen called "interestingly crooked," or appearing dressed as Wagner at a local soiree, or attending mission services, or even writing a few verses of Carmel-style poetry. Although he would later identify himself as a Protestant, his attendance at Catholic services with Veblen led to one of his few recorded comments on Christian religion, an apparent attempt at blending Jesus' teachings with the naturalistic religion of his community: "[Henry] said . . . that the whole law was 'Love thy neighbor as thyself,' & he trusted God was our neighbor."[2] The handful of his poems that survive from 1914 not surprisingly dwell on nature and freedom. One in particular is a kind of bohemian declaration on the refusal of the natural elements to be bound by man's categorical expectations.

> The moon with malice aforethought will shine,
> The sun, also, unpredictably,
> For when the weather man says it's fine
> And he has the elements all in line,
> They break loose from their bonds and are free.[3]

During the summer of 1914, while not spending time around Carmel, Henry was staying with Harry and Henrietta in San Francisco. At this time, Harry began to involve himself more deeply in Henry's life, partly from paternal love and perhaps partly from a desire to leave an artistic legacy for himself. From the 1910s on, as his third wife said, "Harry who failed to communicate his art to the world, lived as an artist through the creative expression of his very own son."[4] Harry nourished that creative expression by giving Henry a base from which to attend more elaborate and sophisticated concerts than he could ever hear in Carmel or Menlo Park. It was in the summer of 1914, for example, that Henry first recalled hearing the music of Schoenberg, the lushly romantic First String Quartet (although a recurrence of chorea forced him to attend the recital on crutches).[5]

Inspired by the comparatively rich musical culture of the big city, the young Cowell produced no fewer than thirty new pieces that summer. He wrote four songs, one of which was his first setting of a poem by his mother. He also wrote a batch of frankly academic piano pieces, among which were an etude, a set of theme and variations, three sonata movements (each in a different key), and four "imitations" of the styles of Chopin, Brahms, Schumann, and Grieg. Also among the pieces he composed were sixteen musical "letters" to Mrs. Veblen. One of these, which he called *Mad Dance* (later renamed *Anger Dance*), was inspired by the muscle spasm in his leg that had kept him on crutches. Cowell saw a doctor who reportedly said that surgery was the only remedy for the chronic pain and spasticity. He urged him to have it done immediately. Cowell declined and on the way back to his father's house imagined the music to the *Mad Dance*.[6]

The work, although not one of Cowell's more celebrated, may be one of the most prescient: a proto-minimalist piece that repeats the same quasi-cadential measures incessantly (see example 11). Cowell begins this B minor piece with a single two-measure idea (A) to be repeated ten times, followed by its transposition at the subdominant (A^1) eight more times. A variant appears for four measures, followed by the return of A (four times), another four-measure variant, then A (four times) and so forth. The mere thirty-two measures of written music expands in performance to a full one hundred measures, most of those being exactly the same and all the others being simple variants (sequences, sometimes slightly altered in pitch or rhythm). The stubbornness of the music depicts well the sense of frustration Cowell must have felt. But the context of the piece also provided him an unusual opportunity to spin a great deal of real-time sound from a minimal idea.

Cowell played *Mad Dance* and other works he wrote that summer at his

Example 11. *Mad Dance* (later renamed *Anger Dance*), opening

second San Francisco recital, July 1914. Walter Anthony of the *San Francisco Chronicle* reviewed the occasion, noting that the young pianist was the son of "Henry Cowell [Sr.], well known to local letters, and Clarissa Dixon, whose identification with Western Art is perhaps even more secure." The review criticized Cowell's poor technique: "That [Cowell] had enjoyed no digital instruction was apparent. That he needed it was." But the review praised Cowell's independence of mind as a composer who wrote things that "older minds would like, but might fear to write." *Mad Dance,* it somewhat ambiguously said, "shouldn't have been written by any one less old than Rachmaninoff or Tchaikovsky. It contained the erotic effort of the former and the latter." In summation, the reviewer uttered what had by now become the standard criticism of Cowell: "The lad . . . is a genius who will surprise you, but who now stands in need of the steadying hand of instruction."[7]

When Cowell returned to Menlo Park in September, he made final preparations to spend his education fund on some kind of formal training. Probably as part of these preparations, he composed his opus 100—a forty-four-page, ten-movement suite he called *Resumé,* which, as the title suggests, was a compendium of his achievements as a composer thus far.

In later years, when his reputation as a modernist was secure, Cowell would blanch at the idea of imitating older composers: "the modernist," he wrote, "believes in actually emulating the old masters—not by trying to imitate their style, as that is *not* emulating them, but to do as they did in creating a new style of their own. . . . If a composer of today really admires [the old masters] he will not imitate their style."[8] But in *Resumé,* as in almost all of the music he wrote while a teenager, Cowell slavishly and systematically echoed the music of the past. Each of the movements is in a different style. The D minor allegretto "Savage" provides the primitivist opening of the suite, using incessant tonic harmony and repeated-note rhythmic figures (example 12). This movement is followed by a pseudo-Bachian "Choral[e]" in E minor—complete with an anachronistic trio section and *da capo* return of the opening chorale material. The third movement, a prelude and fugue, transparently borrows from the opening prelude of Bach's *Well-Tempered Clavier,* yet displays in the three-voice fugue how uncertain Cowell was with both the harmonic framework and the contrapuntal details of the style (example 13). The A minor "Classic Sonata" that follows reveals the lack of development criticized by some of Cowell's hearers—the persistent repeated chords and left-hand figurations, the relatively directionless phrases, and the continual return to a few brief rhythmic figures. The fifth movement, "Folk Music," has been lost.

The next two movements evoke nineteenth-century styles. "Romantic"

Example 12. *Resumé*, "Savage," opening (Reprinted by permission of the David and Sylvia Teitelbaum Fund, as successors to Henry and Sidney Cowell)

Example 13. *Resumé*, fugue, opening (Reprinted by permission of the David and Sylvia Teitelbaum Fund, as successors to Henry and Sidney Cowell)

divides into the submovements called "earlier"—a simple waltz in E♭—and "later," which begins slowly and gradually accelerates into an *allegro non troppo* "development section," so marked (which, in fact doesn't "develop" anything). "Operatic" likewise has a waltz as its first part, then provides a second part made of pseudo-Wagnerian dramatic flourishes.

Cowell titles the final two movements "Oriental" and "Modern." The former predictably uses only the black keys in a *lento placido* pentatonic evocation of the Asian music Cowell had come to know in San Francisco. "Modern" is the only movement in three distinct parts. The first, subtitled "earlier modern, in the form of a sonate in one movement," is, again, a waltz—only now featuring Debussian added-note harmony and Schoenbergian silent depressing of the left-hand keys. Part two is a simple rag in A minor, which is followed by the ostensibly most adventurous part of the whole suite, subtitled "futurist, in form of a coda-cadenza." Surprisingly, this movement omits the clusters that Cowell had used in *Adventures in Harmony.* Instead, its harmony consists almost entirely of augmented triads and quartal chords (each consisting of a perfect fourth and an augmented fourth; example 14). These chords are rapidly repeated and transposed, dissonantly echoing the "Grand Manner" opening of *Adventures in Harmony.* The manner with which the movement closes rounds out the whole suite: what began as primitivist had come full circle as futurist. *Resumé,* if not Cowell's most forward-looking work to date, was his most ambitious. It was a forceful, self-disciplined attempt at showing he had assimilated, more or less, the styles of classical music's great composers. He played it for his mother and Ellen Veblen, who took rhapsodic delight in the work, considering it his best so far.[9]

§ § §

In 1912 a charismatic young music professor had taken a teaching post across the bay in Berkeley. Charles Louis Seeger Jr., though raised in utterly different circumstances from Cowell, had assimilated a similarly quirky mix of vernacular and learned styles. Moving frequently between New York and Mexico, Seeger's parents had brought him up on a mixture of South American folk music and European masterworks. In 1904 Seeger went to Harvard to study music and began to hear the work of modern composers; he especially grew to like Debussy, Mahler, Scriabin, and Satie. In 1908 he graduated magna cum laude and moved to Germany, where he apprenticed in conducting and began to compose what he called "the first American opera of any stature," with a story focussing on the unionization of American workers. In 1911 Seeger moved to New York and in 1912 accepted an offer to become a full professor

Example 14. *Resumé,* "Futurist" (complete) (Reprinted by permission of the David and Sylvia Teitelbaum Fund, as successors to Henry and Sidney Cowell)

teaching music at the University of California at what was then its only campus, Berkeley.[10]

Like Stanford, this university was a relatively lonely and isolated place for its faculty, with no professional colleagues to the north and west, a handful to the south, and many to the east—but hundreds of miles away. Also like Stanford, its isolation made it a perfect place to develop fresh, independent, and speculative ideas. Its landscape was breathtaking: broad hills sloping up eastward from the bay and natural amphitheaters richly vegetated with shrubs, wildflowers, and a strange assortment of palm trees, oaks, evergreens, and eucalyptus. Outside the gates of the rustic campus ran several bustling streets framed by three- and four-story storefronts, the pavement between them crisscrossed with rail tracks and, above them, a network of suspended telephone wires and electric streetcar cables.

When Seeger arrived in 1912, the school had twenty-five music students, but no music department. (He was hired to replace a departing faculty member whose position had been an adjunct to the Department of Agriculture.) Music classes were being taught in various buildings on and off campus. Most of the classes took place in what Seeger called "an old, smelly house on Bancroft [Avenue]."[11]

By 1914 Seeger had established a complete music history course and a large choir that could perform in various styles. At the same time, he became engrossed in social causes, especially those of underprivileged and dispossessed immigrants. His growing social consciousness, especially after the outbreak of the World War, dissuaded him from taking part in what seemed an elitist Western musical tradition. By 1914 he virtually abandoned composing—partly because, as he said, "I could not reconcile the 'ideals' that had dominated my composition up to that time with the growing consciousness of the nature of geographical and social struggles of large masses of people."[12]

Accounts vary as to how Cowell became interested in Seeger's program at Berkeley. As early as October 1913, when he was visiting his father in San Francisco, Henry wrote to his mother that he had "met and pleased" Seeger's colleague E. G. Stricklen, who "offered me the University course he gives at Berkeley, and will introduce me to Seeger, who composes also."[13] But two articles published in the mid-1920s trace Cowell's meeting with Seeger to a chance encounter with a San Francisco Symphony player. Supposedly, the player was walking through the foothills of Menlo Park and overheard Cowell playing the piano in his cabin. In one account, the musician knocked at the door and asked Henry whose music he was playing. Henry answered that he was playing his own pieces, whereupon the musician effusively praised the boy. The player told

Henry Hadley, the symphony's director, about what he had heard, convincing him that Cowell was a genius. In turn, Hadley helped arrange a fund to enroll the young man in the University of California to study with Seeger.[14] The other account of this same episode seems embellished to the point of incredibility:

> One night . . . as the boy sat playing in the dark (they could not afford candles) a well known musician from the San Francisco Orchestra knocked on the door and burst into the room.
>
> "I know all the beautiful music in the world," he cried, "but the music that comes from this cabin I have never heard before. It is powerful yet strange music. Who wrote it? Who plays it?"
>
> "I play it," said the boy. The musician was suspicious and annoyed.
>
> "But who writes it?"
>
> "I write it," said the boy proudly.
>
> The man was furious. He thought he saw a child trying to steal an artist's work. He artistically, temperamentally, exploded. He raged and cuffed Cowell for being a liar. Half terrified, half angry, the boy ran to the piano and pulled from the floor behind it sheet after sheet of his compositions until the musician stood silenced and amazed. . . .
>
> The musician took him to see Charles Louis Seeger.[15]

Both of these accounts may have some basis in fact (although it is doubtful that Hadley was involved with Cowell's education fund). But Seeger himself recalls it quite differently. While shopping around the Bay Area for a music teacher for his son, Seeger said, Harry brought Henry to Seeger's house on La Loma Avenue, Berkeley, during the early fall of 1914. (Seeger even recalls his impression of Henry's father at that meeting: Harry was "a pretty weak sister, just on the edge of silliness.")[16] Henry played Seeger his *Adventures in Harmony* and one of his most recent pieces, the Minuettino, opus 108. Seeger then showed him several of his own pieces, Scriabin's opus 74, some Stravinsky, and Schoenberg's opus 11; of the latter Cowell remembers him saying, "You might like to see how someone else has handled similar problems."[17] Cowell impressed Seeger enough that the young professor agreed to teach him.

Seeger proposed a course of study that showed his growing ambivalence toward musical academics. He recalls that he felt Henry "had gone too far along his own lines suddenly to stop and submit to a system of training which had for some time been showing signs of weakening both in Europe and in America. On the other hand, we did not wish to ignore it entirely, since no substitute was at hand."[18] So Seeger arranged for Cowell to take regular harmony and counterpoint classes with colleagues and to explore "free composition" with Seeger at his home on Thursday afternoons. Through his education fund Cowell had the money to pay for all this (and the train fare to Berkeley). But he lacked the academic credentials—he had never spent more than a week in school. Seeger thought that Cowell showed enough promise to get him "special student" status.

On Tuesday, 15 September 1914, Cowell began classes at Berkeley. For the next two semesters he left his mother to stay at Harry's house from Tuesday through Thursday, taking the train up the peninsula on Tuesday morning, attending classes that afternoon and again on Thursday (including his lesson with Seeger). He studied with a variety of full- and part-time teachers at Berkeley. The most venerable and conservative was Cowell's counterpoint teacher, Wallace Sabin, an Oxford-trained British organist in his mid-forties.[19] Closer to Seeger in spirit was Edward Griffith Stricklen, known to his colleagues as "E. G." Born in Oakland in 1880, E. G. had been trained in local schools, then became a "reader" (just below "instructor") on the U. C. Berkeley faculty in 1912.[20] The composer Leon Kirchner later recalled that Stricklen "sat in a constant cloud of smoke," his features "prominent" and "usually inflamed, whether from allergies or alcohol it was difficult to determine." A fastidious dresser, "self-contained" in his demeanor, Stricklen lived in a hotel room stuffed with books. Kirchner recalls that Stricklen's books, like his conversations, ranged from Schopenhauer to the Cabala. He "displayed an almost compulsive rationalism in class," but at night became "a seeker of divine potencies," a mystical thinker whose interests lay in "the area between the 'phenomenal' and the 'noumenal.'"[21] Given Henry's background, he undoubtedly warmed to this sort of mentor. And Stricklen had another credential, a link to Harry and Clarissa Cowell's literary circle—he was a member of the San Francisco Bohemian Club. Indeed, Stricklen, Wallace Sabin, Charles Seeger, and even Cowell's piano teacher at Berkeley, Uda Waldrop, had all composed large-scale musical works for the Bohemian Club.

In teaching the kind of theory that pertained to modern music, Cowell's professors had little to go on, except for a common interest to justify all harmonic structures by referring to the overtone series (the natural spectrum of higher pitches produced whenever a single tone is sounded). In the latter half of the nineteenth century, British music theorists such as Alfred Day and Ebenezer Prout had tried to show how all scales are derived from the overtone series (although they assumed the validity of equal temperament and picked and chose whichever overtones fit their paradigm).[22] In 1892 Percy Goetschius, the German emigré sometimes referred to as the "father of American theory," presented the idea of having various *ratios* in the overtone series generate all other tones. Still, he would not allow the legitimacy of chords larger than ninth chords. In their book entitled *Modern Harmony in Its Theory and Practice* (1905), Foote and Spalding were more generous, allowing for overtone-based chords that contained elevenths and thirteenths—thus legitimizing the harmonies of composers like Debussy and even Schoenberg.

Continuing in this line of thinking, Seeger and Stricklen jointly wrote the first-year harmony text from which Cowell studied; Stricklen alone wrote the second-year text. In these two slim books—less than forty pages each—Seeger and Stricklen said that they had three aims in their harmony instruction: to explain the logic of harmonic structure, to convey the principles underlying European music, and to instruct budding composers.[23] About this latter aim, Seeger wrote in terms that suggested the premises on which he taught Cowell:

> The young composer [may] be aware of the modern spirit and his relationship to it, whether or not he intends trusting his muse to a guiding intellect, a truant fancy or to somewhat of both. For whether the musician of the older school, who relies upon "pure instinct" or taste for his authority, likes it or not, one can no longer ignore the persistent demand from a younger generation, born and bred in an age of increasing scientific activity, for reasons and explanations instead of the dumb rules and empirical subterfuges which in no great living composer are regarded; further, one cannot remain blind to the forces which set art in motion or to the forces art sets in motion, because, together with the seemingly last gasps of romantic phantasy has appeared a tenuous, at least, scientific explanation for many of the foibles hitherto most jealously guarded by the artistic temperament as strictly private property.

Following this circuitous reasoning, Seeger and Stricklen began the course with two premises. First, music should have "one fundamental scheme" from which rhythm, tone, and form all derive. Second, "a science of harmony may be based upon certain physical laws deduced from phenomena observed in the production of tone"—in other words, the overtone series. Thus, at the beginning of the course, the student was to learn the ratios of the overtone series through the first six partials, knowing that these ratios were the core of the "fundamental scheme" that should govern all aspects of music. These two notions, as we shall see, had an immeasurable effect on Cowell's way of thinking about, talking about, writing about, and writing music for the rest of his career.

Although Cowell learned these two fundamental premises during his first semester, he wrote no particularly ambitious works during those months. From October through December 1914, he recorded in his logbook that he wrote twenty-three pieces. Yet all but one of these pieces—a four-part setting of a poem by Sam Seward—were for solo piano or voice and piano. Of the latter group at least eleven were children's songs, settings of poems from Robert Louis Stevenson's *A Child's Garden of Verse* or from Clarissa's book *Janet and Her Dear Phebe.* Of the entire group of twenty-three works from this semester only eight survive, and five of those are less than seventeen measures apiece.

During the first half of 1915, Clarissa's health steadily declined. Cowell nevertheless continued making regular train trips to Berkeley, returning at night to tend his mother. Under his Berkeley mentors, he began two large-scale works that were completed the following semester: a twenty-three page three-movement sonata for cello and piano (finished in March 1915) and another three-movement piece entitled *Scenario,* scored for two violins, cello, and piano (finished in April). From January through August of 1915 Cowell completed not only these two large works, but a handful of songs, and four small instrumental pieces—now lost except for one (a minuet for string quartet). He also made ambitious plans for new large works, about which his mother boasted in letters to friends, letters that seem to be often fanciful if not delirious. She wrote that in the summer of 1915 Henry had actually composed a five-part orchestral piece for Seeger based on an "outline" by Jaime de Angulo.[24] (No such work survives and Henry never recorded it in his list of works for that year.) In July she had yet another operation, this time to remove five small tumors.[25] By August, Clarissa wrote, Henry had conceived a "bold plan to represent the chief passions, especially the most primal, rising at the last to love universal."[26] Again, it is unclear what work of Henry's fulfilled this plan. To the contrary, Cowell's surviving works from his first year at Berkeley continue in the path he had already begun: short piano solos and songs (especially settings of his mother's poetry), and music for the kids in Carmel.

This fascination with children's music perhaps mirrored Cowell's continuing social isolation. Before college, he had associated almost exclusively with adults—his mother, her literary friends, and local professors. He had not taken part in sports or recreations other than bike riding. "As I child, [I] did not have many playmates," he later recalled, and while attending Berkeley "I did not enter . . . into any college social activities."[27] Moreover, his fellow students at Berkeley viewed him as a curiosity, not only for his lack of schooling and social graces, but for his poor grooming. At the time, Seeger bluntly recalls, Henry "was the dirtiest little shrimp you ever ran into."[28] Back in Menlo Park he kept his hair long and did not shave, prompting some of the neighbors to forcibly shave him.[29] Although he had gradually begun to refine his appearance (partly at Ellen Veblen's urging), Cowell still lived by his mother's teaching on the subject: she forcefully rejected the importance that her neighbors placed on personal grooming, explaining that "Cleanliness may be next to godliness, as we have been taught, but it is not godliness. . . . Appearance is much but character is infinitely more."[30] Now, at Berkeley, three female up-perclassmen complained to Seeger about Cowell's scruffiness, hoping he could get Cowell to clean himself up. Seeger protested that he had tried to do so, unsuccessfully. The young women asked permission to take matters into their own hands. Seeger recalls that they took Henry to the upstairs bathroom of the music house on Bancroft, "gave him soap and a towel and said 'Henry, take a bath.' And he did."[31]

Clarissa's disapproval of male-female relationships also strained Henry's social life. On 7 April 1914 he had written to his mother that he would be attending a dance at the Arts and Crafts Hall in Carmel, apparently his first dance. Henry recalls that he danced with and soon fell in love with a girl about his age (possibly Edna Smith). Upon learning this, Clarissa chided her son, using the same arguments that she had used in abandoning sexual relations with Henry's father: "[My mother], for the first time, gave me a talk on sex matters, one which influenced me very profoundly at the time, on account of the unusually close relation between us. It was only over a period of years, and by very gradual degrees, that I came to realize the unsoundness of her views. She . . . stressed that it was wicked even to think of a girl in that way."[32] Hopelessly devoted to his mother, Cowell tried to cease taking romantic interest in girls.

He did cultivate platonic relationships, however, one of which was with May Glynn. In the summer of 1915 Cowell had begun collaborating with Glynn, a soprano, performing with her and using her home as a studio. By the close of the year, they were placing advertisements in the *Palo Alto Times* for vocal lessons from her and "piano and harmony" lessons from him. In August 1915 they gave a joint recital at Glynn's house, a block away from the Seward home on Kingsley Avenue. In reviewing that recital, the *Times* was quick to point out that Henry was only eighteen years old, had not even had a year's instruction in music, and had written all his pieces on the program previous to any lessons at all.[33] In other words, the university training he had gotten did not affect his choice of repertoire—the old, untutored work he apparently still thought his best.

Within two weeks of this recital, Henry began his second year at Berkeley. Because his classes were now on Monday, Wednesday, and Friday, and because he had to assume more of the housework than ever—cooking, cleaning, and hosting visitors—he traveled back and forth to Berkeley three times a week. And because he had become the sole breadwinner, he also took on nine piano students and two voice students.[34] Clarissa's health continued to fail and on 17 December she went to Peninsula Hospital for still more surgery.[35]

As 1916 opened, Charles Seeger commenced his first course in "dissonant counterpoint." This method was his playfully subversive attempt to stand the traditional methods of writing counterpoint on their head. Seeger had his students deliberately write melodies and harmonies according to a hierarchy of dissonance. Minor seconds, major sevenths, and all compound versions of those intervals were "perfect dissonances," the most "stable" intervals in the system. Next came the "imperfect dissonances"—major seconds, minor sevenths, and all compound forms of those intervals. The weakest of the dissonances, the tritone, he said was "by itself . . . practically consonant."[36] The other intervals were consonances and therefore to be used only transiently, leading on to dissonances. As one would expect, Seeger devised systematic and quite complex methods for connecting and combining these intervals.

But as he had suggested in his theory of traditional harmony, Seeger proposed to derive rhythm from the same "fundamental scheme" as harmony. "Rhythmic dissonance" consisted of superimposed pulsations that followed the ratios of the overtone series. "Mild" rhythmic dissonances occurred when one played 3, 5, 7, or 9 against 2—for example, an eighth-note triplet played against two eighth notes, an eighth-note quintuplet played against two quarter notes, and so forth. "Medium" rhythmic dissonances occurred when one played 4 or 5 against 3. And "strong" rhythmic dissonances occurred when one played 7 or 8 against 3; or, 5, 7, or 9 against 4. Any of these rhythmic dissonances could be used to enliven the texture of a piece just as pitch dissonances could enliven its harmonic fabric.

Cowell did some routine exercises for this course and took detailed notes that he wrote up into short paragraphs. Sometime that spring, after Seward returned from six months in Belgium, Henry asked the English professor to help him make these paragraphs more readable. Seward, who had literally written the book on how to organize one's lecture notes, agreed to help.

From January through May 1916, Cowell logged in seventeen pieces, most of them like the works he had completed the previous fall semester, including song settings of poems by Ellen Veblen, George Sterling, and of course, Clarissa Dixon. Eleven of these pieces are lost, and most of those that survive are quite brief. The one moderate-sized work is the "Quartett Pedantic," a ten-page string quartet manuscript that mixes contrapuntal procedures with the harmonic idiom of dissonant counterpoint. The first movement of this two-movement work divides into two parts. The first features all four instruments playing more or less continuously for forty-three measures in a series of contrasting episodes. Because the ostensible climax, the highpoint of activity and dynamics, arrives at m. 12, the rest of the section seems somewhat directionless. To restore the contrapuntal interest, the second section presents a strict thirty-six-measure canon, using the same one-measure motivic material as the first section. The second movement consists entirely of a series of slow sustained chords for twenty-five measures.

During the spring 1916 semester Cowell also performed perhaps his most important recital so far: a highly publicized concert in Palo Alto High School gym, featuring sixteen of his original works. Although extremely conservative in musical content—at least by Cowell's later standards—the recital was a community event, a time for neighbors to gather and reflect on the fruits of their renowned charity project. In announcing the recital, the *Palo Alto Times* noted that "the boy who has come down from his little home in the hills [to play] original pieces of his own composing" now had obtained "the severe disciplinary training that must be the foundation of every important accomplishment in music." No doubt referring to the patrons of Cowell's education fund, the paper noted that "a growing body of friends has followed these studies in expectation of seeing them develop into musical compositions of genuine significance." This recital would be "the first opportunity in more than a year for Palo Alto to note for itself the progress that the recent months have accomplished." But the recital seemed almost to have been reviewed before it commenced: the *Times* published the entire program under the headline "Local Musical Genius Gives Recital Tonight." The final review, not surprisingly, again proclaimed Cowell a "genius," one whose compositions "are chiefly remarkable for their striking originality and freshness of appeal. . . . [their] wealth of new and distinctive rhythms, chords and melodies." Among the favorites of the evening, according to the reviewer, were the *Anger Dance* (formerly *Mad Dance*) and the *Savage Dance*—both written before Cowell had begun his studies at Berkeley—and the three Clarissa Dixon settings that concluded Henry's performance. The last of these, a setting of *My Auntie* from *Janet and Her Dear Phebe,* was his mother's most forceful anticlassicist statement. This piece, the *Times* reported, was "most descriptive and had to be repeated."[37]

It was perhaps a touching tribute, this encore ovation for the union of a mother's poetry and son's music. The sixty-four-year-old Clarissa's body was now riddled with cancer. Three months later she died. The *Palo Alto Times* lamented that "a brave, gentle life has gone out." It praised Dixon's legacy: "With a childlike directness of vision she saw the evils of her times and enlisted on the side of freedom, justice and every organized movement that sought to lift the human mind from its dark traditions."[38] The *Times* also printed a poem, one of her last, written within the month. The poem, "Capriccioso," bespeaks the same dreamy self-absorption, desire to transcend boundaries, and pursuit of boundless potential that had characterized her last years with Henry:

> Am I new?
> Some part of me is older than the planet,
> Burdened heavily with experience,
> With chaotic, formless, blundering, unappropriated knowledge.
> Am I old?
> Something that is part of myself is lulled by the vagueness of the
> newborn.
> Daily I pass through raw fields of disturbing knowledges
>   to flat, insipid, tranquil infancy;
> Yet, other times, as one somewhat more grown, though knowing
> nothing,
>   I am vivid with amazements, curiosities,
> Bounding to worlds beyond limits,
> An explorer bent upon discovery,
> To whom liberty, itself, is not free enough.
> Space is not wide enough.
> Knowledge is of the future.
> Nothing is finished.
> Few things are begun.

On May 17, two days after she died, Henry and his half-brother, Clarence Davidson of the *Des Moines News,* held a small, private burial service in Palo Alto. Henry then left Menlo Park to live for the time being at Jaime de Angulo's house in Big Sur, where his secret patron Edna Smith, having just closed her school in Carmel, was also staying.[39] In June his visit was "cut short" by a call from Berkeley to be a reader for summer school classes, his first job as a bona fide academic.[40]

Henry never seems to have spoken of his mother's death. While they were extraordinarily close, Cowell must have felt some relief at her passing, given the wrenching demands on a teenager to be her constant caretaker and the recipient of her most repressive views. Yet Henry must also have felt her continuing presence in his life, given his remark in 1932: "I have never been able to feel a sense of separation through death."[41] In any case, the demands of the summer teaching job and the emotional toll of Clarissa's death seem to have combined to temporarily halt Cowell's composing. That summer he wrote only one piece, a song (now lost) entitled "Children Shall Cry."

Clarissa's death meant that Henry could now study, create, and travel, freed from the responsibility of feeding and caring for an invalid. Seeger suggested that Cowell enroll that fall at the Institute of Musical Art (later renamed the Juilliard School) in New York, founded and directed by Frank Damrosch. Seeger had close ties to the institute, then a conservatory housed in a five-story brick building on the corner of 122d Street and Claremont Avenue. He had worked there as an accompanist and in 1911 met his wife-to-be Constance there; she had been a scholarship student at the institute, a protégé of Damrosch himself. Although Cowell had formerly determined never to return to New York, he honored Seeger's advice and, with the help of his education fund, enrolled at the institute.

He could scarcely have been prepared for the institute's rigorous, musically orthodox regimen. As Damrosch explained on the school's opening day in 1905: "There is a need . . . for a music institution, which like any of our higher institutions of learning should be in a position to say, 'Thou shalt learn these things'; that the institution should direct the study of the student, and not the student the work of the institution."[42] Damrosch insisted that his school teach students the canons of proper music-making and promote musical respectability. The academic curriculum was led by German scholars such as Percy Goetschius and Henry Krehbiel, whose artistic values resembled those of Henry's old violin teacher more than those of California bohemianism.

About six hundred (mostly well-to-do) students were enrolled at the institute when Cowell arrived—a late arrival, as it turned out, since the term had begun in mid-October, and school records show Cowell did not enroll until November. It is not clear at which level of instruction Cowell enrolled, but the institute assigned him, like every student, to a prescribed set of courses. Cowell bristled at this, as well as to the musical conservatism that surrounded him, a far cry from what he had known at Berkeley: "Everyone here composes along old lines, or merely stupid new ones, using discords without reason."[43]

But, as when he was a boy, Henry soaked up the cultural life of New York. He saw the Ballet Russe perform Stravinsky's *Petrushka,* the music of which he considered "unmentionably lovely . . . so strange, yet lyric."[44] He heard Paderewski play and wrote to Veblen enthusiastically about the pianist's virtuosity.[45] He attended a Metropolitan Opera performance of Wagner's *Tristan und Isolde* and excitedly wrote that "I never enjoyed music as I did last night . . . for while in a concert they mix bad and good, this is great from start to finish."[46] Above all other performers and composers, however, Cowell was taken with the radical young composer-pianist Leo Ornstein.

It is difficult now to imagine how much attention Ornstein received in those years—international tours, controversial reviews, lengthy articles about him in prestigious journals such as the *North American Review,* the *Onlooker,* the *Dial,* and the *Musical Quarterly,* at least one book chapter about him and then even an entire book—all before 1920. Less than five years older than Cowell, Ornstein had become known as a "futurist" pianist, whose self-performed compositions portrayed the speed, aggression, and mechanization of modern life.[47] His most daring piano technique was to rapidly repeat closely spaced "chords" made out of seconds. As the *Musical Quarterly* explained in 1918: "Ornstein gives us masses of shrill, hard dissonances, chords consisting of anywhere from eight to a dozen notes made up out of half tones heaped upon one another."[48] To play such chords, according to the London *Daily Telegraph,* Ornstein would place the fingers "close together, stiffening the hands and striking alternately down on the keyboard perpendicularly in ramrod fashion as hard as possible [and] slapping the upper notes . . . in the bass."[49] The effect of this was clear to the critic Lawrence Gilman: "sometimes . . . it seems as if a maniacal rage possessed [Ornstein], and you think he must surely be beating the keyboard furiously with both fists."[50]

Ornstein's clusters—as heard in pieces like his "Wild Men's Dance," published in 1915—generally differed from the broad gong-like chords of Cowell's *Adventures in Harmony.* Ornstein preferred only two or three adjacent seconds at once, which often appear as clumps of notes within larger chords, played rapidly. But Ornstein's explanation of how he came upon these clusters did resemble Cowell's: the clusters came to his imagination first, uncontrollably, and he transcribed them to the keyboard.[51] He had little interest in the sort of clusters Cowell had tried, however, as he later explained: "By the time that you put so many minor seconds together, the inside would become absolutely muddy and would become black."[52]

Ornstein had not only perfected new ways of playing the piano, he had also mastered the art of attracting an audience amid the glutted musical marketplace of New York City. When, in November 1916, the pianist performed a Saturday afternoon recital at Aeolian Hall, the *New York Times* reviewer was bewildered by it. But, he wrote, Ornstein had discovered how to make a name for oneself in an otherwise routine musical world: "For any pianist to delight, puzzle and amuse an audience is distinctly something, and Mr. Ornstein should be counted a happy young man that he has found the way."[53] Ornstein himself was well aware that the sideshow atmosphere of his concerts had secured his reputation. In 1916 he described his first "futurist" recital in this way: "The crowd whistled and howled and even threw handy missiles on the stage . . . but that concert made me famous."[54]

Soon after Cowell arrived at the institute, he began to write to Ellen Veblen admiringly about Ornstein, praising his piano technique, the brilliance of his compositions, and telling how much he would like to meet him and study with him.[55] After hearing Ornstein play in his November 1916 Aeolian Hall recital, which included works by Korngold, for example, Cowell wrote to Veblen that Ornstein's technique was better than Paderewski's, that it was "so fine that it is like a magnificent structure." Moreover, Korngold's compositions "sound very pale beside the really magnificent work of Ornstein."[56] In March 1917 Cowell explained to Lewis Terman more about his interest in Ornstein's compositions. After attending a concert (not by Ornstein), Cowell said, he started reading a magazine to help him relax. The magazine contained an article on Ornstein, including some fragments of his compositions as illustrations. Terman quoted Cowell as saying that this article and musical excerpts "aroused me to such a pitch of excitement that I could not sleep at all. I lay awake all night thinking of the genius of Ornstein."[57]

Cowell hoped to meet Ornstein and would later tell a newspaper reporter how he was finally able to do so. The reporter wrote: "A musician spoke to Ornstein of Cowell, but he refused to meet him [until] the musician said: 'Leo, you are foolish; this young man is more modern in his compositions than you.' This interested Ornstein, who arranged the interview and was so enthusiastic and excited that he declared: 'These are the most interesting compositions I have seen by any living American.'"[58] Cowell elaborated on the meeting to Terman. Ornstein's manager initially scheduled a two-minute appointment for Cowell to meet Ornstein. At that appointment Ornstein took some of Cowell's scores and asked him to come to his room (behind a hardware store on Forty-second Street) at 6:30 that evening. When Cowell arrived, Ornstein had already spent two hours practicing the younger composer's pieces. Terman quotes Cowell as saying that Ornstein considered Cowell's music "crude, but that the material was there. That H. must learn what to leave out. That altho H. was working in the dark, he needed only to find himself. He let H. know that he consid. him far more promising than Levitzky (another youth now coming into national prominence as a pianist and composer)—In fact he threw Levitzky's music in the waste basket before H's eyes."[59]

Henry Cowell, of course, had been interested in musical "futurism" at least two years before he met Ornstein (as shown by his "futurist" movement for *Resumé*). In December 1916, however, shortly after his meeting with Ornstein, Cowell produced a new cluster piece, entitled *Dynamic Motion*. At first he marked the pencil draft "Largo," putting the work in the same class of brooding, emotive music as Chapter III of *Adventures in Harmony*. But Cowell then crossed out that tempo marking and replaced it with "Allegro." He went on to explain that the piece was a tone painting, a musical representation of a New York subway.[60] It was typically futuristic imagery, and, unlike the placid gonging effects of *Adventures in Harmony,* the jarring angularity of this new cluster piece could truly unnerve his audiences and possibly make its author, like Ornstein, "famous."[61]

Dynamic Motion is the reincarnation and metamorphosis of his earlier hand and arm chords. A rapidly arpeggiated cluster, for example, is produced by a tilting of the arm. Sympathetic resonances are produced by silently depressing low clusters. Octave and two-octave clusters are divided into their most logical pianistic components—white keys and black keys. Large bands of pitch alternate rapidly between diatonic collections and their complementary pentatonic; and when white+black–key macroclusters are called for, both arms are used, a departure from his earlier one-arm approach.

Beyond its innovations in technique, *Dynamic Motion* shows Cowell using clusters to try and overcome the fault that Redfern Mason and others had seen in his music, lack of development. In mm. 13–16, for example, Cowell executes what would become an essential part of his later method—a progressive widening from micro- to macroclusters in order to give rhetorical weight to small gestures. In the same vein, the motivic major sevenths of mm. 29–30 immediately reappear as alternating white- and black-key clusters in mm. 31–32.

We should note, however, that, despite the great leap forward made by *Dynamic Motion,* Cowell's compositional logbook shows that, immediately after writing the piece, he abandoned its techniques for almost a year.[62] Not until November 1917 did he produce successors to *Dynamic Motion,* five of them written within a two-month period. Cowell entitled them: *What's This?, Amiable Conversation, Advertisement, Antinomy,* and *Time Table.* Collectively he called these the "Five Encores" to *Dynamic Motion* (although in practice he freely interspersed them in his recital programs; they were not just encores). Some of these "encores" extended the pyrotechnics of *Dynamic Motion.* For example, in *Advertisement* he specifies that a running cluster passage is to be played by the fists; in *Antinomy* he calls for a two-arm cluster tremolo (example 15). These two pieces (the third and fourth "encores," respectively) also codified the bravura techniques of his futurist style. These techniques were: measured arpeggiations of smaller clusters (up to five notes, played by the fingers of one hand);[63] unmeasured arpeggiations of larger clusters (a twelfth or more, played by tilting the forearm against the keys); microcluster filigree (played by alternating fists); and macrocluster filigree (played by alternating forearms). These techniques are sometimes used for development, but usually not.

With the Five Encores, Cowell apparently learned that he could create whole

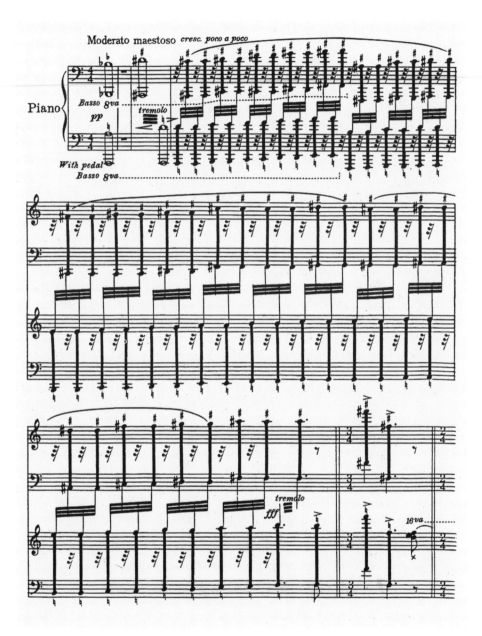

Example 15. *Antinomy,* opening

works simply by transposing his basic cluster techniques into disparate registers and then juxtaposing them with more conventional passage work. The resulting pieces were improvisatory, shallow in structure. Correspondingly, he tended to give such new works offhand titles, drawn from casual speech or jargon: *It Isn't It, Conservative Estimate, Well?* and *Seven and One Fourth Pounds* (the last of these, from 1922, a reference to the birth weight of Sam Seward's newborn daughter, Jean).[64]

Later, in his quest for a place in history, Cowell persistently rolled back the dates of these and a number of other cluster pieces: compare the dates he assigned to them on work lists for the American Composers Alliance and the Pan American Union in the 1950s with the dates he gave them in his logbook of compositions (table 1). Although Charles Seeger recalled that Cowell showed him pieces with large clusters when Cowell was his student (1914–17), all of the pieces Seeger recalled *by name* are dated in Cowell's logbook December 1916 and later—that is, after he went to New York and became infatuated with Ornstein.[65] The few available programs and reviews of Cowell's recitals during 1914, 1915, and most of 1916 also name no cluster pieces, except for *Adventures in Harmony,* and even that is not named after 1914. Far from shocking his audiences with clusters, Cowell in his late teen years wrote and performed primarily simple song accompaniments, children's music, and pieces in imi-

Table 1. Dates Assigned by Henry Cowell to His Early Cluster Pieces

Piano Works	CD[a]	ACA/PAU[b]	PMHC[c]
Tides of Manaunaun	Not listed	1912	1911–12
Advertisement	Nov. 1917	1914	1914*
Dynamic Motion	Nov. 1916	1914	1914
Amiable Conversation	Nov. 1917	1914	1914*
What's This?	Nov. 1917	1914	1915*
Antinomy	Dec. 1917	Not listed	1914*
The Hero Sun	1922	1915	Not listed
The Voice of Lir	Nov. 1920	1915	1918*
Exultation	May 1921	1919	1919*

a. "Compository Dates," holograph notebook of Henry Cowell, in Cowell Collection, New York Public Library, Music Division; typescript in Joscelyn Godwin, "The Music of Henry Cowell," Ph.D. diss., Cornell University, 1969, 403–23.

b. "Catalogue of Henry Cowell Compositions," *Bulletin of the American Composers Alliance* 3, no. 4 (Winter 1953–54): 6; "Chronological Catalog of the Works of the North American Composer: Henry Cowell," *Composers of the Americas: Biographical Data and Catalogs of Their Works* (Washington, D.C.: Union Panamericana, 1962), 28.

c. Notes to *Piano Music by Henry Cowell: Twenty Pieces Played by the Composer,* Folkways Records Album #FG 3349 (1963). An asterisk (*) after a date means this source says "about [the given date]."

tation of classical masters. Now, in New York, he found in Ornstein a mentor and inspiration for what his career would shortly become.

But after all, that was not what he had gone to New York to find. His actual schooling, paid for by Seward's fund and arranged for by Seeger, turned out to be a dismal failure. Not only was Cowell unimpressed by the young composers at the Institute of Musical Art, he felt he was learning little and that there were "better advantages" for him back in California.[66] He would later tell Terman bluntly that the teachers at the institute were "rotten," "utterly ignorant" of theory, and incapable of teaching him anything.[67]

Cowell was more reticent about his social status. As a bohemian from California, he was socially unprepared for life among the rich students at the institute. He was chronically lonely, a fact about which Veblen remarks in all of her letters to him during these months. Cowell complained to Veblen of the "severe personal treatment" he was getting: "The people there are all cads. . . . I don't know how long I can stay there."[68] Veblen worried that some of this was because of his poor personal hygiene. Tactfully, but firmly, she advised him to "please do keep punctiliously clean, never wearing undergarments at night worn through the day, and changing them anyway once in a week, and keeping your shirt cuffs up with elastics or something, and your hair convenient. I ought to beseech you this in every letter, for you should devote five minutes to prayer on the subject every morning—Just for the sake of being inconspicuous."[69] It is not known whether Henry followed her advice.

The one saving grace of his social life turned out to be none other than Edna Smith, who had enrolled at Columbia University that fall. With their Carmel past in common, Henry and Edna now took solace in each other. She introduced him to her well-to-do friends (one of whom, he wrote excitedly to Veblen, knew Ornstein) and he actually changed his mailing address to hers (although he probably did not live with her). While Cowell, then as always, spoke little of Edna, Ellen Veblen sensed that he felt something special for her. "This Miss Smith friend must be exciting," she wrote.[70]

But even his closeness with Edna was not enough to persuade him to stay in New York. Ill-suited both intellectually and temperamentally to the institute, Cowell became exasperated at receiving his harmony assignments back covered with blue-pencil corrections. So he tried an experiment, turning in a Bach choral harmonization as his own to see how it would fare. When it too came back covered with blue, Cowell showed it to Damrosch, told him that his teachers were wasting his time, and asked for his tuition deposit back. Incensed, Damrosch said that Cowell was ungrateful and that the school wanted nothing more to do with him. When Seeger heard that Henry wanted to come back to California, he told Veblen, "What would he have to come back to? Just the same that he left." Seeger added that, even if Henry didn't learn what he hoped to at the institute, he would at least have the "glamour of having studied in New York."[71] But Cowell wanted to resume his studies with Seeger (who, as it turned out, would leave Berkeley himself in 1921 to teach at the institute).

§ § §

During his time at Berkeley and at the Institute of Musical Art, Cowell was also quietly attending another "school": the Temple of the People at Halcyon, California, near Pismo Beach, which he officially joined after his mother died in 1916. Cowell had been introduced to this theosophical community by John Varian, a quirky and somewhat pompous Irish poet who led the "Temple Square" group in Palo Alto, devotees of Madame Blavatsky's "secret doctrine," an eclectic mix of Asian religions, pagan philosophy, and Western science.[72] Those devotees included not only Ellen Veblen, but also "professors and students from Stanford, writers, artists, musicians, local business and professional men, and a spattering of dreamers and idealists."[73] In 1913 Henry met Varian not through Veblen but through his son Russell. Cowell, as he had learned to do in Carmel, wrote Russell a piece of music to enhance their friendship.[74] An article written years later as part of a tribute to John Varian explains what happened next:

> One day at the door of a rose-clambered cottage in Palo Alto there came a knock, and from inside there answered Mr. Varian's cheery, "Come in!" And a boy about fourteen, short of stature and with a tousel of hair and a shy manner, entered. Mr. Varian looked at him and knew him, for he had heard of this boy composer who lived in a tiny cottage up back of Menlo with an invalid mother; sold lily bulbs for a few scant dollars and wrote music. The boy took a chair at Mr. Varian's bidding, stuck his heels over a rung, laid a MS roll across his knees, and, looking up at Mr. Varian with an introductory smile, said, "I have written a sonata to Russell."
>
> Now, Russell is Mr. Varian's eldest son. . . . He, about twelve years of age, was then freckled along with his red hair and primitive celtic features; had grown much of his present six-feet-oneness and was in the midst of being quite awkward about it, and having a soul wholly unborn to the romance of musical composition. He came in at the call of his dad from the yard where he was in the midst of making a flying machine out of a cigar box and some rubber bands, and he proceeded forthwith to expound the wonders of his invention right over the unsuspecting MS. If you had seen you would have smiled, but— one look taken more deeply and the smile would have died. For that boy, stand-

ing there with the other boy and the poet father was a sign and a symbol; a part of the new Cosmos to be born. There was distinction in all three.[75]

Cowell soon began attending Temple Square meetings. Member George Harrison recalled that Cowell spent most of his time talking to the "grown-ups," something to which he had by now become accustomed.[76]

In 1914 the Varian family moved from Palo Alto down the coast to Halcyon to join the Temple of the People, who lived there as a colony. John explained to one of his colleagues that he wanted to work with Dr. William Dower, the group's co-founder, and Edgar Cheetham, the temple's music leader. Both men were estimable and progressivist musicians: Dower had created a system of attaching musical symbols to word sounds; Cheetham not only studied Hindu music with its long strings of rhythms but also played with two metronomes set at different tempos, in what Russell Varian called a "compound rhythm stunt."[77] More to the point, both men were working on settings of Varian's strange Irish myth texts.

Soon after the move, John Varian wrote to Cowell and invited him to "stray down this way some day & stay round. . . . If you do drop in there is room somewhere in our diggings & you wont have to sleep in the pig pen either."[78] Because of his mother's illness and his school commitments, Cowell declined the invitation until after Clarissa's death. In August of 1916, along with Charles Seeger and Jaime de Angulo, Cowell walked and rode mules for days through the woodlands and foothills beside the coastline to reach the beachfront town of less than a hundred people, living in modest cottages and raising vegetables, sugar beets, and flower seeds.[79] There the three men hoped to see a temple pageant with a text by Varian that was being performed. When they arrived, they had missed the pageant; their journey had taken longer than expected. But Cowell had found a new home.

The members of the community to which Cowell was drawn through John Varian virtually adopted the young composer, and he them.[80] A few weeks after the summer 1916 mystery play that Henry had missed, the official magazine of the Temple of the People reported that Cowell—a composer of music "of such high and unusual order that it has attracted wide attention on the Pacific Coast"—had just spent a month affiliating with the Temple.[81] The report also mentions that Cowell had given a series of eight lectures on music for the colony. A friend of Varian's recalls that, in Varian's living room, Cowell taught a class in harmony "to anyone who was interested." She adds that "he was a good teacher. . . . I remember we all had note books & his telling us about counterpoint."[82]

John Varian reported that Cheetham was "deeply in love with" Henry and considered that the young composer had "the Karma" for the music of the temple. And indeed, Cowell's cluster concept from *Adventures in Harmony* seemed perfectly suited to the renovation of Halcyon's music. Varian, who directed the temple choir, described music at the temple before Henry's arrival as "sangtified raggtime" and "rehymnafied hymn music" (although he observed that "if the Lord can stand it I can & it seems to do some folks good").[83] According to Seeger, Cowell heard that music and said to the Halcyon congregation, "You ought not to be singing those hymns. They have nothing to do with the oneness of man and the universe. You ought to sing my music." They asked what that music was and he played, in Seeger's words, some of the "elbow music," which they then adopted.[84] Thereafter, from New York, Cowell wrote to Varian that the music at Halcyon was now more progressive than that of the metropolis he had entered: "You have heard and are hearing more of the best present day music in Halcyon than is produced in all this big city."[85]

At first, Cowell hid his membership in the Temple of the People from his surrogate mother, Ellen Veblen. Although she was sympathetic to the group at Halcyon, and even owned a cabin there, he apparently feared that she might think the group would warp his independence of mind—a true bohemian would not subscribe to a group, no matter how avant-garde in its thinking the group might be. In October 1916, however, he wrote her from New York that "I have joined the Temple. I really had joined it when I saw you, but somehow I couldn't make myself tell you. Don't be very scared at this. It only means that the Temple doesn't make you believe anything didactic when you join it." He went on to explain why he had embraced this particular sect, yet intended to maintain his freedom of thought: "I never could join anything where you had to believe something. But they present instructions to you, to take as you will and these are so logical, so scientific, and so nearly in accordance with my own experience, that I felt like persueing them further."[86]

With Cowell's music now accepted by the temple, John Varian suggested that he and the teenage composer should work together, Varian supplying the texts, Cowell the notes. "If you wished I could supply you with other verses to put a music soul into as I have a lot written[.] But the best way would be for you to come down & read them with me." He then describes his texts: "I have one to the sea fog mysteries & one to the night spirit & two to a wave of the ocean of Life &c &c."[87] Soon Varian proposed an enormous, hyper-Wagnerian collaboration with Henry: "I see that I have a whole cosmos full of the best kind of material for you to make music to. . . . I see now that I can easily supply you with perhaps 40 or 50 operas for the open air or indoors & every one connected

up before & behind with the others & every one vital & independent in itself."
The first of these was to be nothing less than an epic depiction of "the greatest battle between light and darkness of all the Irish mythology."[88] He wrote
to Cowell at length and in great detail, explaining the relation of his work to
specific Irish myths. The result was *The Building of Banba* (the latter word of
which Varian sometimes spelled "Bamba," and which Cowell always did),
produced at Halcyon's summer convention in 1917.

Cowell's music for *Bamba* was relentlessly simple—perhaps, as Steven
Johnson points out, because of the limitations of Halcyon's amateur performers.[89] But the movements associated with the character of Manaunaun, the
warrior sea-god of Irish myth, use clusters in the way Cowell had used them
in *Adventures in Harmony.*

The Tides of Manaunaun, now probably the best known of Cowell's cluster
pieces for piano, was the play's prelude. It combined a diatonic treble tune—
essentially a pseudo-Irish waltz—with slowly throbbing cluster figures in the
bass (example 16). With these minimal materials, *Tides* shows how nicely Cowell's musical training had allowed him to advance beyond earlier cluster works
like *Adventures in Harmony* or even *Dynamic Motion.* He builds a form primarily by changing the nature of the clusters: first left-hand chromatic one-
octave clusters, then left-arm chromatic two-octave clusters, then left-arm two-
octave clusters alternating between white and black keys, then larger than

Example 16. *Tides of Manaunaun,* opening

two-octave chromatic clusters, returning (in a kind of coda) to the original one-octave clusters. What makes the piece most interesting, however, is the parade of climaxes at different points. It reaches its high point in register at m. 18, in left-hand activity at m. 22, and in dynamics at m. 24. And while the "tides" per se might seem to be depicted by the clusters in the left hand, a kind of tidal motion appears in the melody as well: when echoing a melodic idea, Cowell usually reverses its direction, creating a constant ebb and flow.

Other numbers in *Bamba* also feature clusters. Manaunaun's first song includes a fast series of whole steps followed by the notation "etc to" and a two-octave cluster (F_2 to F_4). In "Building the Dream of Oma," the piano plays chromatic octave triplets, with the first octave shown as an octave cluster, but the others not. And throughout all of Manaunaun's songs appear low, slowly throbbing one-octave clusters that recall those in *Adventures in Harmony*, as had appeared in the prelude, *Tides of Manaunaun*.

The pageant was produced in a field near the beach, the makeshift stage lit by automobile headlamps covered with cellophane.[90] An anonymous writer described the spectacle under the title "Oberammergau in America":

> Presently music joined itself to the lights—rather queer music, a piano out of doors, played boldly and freely, the high cry of a man's dramatic tenor, then a crash of chorus, accompanied with flares of red, green and yellow light. We headed toward it [from the highway], and presently found other machines moving swiftly in the same direction. With them we came on the extensive grounds of an old-fashioned California mansion, where some hundreds of people sat in utter silence watching what went forward on a two acre out-door stage, the audience in the star-lit dark, the stage expanding and contracting, appearing and disappearing in the varying moods of flames and lights cleverly manipulated. A little watching and listening proved that the lights and the music played together, in harmony with the tale there unfolded, and with the slight gesturing and posturing of the actors and chorus.

The story being enacted in all of this, the writer explained, was "nothing less than the story at once of the creation of the Universe out of chaos and the parallel evolution of the human soul, a theme vast enough for the great out-door stage, with the sky for a dome, and the booming undertones of the ocean for majestic accompaniment to the lesser but harmonious human music, a theme vast enough for the New Age being born in bloody travail, and for this Western world, completing the circle mankind has put around the globe."[91]

The photographer Edward Weston, however, upon visiting a revival of the pageant a few years later, called it "so poorly produced that one could not tell if it had possibilities or not. . . . I have my doubts about the esoteric when it does not include the aesthetic!" He thought the acting "awful" and the singing "staged bellowing." Finally, he attacked the extremely conservative style of the music: "I had hopes this might be a new note, or new music from Henry. But no, much of it sounded like old church hymns poorly sung."[92]

Unfortunately for Cowell the spectacular premiere of *Bamba* was marred by the angry departure of Ellen Veblen. Since Clarissa Dixon's death, relations between Cowell and Veblen had grown increasingly strained. According to Sidney Cowell, Veblen wanted Cowell to move in permanently with her, but he refused.[93] When he went to New York, she wanted to go with him, but he again refused. At some point she, like Henry, joined the Temple of the People. But in time Varian warned Henry that Ellen was "a Temple member inhibited by jealosys & prejudices" and that she was "a big soul . . . with queer karma." Varian hoped that with "wisdom & brooding" she would "become much more ballanced."[94] Despite some sort of ongoing "treatment" at the Temple Sanitorium, Veblen suddenly left Halcyon two days before the premiere of *Bamba*. "Poor frantic woman," Agnes Varian reported in her diary, Veblen was "heart broken because Henry is not what he was 3 years ago, & blaming it on the Temple." Agnes thought it "very tragic, but quite beyond help. Life moves on for him, but she looks backward."[95]

Beyond giving Cowell a mythic context for his music, John Varian also freed Cowell's mind to reexamine musical instruments, especially the piano. On the one hand, Varian worked for years building what he called "the big harp keyboard."[96] It was to be a replica of the Harp of Life in Irish mythology, the subject of the temple pageant he had written for the 1916 conference. "That harp," he had written, "is indeed a gigantic mystery of Imagination [with] its keyboard above the farthest stars upon the ridge of Heaven, and . . . its strings strung across Time and Space and Eternity, and . . . its sounding board the very Soul of Cosmos itself!"[97] Varian worked for many years on his replica but never completed it.[98] He not only discussed this instrument frequently with Cowell, he also wanted Cowell to someday use it himself. In 1917 he told the composer that if the harp had "as much sound [as] I expect and you learned to master it, you can easily get known all over the world and make as much noise over it as the war."[99]

On the other hand, Varian's obsession for attaching a keyboard to a harp was matched by his ideas for attaching other things to a piano. In some notes written apparently in 1916, Varian proposes four broad modifications: a "drum piano," a "bar piano," a "bell or gong piano," and a "rotary piano." The first, as the name suggests, would have tuned drums instead of strings, the second steel bars instead of strings," and the third tuning forks or heavy bells to provide outdoor music "that could be heard for miles." The rotary piano kept the strings but discarded the hammers: each keystroke would initiate "a rotary action instead of struck action, consisting of rotary brushes like those used in burnishing. Many more strings used at treble & base to reinforce sound[;] this can be accomplished by setting them in a curve above the brush so that when it is lifted it will meet them all at once. To increase the power of piano more strings to each sound can be used all along the instrument[,] dampers &c as in ordinary piano."[100]

Varian's strangest plan was to attach a keyboard to a huge set of audion bulbs that would resonate in what he called a "harmonious speaking cave"—"a cavern built of concreet as large as possible in shape to correspond in principle to throat nose mouth and skull." The cave would have a throat shape at the back, a kind of soft palate made of celluloid, a flexible tongue capable of making phonemes, and two players, one to control the phonemes, the other to control the pitch. Varian gave detailed instructions as to how one might build this cave (which he insisted must be heard only from a distance). In 1918 he even began to build a prototype from a barrel, but at some point abandoned it—or perhaps turned it over to his son Russell.[101]

Russell Varian, about two years younger than Henry, had inherited the libertarian traits of his father, enough so to reject even the dogmas on which he had been raised. In a letter to Henry, he wrote a kind of manifesto for bohemianism, one that seemed to harmonize completely with Cowell's own beliefs: "I think that anyone who can be completely classified as a Socialist, a Theosophist or any other ist or ism is a follower of beaten paths. Possibly it is best that the average man should be a follower of beaten paths, for if he is unable to steer by the stars, he is better on a path even if it is a cow path. But on the path he'll find nothing new, and he'll be all his life an artisan. Writers and other producers of new things don't come from this class." Russell went on to explain that most path-followers did not so much revere the path as fear the discoveries they might make should they veer from it. The answer to this fear was a new kind of education: "I think a course in Practical Vagrancy, or something like that would do more toward broadening college men out into writers than the abolition of English Departments. After all, it isn't that these fellows can't write, but they havn't anything to write about that hasn't been all written before."[102]

Henry Cowell resonated to this kind of thinking and joined with Russell Varian in a variety of rhythmic experiments that combined the "stunt" work of Cheetham with the theories of Seeger. One such experiment was the creation of a barrel that, with the assistance of carefully machined gears, could play "dissonant" cross rhythms. Cowell discussed the rationale behind such a device in a December 1916 letter to Russell from New York.

> As nearly as I can figure, you got that idea [of cross rhythms] about the same time I was working out some remarkable new rythmic s[c]hemes. I wonder whether our ideas are similar, and if they're not, how they will fit.
>
> . . . About rythm again, you are right in supposing most rythms to be intirely monorythmic. As a matter of fact, the music of counterpoint is quite complex comparatively and the contrapuntal style was developed rather early. . . . Anyway, Counterpoint is practically built on rythms working against each other, almost entirely, however[,] in consonant ratios, that is, either 2 or 3, or 4 notes against one, which, in tonal ratios would be the same as the octave, the fifth, and the octave above again.[103]

Cowell also alludes to the use of two "rates of speed . . . in counterpoint to each other." He elaborates: "Another interesting counterpoint with rythm would be to have one steady movement getting steadily faster against another getting steadily slower. This, of course, opens up an endless field for development. . . . A lot of new kinds of notes will have to be invented to write this down, as it is impossible with our limited present supply."

In his response, Russell explains, "My Idea is to introduce the same ratios between a group of rythms as would exist between the notes of a chord, and changing as the chords do in a piece of music, only necessarily much slower. Perhaps a fixed ratio of rythms moving regularly at different speeds through a whole movement of a composition, or being altered a part at a time through the movement."[104] Such Seeger-like ideas would eventually be credited to neither Charles Seeger nor Russell Varian, but to Henry Cowell alone.

§ § §

If Ornstein had inspired Cowell and given him a template for a career playing cluster music, Seeger and the Varians had filled his mind with "scientific" ideas and speculations. Cowell had by then developed with (or borrowed from) his teachers essentially all the modernist techniques, ideas, and theories that would fuel his best-known compositions. What he got from Seeger alone is incalculable. Indeed, Seeger would later claim that Cowell "swiped many of his best (and some of his worst) 'ideas' from me, and occasionally acknowledges it."[105] For his part, Cowell said vaguely that Seeger "has rarely been given public credit for the ideas which he has initiated."[106]

But Seeger gave Cowell more than ideas. He gave him an actual method to shape his career as a modernist composer. Seeger taught Cowell that if he wanted to explore a new technique, he must first do so systematically. Second,

Seeger taught him that he should create a specific repertoire for any new technique. Finally, Seeger said, Cowell must be able to perform the repertoire himself and not rely on someone else to do it.[107] That confirmed to Henry what he had witnessed firsthand in the person of Leo Ornstein.

Varian and the Temple of the People complemented Seeger's tutelage yet fueled Cowell's imagination in a way Seeger never could: with mysticism and mythic poetics on the one hand and the bent for scientific experimentation on the other. Even with his breadth of learning, Seeger was a rather single-minded scholar, a musician who wanted to systematize, codify, and catalog everything musical. Cowell's mind preferred to roam among many fields, from literature, to philosophy and science, to botany and entomology, with a restless and searching intellect that embraced order at the same time as it threw off constraint. The playful breadth of his intellect made Halcyon an apt home. As Sidney Cowell later said, not one of the father-figures in Cowell's life could offer Cowell "the broad humanistic thinking that John" did.[108]

In going from unschooled prodigy to well-schooled adult, taught by both poets and professors, Cowell got just enough education to confirm to himself that he didn't need any. He would later explain with evident pride concerning his early music: "This music was not written according to rules, and it did not come about through study, but through direct interest. And since it was written without reference to rules, it can hardly be said that the rules were broken by it."[109] Of his later music he would declare: "I do not compose according to any set scheme. I do not compose while either in an emotional or intellectual fever. . . . I do not follow any formula. . . . I do not try to follow the style of any other composer old or new."

If it was Lewis Terman who indirectly sparked Cowell's formal education, it was also Terman who gave Cowell the license to transcend it. By officially deeming him a "gifted" child, Terman set the tone for future pronouncements of Cowell as a "genius," a person for whom education was merely an embellishment, even a kind of pollution. As a certified "genius," Cowell would eventually owe his greatest glory to the neglect of schooling. And as a "gifted" child, Cowell would only distantly acknowledge the gifts of the scholarly community that adopted him, the artistic enclaves that nurtured him, and the parents who had predestined him for the fame to come.

With his plump cheeks, wide eyes, and curly locks, the infant Henry Cowell was
reputedly a model subject for San Francisco photographers at the end of the
nineteenth century. This ca. 1895 shot is one of the many taken of him as a young
boy. (Cowell Collection, Music Division, New York Public Library for the Performing Arts, Astor, Lenox and Tilden Foundations. Used by permission of the
David and Sylvia Teitelbaum Fund, Inc.)

Henry's mother, Clarissa Dixon Cowell, around the time of his birth (1893). A radical thinker, lecturer, and writer, Clarissa shaped her son's independent outlook and experimental turn of mind. (Cowell Collection, Music Division, New York Public Library for the Performing Arts, Astor, Lenox and Tilden Foundations. Used by permission of the David and Sylvia Teitelbaum Fund, Inc.)

Henry's father, Henry Clayton Blackwood Cowell (better known as "Harry"), standing outside the homestead in Menlo Park he had built at the turn of the century. This is the house in which the composer was born and in which he lived more or less until his incarceration in 1936. (Cowell Collection, Music Division, New York Public Library for the Performing Arts, Astor, Lenox and Tilden Foundations. Used by permission of the David and Sylvia Teitelbaum Fund, Inc.)

In 1902 Cowell began violin lessons, which fared well until an argument with his teacher ended them. (Cowell Collection, Music Division, New York Public Library for the Performing Arts, Astor, Lenox and Tilden Foundations. Used by permission of the David and Sylvia Teitelbaum Fund, Inc.)

One of the few photos of Henry with other children, in this case some cousins, with whom he lived briefly in 1907. Cowell would later explain that he had few playmates his own age but was constantly surrounded by his mother's older friends—bohemian writers, painters, photographers, and musicians. (Cowell Collection, Music Division, New York Public Library for the Performing Arts, Astor, Lenox and Tilden Foundations. Used by permission of the David and Sylvia Teitelbaum Fund, Inc.)

The two Henry Cowells, father and son, ca. 1912. (Cowell Collection, Music Division, New York Public Library for the Performing Arts, Astor, Lenox and Tilden Foundations. Used by permission of the David and Sylvia Teitelbaum Fund, Inc.)

As a young composer, Cowell methodically worked on his music during a set hour each day. This shot of him (ca. 1912) was probably taken by his friend and financial patron Ellen Veblen. (Cowell Collection, Music Division, New York Public Library for the Performing Arts, Astor, Lenox and Tilden Foundations. Used by permission of the David and Sylvia Teitelbaum Fund, Inc.)

Ellen Veblen, patron and friend of Henry Cowell and his mother, Clarissa. This photo shows Veblen speaking to a group of children around the time she met the Cowells (ca. 1910). (Carleton College Archives)

This photo, ca. 1914, shows Cowell working at the trade he had invented for himself: finding and digging up rare plants in the foothills, then selling them to the well-to-do around Stanford. (Cowell Collection, Music Division, New York Public Library for the Performing Arts, Astor, Lenox and Tilden Foundations. Used by permission of the David and Sylvia Teitelbaum Fund, Inc.)

Cowell at the Forest Theater's production of *Creation Dawn*, 11 August 1913. (Forest Theater Scrapbook, Henry Meade Williams Local History Department, Harrison Memorial Library, Carmel, California)

An early photo of the Forest Theater in Carmel (ca. 1911). Cowell wrote his first work to use "tone clusters" as a sixteen-year-old in Carmel, June 1913; two months later he used clusters in the music he wrote for Takeshi Kanno's *Creation Dawn*, a mystical outdoor drama produced at this theater. (Forest Theater Scrapbook, Henry Meade Williams Local History Department, Harrison Memorial Library, Carmel, California)

Sporting fancy new clothes (partially supplied by his Carmel fans) and trimmed hair, Cowell had this promotional portrait taken for use in newspaper notices and recital programs in the late 1910s. (Cowell Collection, Music Division, New York Public Library for the Performing Arts, Astor, Lenox and Tilden Foundations. Used by permission of the David and Sylvia Teitelbaum Fund, Inc.)

A 1915 view up Telegraph Avenue, the main thoroughfare of Berkeley, 1915, when Cowell studied at the university there. (Michael Hicks Archives)

Composer, musicologist, educator, and social activist Charles Seeger, 1921. Seeger instilled in Cowell many of the ideas for which the younger composer would become famous. (Courtesy of Seeger family)

John Varian was perhaps Cowell's greatest inspiration in the 1910s–1920s, providing the young composer with the Irish myths and poetry on which Cowell based much of his best-known music. Varian also gave Cowell ideas for musical experimentation and introduced him to the theosophical commune at the Temple of the People, which Cowell joined in 1916. (Varian Papers, Stanford University Archives)

Samuel Seward, who helped Cowell write his early essays on music—which resulted in his treatise *New Musical Resources*—and organized a fund drive to help the composer get formal music schooling. (Courtesy of Jean Seward Uppman)

Cowell, ca. 1916, on the dunes near the Temple of the People at Halcyon, California. (Cowell Collection, Music Division, New York Public Library for the Performing Arts, Astor, Lenox and Tilden Foundations. Used by permission of the David and Sylvia Teitelbaum Fund, Inc.)

Cowell, ca. 1916, in a typical bohemian pose: wearing walking shoes and a day's growth of beard, slouching and reading. (Cowell Collection, Music Division, New York Public Library for the Performing Arts, Astor, Lenox and Tilden Foundations. Used by permission of the David and Sylvia Teitelbaum Fund, Inc.)

He THUMPS his Way to FAME

By MARION TODD

In the 1920s, adulatory—or mocking—articles about Cowell appeared in many newspapers and magazines. They often featured a promotional photo of him playing tone clusters at the piano and occasionally included a caricature of him doing battle with the instrument. This typical example appeared in *Collier's*, 2 May 1925. (University of Utah Library)

In the 1920s and 1930s Cowell drove tirelessly around the country giving recitals and lectures wherever he could. Here, ca. 1935, he strikes a pose beside the "jalopy" that he drove. (Cowell Collection, Music Division, New York Public Library for the Performing Arts, Astor, Lenox and Tilden Foundations. Used by permission of the David and Sylvia Teitelbaum Fund, Inc.)

The morning after his arrest, 22 May 1936, the police took Cowell home to retrieve some personal belongings before going to jail. The *San Francisco Examiner* photographer waiting at his house persuaded Henry to sit at the piano for this last shot before his four-year imprisonment. (Courtesy of San Francisco Examiner)

4

The Work of Exploration
Has Just Begun

When the United States entered the Great War on 6 April 1917, most young men of Henry Cowell's age suddenly faced the draft. Thousands enlisted, many of them college students, eager to serve their country in a manly way, but hoping for safer assignments than conscripted men received. Cowell, however, escaped the draft, declaring himself a subject of Ireland, because his paternal grandfather was the Dean of Kildare.[1] The invocation of Ireland was a particularly sensitive matter, because in pursuit of "home rule," the Irish had set up their own provisional government in defiance of England and refused to join with the mother country in declaring war on Germany. Because England knew that forced conscription of the Irish might inflame the empire, the United States avoided calling up Irish men. Thus the heritage that Henry's father had fled in pursuit of the bohemian life now enabled the son to perpetuate that life for himself. As many of his peers went off to war, Cowell could live as he had lived, writing experimental music, teaching summer school, and visiting the beach at Halcyon.

During the fall of 1917 he wrote several small pieces that broke new ground. In his Quartet Romantic, a brief two-movement piece scored for two flutes, violin, and viola, Cowell tried for the first time methodically doing what Seeger had proposed and Henry had discussed with Russell Varian: using the overtone series to generate rhythms. To write this piece, Cowell composed a simple four-part diatonic chorale in C major (example 17). He then converted the pitches into rhythms by translating the four parts into the numbers of the harmonic partials that would produce them (with one *beat* of the original chorale's rhythm now equal to one measure):

mm. 1–4	mm. 5–6	mm. 7–8	mm. 9–10
G = 6	A = 13 ⅓	B = 15	C = 16
E = 5	F = 10 ⅔	G = 12	G = 12
C = 4	C = 8	D = 9	C = 8
C = 2	F = 5 ⅓	F = 5 ⅓	E = 5

But even though a diatonic chorale was the basis of the rhythmic proportions, he used these rhythms to set freely chromatic material.[2]

After completing this quartet Cowell began writing a set of (cluster-free) piano etudes that he called "Ings" (because the title of each ended in "ing"). Each "Ing" focused on a specific technique or texture, creating what Godwin calls a "self-consistent, monothematic miniature, or character piece which is an exploration, within strictly defined limits, of a specific mood or a particular compositional device."[3] In "Floating," for example, the right hand plays a continuous stream of major thirds, mostly in eighth notes, but sometimes in eighth-note septuplets. The left hand plays a long, languid melody in quarter notes, with an occasional accompaying chord. "Frisking" puts the right hand in D minor and the left more or less in G♭ major, with both hands playing in the same meter (3/8) but displaced by an eighth note. Each of the other "Ings" written at this time employs a similar single-mindedness and Cowell might have kept writing such pieces indefinitely. But events of 1918 hindered him.

In February of that year the British and American governments forged a reciprocal pact requiring young men to either return to their native land or submit to the draft in the country where they lived. Knowing that enlisted men stood less chance of seeing combat, Cowell did not wait for the draft. He enlisted on 23 February and was assigned to the United States Army Ambulance Corps at Camp Crane, Allentown, Pennsylvania. There he would be trained, he thought, to carry the wounded from battlefields in France or Italy. Instead, he found himself again immersed in music.

Henry was probably unprepared for the bustling intellectual community that

Example 17. Chorale basis for *Quartet Romantic,* mm. 1–8

existed at Camp Crane. Most of the men there were college students or even professors, including Sam Seward, who had come there the previous June. Like Cowell, they had enlisted in hopes of avoiding the battlefield. So strong were the academic roots of Camp Crane, the enlistees were billeted according to the university they had attended—University of Virginia students formed a unit, Brown University students another, and so forth.[4] The people of Allentown virtually adopted the men, inviting them for meals, giving them gifts, and welcoming them into their homes and families. (As one woman recalled, "if you think the Allentown girls did not have fun, you'd better think again. Why[,] I had so many dates there weren't enough evenings in the week for them so I had luncheon dates [as well]."")[5] The *Philadelphia Record*'s description of Camp Crane in 1917 calls it "the most cheerful place you ever saw," a place where "the fellows set to work with a will" transforming the sheep and cattle pens that had stood on the spot until then into a set of "breezy cubicles—roofed over but exposed to the winds on all four sides—in college fashion, with pennants and posters and humorous signs. Here they play cards and yarn and loll in 'dorms' or 'Gold Coast' diggings."[6]

Cowell, of course, had never fit in with the well-bred college crowd and probably did not now—especially after being assigned to kitchen patrol, a demeaning job but one for which he was well suited after years of cooking for his mother. As a cook Cowell had the privilege of going on overnight leave to New York City once every three days. When there, he wrote to Harry, "I see Ornstein, & one Mr. [Carl] Ruggles, a fine composer, who is helping me in orchestration. My symphony is finished & I am sending it to Seeger."[7]

Upon learning of Henry's new military assignment, John Varian wrote Henry a long letter. Commenting that kitchen patrol was "pergatory," Varian added that "of course pergatory is not a bad place even some of the Irish saints went there & had a hell of a time."[8] Varian went on to say that "it was just the same to be sending you off as one of my own boys there is surely a very old bond between us"; "be sure that you are always my boy," he added, "no matter what kind of hell" Cowell might encounter. He then spent two pages ruminating on the Bolshevik Revolution: "Poor Russia, she is . . . crucified for her great ideal forsaken by all except her working folk & all the nations against her. . . . no matter what happens Russia has won. The Child of Freedom is born & even if the present effort is swept away the child will grow." Despite his hatred of the hell of war, Varian thought that the army would be for Cowell "golden in experiance," because "mother nature looks out for her lovers & gives them a pretty tough time to develope their vital strength of character & bring outward the latent heroism." Henry would be able to find new ideas if he would listen to "the music of what happens." In the end, "When you come back our boy will be a man filled with a deeper tone of Humanities Music. Even if you must be silent a few years it only strengthens the music in you."

As it turned out, Cowell was far from silent. The USAAC Band (the band of the United States Army Ambulance Corps), which had been formed when Camp Crane opened, was shipped out with the Italian Contingent about three months after Cowell arrived at the camp. Section 507, to which Cowell belonged, was detailed to reinstitute the band. Cowell was placed in immediate charge of organizing it. When Sergeant Theodore G. Otto, the former bandmaster, was renamed to that position, Cowell became an assistant bandmaster, music copyist, and flutist. At the time their official photo was taken the band numbered a total of fifty-three.

The band was active and vigorous, playing for parades and shows at Camp Crane and elsewhere (on at least one occasion in Atlantic City). As their notoriety increased, Lieutenant Colonel C. P. Franklin, chief executive officer of the camp, invited John Philip Sousa to come to camp and hear them. He did so, but one member wrote, "I do not recall that [he found] our playing so meritorious."[9] Orchestral composer and conductor Victor Herbert also visited the camp and guest-directed the band, wincing enough through their sound as to ask a second violin player not to play at all.[10]

The band pleased the commander, however, and he tried to advance their work. For months the players had apparently used their own instruments, a motley assemblage of professional, second-hand, and student models. In October 1918, Colonel Franklin bought them all new instruments. When the armistice was signed the following month, Camp Crane's future looked bleak. The band was forced to dissolve as some of its members joined other branches of the service, some were discharged, and the rest, including Henry Cowell, were transferred to General Hospital #5 at Fort Ontario in Oswego, New York, apparently as part of a deal. Cowell recalls that the commander at Fort Ontario would pay the unpaid balance on Franklin's batch of new instruments if he could have a band for his post.[11]

Unlike Camp Crane, Fort Ontario was a venerable old army base, built on the Oswego River near Lake Ontario in 1755 as a companion to Fort Oswego on the river's opposite side. When the Great War began, representatives of the War Department inspected the fort and decided to turn it into an army medical center. But its decades-old buildings had been designed to house only four hundred men—a number that more than doubled in 1917, prompting Congress to send money for more buildings. Almost as quickly as the building stopped, the war was over and, perhaps for the first time, this bustling military hospital could afford the luxury of a band.

Cowell could not immediately resume his band duties at Fort Ontario because he came down with chicken pox, which, perhaps due to his isolation from fellow children, he had never before had. In January 1919, in the midst of the sickness, Cowell replied to a letter from Russell Varian: "My head having been filled full of much rubbish, has been constantly vomiting, and is now ready to hold ideas once again. . . . Being in bed [I begin] to seriously consider the mechanistic development of musical technology and other charming points. . . . I have been longing for a little reciprocating of ideals, [and] so your letter felt like a delicious hot tamale on a goulash-oppressed tongue."[12]

While Cowell had written some of his most adventurous music in the months before enlisting, he now could only write small, simple, and mostly serviceable pieces. His personal records show that he wrote about twenty-four pieces from February 1918 through May 1919, the month he was discharged. Eleven of those have been lost. Of the other thirteen, five are instrumentals (two for solo piano, two for piano plus a string instrument, and one march written for the band at Fort Ontario). The eight others are short songs for voice and piano, ranging in length from nine to thirty-six measures and drawn from a variety of sources, including children's verse from Robert Louis Stevenson and political writings of John Varian. Cowell's setting of the latter's "Democracy" typifies the plain, seemingly non-emotive way he set texts during this period (and indeed, often throughout his career).

> Democracy, thou flaming vision-dream,
> Haunting that age-long path of blood-filled years,
> Beckoning us on about the heights
> Thy mighty hands, thy starlit eyes gleam
> Through the smoke and pain and tears—
> We here below, bloody with human death
> War again with brother man.
> Above, your stars and beckoning hand
> Point us the road again, Almighty One.

In a handwriting that shows haste, Cowell dashes through Varian's text in a mere twenty-nine measures of D major in common time (allegro). The piano part consists primarily of thickly doubled triads and seventh chords in half notes, while the voice sings what begins as a garden-variety hymn. After two four-measure phrases, the voice begins a long, directionless eight-measure phrase, then a three-measure phrase. Suddenly, on the words "War again with brother man," Cowell inserts a very different three measures marked *presto*, with the piano playing repeated chords in triplets and the voice climbing to a high sustained G♯. The last phrase returns to the original style for seven measures, with the voice beginning and ending the phrase on a high A—far beyond the reach of the medium-range hymn tune that began the song. Overall, the song shows Cowell setting Varian's text somewhat perfunctorily, yet with an odd, semi-proletarian agenda: he begins it as though it were a hymn for the common man, then interrupts it with, in effect, a heated parlor song. He ends it with more hymning, but in a very high range the common man could not commonly execute.

§ § §

When in May he was finally discharged, the bohemian Cowell returned to his home transformed. He had a stronger personal regimen. The army had made him, for perhaps the first time in his life, part of a team. It had given him real public responsibilities. And while some of it augmented the cynicism toward state-run enterprises that his parents had instilled in him, the army experience almost surely heightened his sense of patriotism. All of these traits would affect his career thereafter, whether as a composer, an entrepreneur, a teacher, or a writer. John Varian's prophecy had come true.

Now, with Cowell on his own again, Varian offered fresh counsel to prepare Henry for his return to life as an artist. Varian worried that his "boy" might be seduced by the musical orthodoxies of big cities. He called places such as New York and Paris "has beens" that "will have somewhat the effect of university englush upon a Poet." The place for Cowell, claimed Varian, was in California, where "the great movement is to be. . . . what you want in reality is not so much to be with musicians as to be in a spiritual atmosphere all the time. Us kind of folk who are sucking in the new vibrations in Art should get into the purer life currents & not the putred ones." But, no matter where Cowell was, he warned, "You will have to depend on yourself & a very few other musicians to develope your music. . . . you will have to forget the public & their demands altogether & only write to your best idea."[13]

Few events could have illustrated so pointedly Varian's warnings against the musical establishment as Henry's encounter with Sergei Rachmaninoff, who in the summer of 1919 moved to Menlo Park. Hoping for some tutelage and encouragement Cowell went to Rachmaninoff's house, taking with him a pile of manuscripts. Rachmaninoff chose to look only at one: "Fleeting," one of the "Ings" and indeed the "Ing" that most resembled Rachmaninoff's own writing. Cowell recalls that Rachmaninoff "looked at it intently with no comment for two hours, upon which he marked tiny red circles around 42 notes, saying 'You have 42 wrong notes.'" Sensing Cowell's dismay, the older composer added, "I too have sinned with wrong notes in my youth, and therefore you may be forgiven." Cowell asked what was wrong with those notes. Rachmaninoff replied that they were "not within the rules of harmony." Cowell then asked if composers still needed to follow those rules, whereupon the older composer replied, "Oh yes, these are divine rules."[14] Probably no reply could have struck Cowell as so nonsensical as that one.

For the rest of 1919, Cowell tried to set forth a new corpus of rules that could match and overtake the old "divine" ones. With his mind clear and "ready to hold ideas once again," he carefully revised and collated the essays written with Seeger and Seward into a small book. To accomplish this he again worked closely with Seward, so much so that Seward's fiancée recalls she had to compete with Cowell's manuscript for attention from her husband-to-be.[15] By the end of the year, Henry had typed and revised until he at last held in his hands a complete draft of the book manuscript entitled "New Musical Resources." It was at once a tenuous, dramatic, cocky, and sometimes illogical jumble of ideas, full of promise for the progress of music and the scientificizing of aesthetics. In it he recapitulated many of the theoretical notions he had discussed at Berkeley and Halcyon. He also outlined many techniques he had already used—from as far back as *Sounds from the Conservatory*—and would keep using during the noisy, novelty-driven epoch of the Roaring Twenties. When, after some dramatic revision, he finally got it published at the end of that decade, its sales would flop. Yet it would become perhaps the most celebrated failure in music literature and the most influential book on composing written during the twentieth century.[16]

Cowell's forty-one-page typewritten manuscript contains nine chapters.[17] The opening three deal with pitch. The first, drawing on Cowell's training with Stricklen and Seeger, traces the evolution of Western harmony via the increasing acceptance of intervals in the overtone series (and even of the "undertone series," which he claims has been scientifically proven to be audible). The second chapter discusses "polyharmony," a term that he got from Schoenberg via Seeger. (Stricklen had called this harmonic phenomenon "double chords.")[18] In this chapter he claims that the superimposing of different chords has always taken place: since the overtone series—which is, in effect, a big "chord"— is audible in any single note, the playing of two notes together actually yields the sound of two chords. Polyharmony, then, the literal playing of superimposed chords (which he called "polychords"), is simply making explicit what one already hears in multilinear music. In the third chapter, Cowell treats "dissonant counterpoint," Seeger's reversal of old contrapuntal rules in which consonance now resolves to "dissonance," which is really a more complex form of consonance, one founded in the more remote overtone relationships. This, he postulates, is how harmony should proceed in the modern age, which should now welcome those more remote relationships. Strangely, given Cowell's discussion of these techniques here, he actually used true dissonant counterpoint and polyharmony in only a few of the pieces for which he is well known. He is far better known for his exotic rhythmic devices and tone clusters, both of which he deals with at length later in the manuscript.

The next five chapters all deal with ways of transposing overtone-ratio-based thinking into the realm of time. The first of these, entitled simply "Rhythm," transposes the overtone-ratio basis of pitch relationships back into the realm of pulse. (Pitch, after all, he points out, is simply very fast pulse.) Modern composers, he suggests, should divide whole notes into equal parts by divisors other than two (or multiples of two). These divisors should reflect the same sorts of ratios as one encounters in the overtone series. That will allow the composer to create true overtone-like "harmonies" of rhythm by superimposing the different equal divisions, a technique Cowell would later call "cross time."[19] For example, just as the combination of the third, fourth, and fifth partials in the overtone series produces a major triad, one can produce an analogous effect in a (3/4) measure of music by playing three against four against five. In this regard, Cowell argues for the use of real fractional terms when referring to complex divisions of the whole note: the members of "eighth-note triplets," for example, are really "twelfth-notes," since there are twelve of them to the whole note. Somewhat less persuasively, Cowell argues the need for newly shaped noteheads to denote a fuller spectrum of fractional values.

The next four chapters develop and extend the essential idea of overtone-based rhythm. The chapter entitled "Metre" proposes creating *metric* harmonies—that is, superimposing time signatures with the same denominator but differing numerators (a technique Cowell would later call "cross meter"). In such a case, to vary our earlier example, one could create a "major triad" of meter by superimposing 3/4, 4/4, and 5/4 (the quarter note being equal in all voices).[20] The next chapter, "Metre and Time Combinations," suggests combining the previous two effects (i.e., cross time and cross meter): vary the fractional divisions of whole notes to produce, in effect, different "pulses," but also vary the pattern of downbeats for each pulse. Thus, one could hypothetically play third notes against quarter notes against fifth notes, but group the third notes in groups of five, the quarter notes in groups of three, and the fifth notes in groups of four—a feat not only very difficult to play but also hard to notate. It can be expressed as 5/3 against 3/4 against 4/5, but would require Cowell's alternate-shape noteheads to clearly express. Such a situation, where neither pulses nor downbeats line up, Cowell would later call "polymeter" (a term that has since been widely adopted, but rarely with the narrow definition Cowell gives it).

In the next chapter, "Tempo," he proposes keeping the unit of the beat constant among voices but varying the tempos via metronome markings (e.g., $\quarternote$ = 60 against $\quarternote$ = 75, which expresses a 4:5 ratio, equivalent, in overtone terms, to a major third). He would later explain, without any elaboration, that "music which is to convey more than a simple emotion, can be written far more effectively by using different tempos in its different parts."[21] Finally, in his last chapter on rhythm, Cowell suggests using different rhythmic ratios—whether through contrasting divisions of the whole note, contrasting meters, or contrasting tempos—to express all the intervals available in the chromatic scale.

The last chapter of "New Musical Resources" treats the subject for which Cowell would always be best remembered. No technique of Henry Cowell's was more celebrated or vilified than his tone clusters. Modern music theory or history textbooks, even when they ignore Cowell's theories of rhythm, dissonant counterpoint, and so on, describe his tone clusters. In his comprehensive book on American music, Gilbert Chase puts it bluntly: Henry Cowell is "The Cluster Man."[22]

But Cowell's book chapter on clusters was, if nothing else, a fervid attempt to tinge with academicism something far more intuitive and primal. Tone clusters, he writes, are built from major or minor seconds, derived, of course, from the overtone series. (Indeed, he says, the overtones of simple chords already create "clusters" that are "plainly audible to a sensitive ear.") As the intervals of triads vary, so do those of clusters: "there is an exact resemblance between the two systems, and the same amount of potential variety in each"—a principle that is, of course, self-evident if major and minor thirds in triads are compared to major and minor seconds in three-note clusters, as Cowell does here. Thus, he writes, there are four clusters that "are the basis of all larger clusters"—two minor seconds, a minor + a major, a major + a minor, and two majors. These "basic" clusters, of course, are what I earlier called "microclusters." They are common to virtually every twentieth-century composer's work. (Indeed, Cowell refers to the presence of such clusters in the music of Schoenberg and Ornstein.) But they are probably the least noteworthy harmonic elements in Cowell's music.

In his manuscript Cowell also makes some circular suggestions about how to use clusters. Consider the following: It is acceptable, he writes, to alternate clusters and other kinds of chords, but it is "often better" to maintain a succession of clusters. Why? "For the sake of consistency." Also, one may use simultaneous clusters. Why? For "harmonic effect." At other times Cowell's arguments are merely fastidious. For example, he notes that the white keys of the piano offer seven different "cluster chords"—C to C, D to D, E to E, etc.—while black keys give five possible; and as for the motion of one cluster to another, he says, it "must be up or down the scale, as in melody."

With his manuscript Cowell attempted to legitimize clusters. But the theory and the practice were strangely discordant. Throughout Cowell's works, clusters are clearly not "built" from seconds but are the result of *filling in* larger intervals. His music likewise gives no indication that large clusters derive from four "basic types." On the contrary, the basic cluster of Cowell's works is the chromatically filled octave; smaller clusters are either *subsets* of that basic cluster or act independently as microclusters. Cowell's extant sketches suggest that even the specific interval of the cluster is not nearly so important as its registral placement and percussive effect.[23] Finally, the black-key "clusters" that appear in virtually all of his cluster pieces are not clusters at all by any of his definitions of the term, because they consist of both seconds and thirds.

The irony of Cowell's cluster theory is that the clusters most prominent in his own music derive not so much from the more remote overtones as from the least remote. That is, the complicated ratios of the higher overtones are typically employed as coloristic fillings of the most basic interval, 2:1, the octave. In all of Cowell's cluster music the octave is as much the intervallic source as is the second.

§ § §

After completing his manuscript, Cowell followed the counsel that Seeger had given him: having devised new techniques, he had to write pieces to illustrate those techniques and then perform them himself. While writing the rhythm chapters of "New Musical Resources," Cowell tried expanding the cross-time technique he had used in the Quartet Romantic into a more elaborate polymetric scheme in the very brief Quartet Euphometric for string quartet (1919). In that work he leaves behind the constancy of the meter-bound pulsations in the earlier quartet in favor of frequently changing superimposed meters, sometimes irrational ones (e.g., 6/20). The difficulty of managing such a compositional process—especially for someone used to a more spontaneous and improvisatory way of composing—becomes evident in the abrupt shifts and stuttering quality of the counterpoint: once things get genuinely complicated, voices drop out, the motion stops, and he starts over with a new idea.

Cowell could not, of course, perform these pieces himself and it is uncertain whether he even tried to get them performed. (Quartet Euphometric is not known to have been played until 1964; Quartet Romantic was not performed by the instruments Cowell designated until 1978, thirteen years after his death.)[24] Clearly neither work was feasible to program: one was for a nonstandard ensemble, and the other was too short (less than two minutes in length) to entice a string quartet to invest the time it would require to prepare the piece for a recital.

What Cowell could perform was solo cross-time piano pieces, the best example of which was *Fabric*. Cast in a chromatically wandering B♭ minor, the three-voice, twenty-one-measure neo-romantic piece requires the player—i.e., Cowell—to play within each measure three rhythms at a time, always in ratios of 5:6:8, 5:7:8, 5:6:9, or 5:7:9 (ratios the sound of which he had learned with Russell Varian via their multi-sprocketed barrel). When he played the piece in recital in the 1920s, Cowell pleased the critics. Some saw in the piece a welcome alternative to the more gymnastic piano techniques for which he was becoming notorious. In *Fabric*, a Carmel critic wrote, Cowell had "adopted . . . a form which brings into use the development of thematic material in a more polyphonic way."[25] The *Los Angeles Times* called the work a significant "prophecy" of music's future, rooted in the science of tone.[26] The composer Marc Blitzstein, however, disapproved of the piece, citing it as yet another example of Cowell's "academicism," in finding new techniques and terms for their own sake. "*Fabric*," he wrote, while "purporting to be a demonstration of polyrhythms . . . turned out to be an inoffensive, romantic little morceau, with the old-style *rubato* mathematically calculated."[27] Blitzstein, like many listeners, preferred Cowell's poetic and often bombastic cluster pieces, which could immediately captivate one's attention by the sheer power of their sonorities.

It is quite clear that Cowell's cluster pieces broke down into two main types: the virtuosic futurist pieces such as *Dynamic Motion* and its Encores and the resonant mystic pieces written under the spell of John Varian, all of them from the late 1910s through the 1920s. Clearly Cowell preferred the mystic pieces, perhaps because they allowed the clusters to yield their full harmonic sensuousness and perhaps because the Varian-inspired titles were evocative. Most of his piano works connected with Varian and the temple more or less echoed *Tides*. These works depicted different aspects of Irish mysticism and myth, under titles that included *The Hero Sun, The Voice of Lir, The Vision of Oma,*

The Vron of Sorrows, The Fire of the Cauldron, The Harp of Life, March of the Feet of the Eldana, The Trumpet of Angus Og, March of the Fomer, The Battle of Midyar, and *Domnu, Mother of Waters.* The mystic style of these works relies on a small repertory of cluster techniques. It forgoes the rhetoricism and virtuosic devices of the futurist style almost entirely in favor of low, gonging clusters, macrocluster backbeats, measured arpeggiations of large clusters, and slow scalar passages in two-octave clusters alternating black and white keys (played with only *one* arm).[28]

The mystic-style clusters usually accompany a traditionally harmonized modal tune. In other words, these Varian-inspired works exchange the abrupt juxtapositions of his futurist style for a superposition of two musical layers—one, Irish folk music; the other, primal throbbing.[29] In this way, the pieces expressed a peculiar aesthetic based on one of Cowell and Varian's favorite Irish legendary figures, the father of the gods, Lir. Because he had only half a tongue, only half of Lir's directions for creating the universe could be understood, went the legend. Thus, "for everything that has been created there is an unexpressed and concealed counterpart."[30] The simple tunes and harmonies represented the understood; clusters, the incomprehensible mystery. One of the mystic clusters pieces, *The Voice of Lir,* overtly portrayed the half-tongued god. As in *Tides,* Cowell chooses musical elements that well suit his programmatic scenario: the well-defined, "legible" right-hand modal material depicts Lir's clearly understood orders, whereas the low clusters represent the "concealed counterpart" to those orders. As Steven Johnson points out, *Lir,* like other mystic-style pieces, also features the same dramatic trajectory found in *Tides.*[31]

If his futurist cluster pieces had evoked the drama of modern life, his mystic cluster pieces evoked a slower, subtler cosmic drama, in which one sensed something ineffable struggling to achieve a voice. But when compared with Cowell's futurist style, the mystic style seemed regressive—"audaciously conservative," Nicolas Slonimsky called it.[32]

For all of these cluster pieces, Cowell devised a new notational system. As we saw, *Adventures in Harmony* used conventional noteheads for both micro- and macroclusters. Since the noteheads were too numerous and dense to be written out continually, Cowell used the shorthand "simile" or "sempre" (and the colloquial "like last") in connection with the verbal notations "hand" and "arm." It must have been clear to him even then that, if he were to continue using clusters, he would have to create a simpler way of signifying them. Measured arpeggiations and microclusters, even those to be played with the fist, could still be written with normal noteheads, but chromatic clusters of an octave or more posed a problem that only a new notation could solve.

Figure 1 shows the progress of his attempts to create just such a notation. Sometime in 1916, probably while working on the pencil score to *Dynamic Motion,* he created his first type of new symbols for clusters. According to this notation, the sort of cluster to be played between two pitches was signified by right-angled brackets protruding from the stem to the left, to the right, or both. Even in his pencil score to *Dynamic Motion,* however, he began to vary this notation by relaxing the angles; by the time of *Building of Bamba* the lines were all completely rounded.[33] Probably around 1920, Cowell devised his second and considerably simpler type of symbols for clusters: upright cigar shapes, topped by a sharp or flat if a black-key cluster was called for, topped by a natural sign if a white-key cluster. He would use this notation in manuscripts of the 1920s—including the final draft of *Dynamic Motion*—as well as in a chart of cluster techniques probably prepared for lectures at Halcyon.[34]

If the rhythm pieces were illustrations of "New Musical Resources," the cluster pieces were refutations of it, since they usually failed to follow the manuscript's "rules" or behaved in ways not mentioned in the manuscript. Both the rhythm pieces and the cluster pieces epitomized one aspect of Cowell's aesthetic: Cowell worked best when a piece was *about* something, but only one thing. Each of the pieces related to "New Musical Resources" behaved in one of two

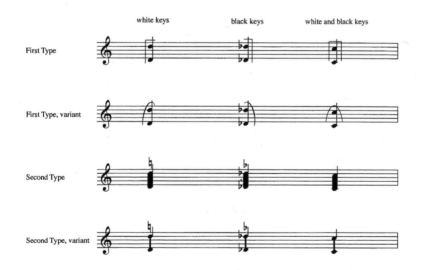

Figure 1. Cowell's Cluster Notation

ways: either it realized a specific formula and then, having done so, ended, or it started with a poetic image or mood, then used simple resources to evoke it.

§   §   §

Cowell's new music was destined to flourish in the 1920s, a decade that would become legendary for thriving on novelty, new ideas, freedom of expression, and gadgets. With much of the Western world still buoyant from the postwar boom and the end of combat, the year 1920 opened what one historian called a "free-form age, an age of experiment."[35] In such an age avant-garde musical culture took wing: in 1920–21 alone the first commercial radio station went on the air, a German modern music journal (*Melos*) went on sale, Tristan Tzara gave the first dadaist performance, Leon Theremin built the electronic instrument that would bear his name, and Edgard Varèse started the International Composers Guild in New York City, an organization dedicated to promoting the performance of experimental music in America.

With such headiness for the avant-garde surrounding him, Henry Cowell experienced his own personal breakthrough, the first biographical article about him in a major New York newspaper. In January 1920 the *Globe and Commercial Advertiser* spent sixteen lengthy paragraphs extolling the twenty-two-year-old, reviewing his life, praising his quest for modernism, telling anecdotes of his childhood, and focusing on his acquaintance with kindred spirit Leo Ornstein. The article ended almost better than Cowell could have hoped for: "Personally after hearing Cowell I am convinced that he is the coming musician of America. He is original. He is modernistic, as for instance in his strange 'The Tides.' But he is also as classical as could be desired in other music. . . . I predict for Cowell a most brilliant career. He is a modest, quaint character. You only need to see him to know that he is genuine, different, musical, and poetical."[36]

The article coincided with Cowell's return to New York, where he spent the first months of 1920 putting aside his experimentalism in order to learn the "divine rules," studying counterpoint with R. Huntington Woodman, learning to write inventions, fugues, and even a double fugue (as he proudly announced to Ellen Veblen).[37] More important to his career, he also played in at least two recitals in the first three months of the year. In January Cowell met Ethyl Leginska, an inveterate fan of Ornstein and a performer of his music. After he played some of his music for her, she said that *Antinomy* was "better than anything [Ornstein] ever wrote."[38] In a few weeks, Leginska asked Cowell to replace Ornstein at a Steinway Hall modern music concert she had arranged, because the better-known virtuoso had come down with the flu. At the concert Leginska took the audience and reporters in attendance by surprise when she publicly announced that Henry Cowell was a better composer than Ornstein.[39] The critics loved Henry almost as well, praising his "extremely futuristic compositions" and calling his ideas "original, to say the least, and he treats them novelly."[40] A few days after this concert, Henry got a letter from his half-brother, Clarence, who asked him to give up music and go into business with him. Not surprisingly, Henry declined.[41]

When he returned to the West Coast in the fall of 1920, Cowell felt emboldened for the first time to charge admission to a recital.[42] His audiences correspondingly seemed to take him more seriously, as suggested by Russell Varian in a letter to his parents: at a Palo Alto concert, "Henry played some of his piano music including some of the elbo music, and got away with it without a laugh."[43] The local newspaper critics were also impressed, hailing his talent, again calling him a "genius," defending the logical soundness of his ideas (especially of clusters), and forecasting a great future for him. Only Redfern Mason continued to find fault: Cowell's compositions are "more remarkable for occasional daintiness of fancy and episodic picturesqueness than for logical sequence, or organic unity." Undoubtedly because Cowell's musical single-mindedness still vexed him, Mason wrote, "It is in the smaller forms that Cowell is at his best."[44]

Meanwhile, Cowell was writing a basic piano course for the children of Halcyon. In October 1920 he sent the first chapter to the wife of Dr. Dower, hoping to prepare a new lesson each week, and pledging to correct the children's written assignments (though not grade them), on the premise that his corrections would make the children work harder. He wrote happily about his desire to start at the simplest level, then proceed by slow degrees: "I hope it is the right thing. It is for children, and begins at the very beginning. Probably most of the Halcyon children know these things already, but it won't hurt them to review. The language tries to be simple, even at the expense of extreme accuracy."[45]

The course, for which he eventually wrote ten lessons, begins by describing the piano keyboard, the names of the keys, rhythmic values, and so forth. Subsequent chapters treat fingering, clefs, basic musical symbols, basic articulation, and dynamics. The most interesting portion of the course comes in lesson 3, under the heading "Tones and Melodies." He begins by describing "how a tone is made," in terms that these beachside children could understand: "When the hammer in a piano hits a string it makes the string vibrate (to vibrate is to swing back and forth very fast), and the string vibrating makes waves through the air, which, if we could see them, would look a little like waves in the sea, only so tiny that there might be several hundred to an inch. These waves hit our ears and make there what we call sound or tone." He goes on to describe some basic frequencies, then invites the children to place their fingers on the string to feel the vibration: "If you watch a low string after the hammer hits it you can see it vibrate, and if you put your finger on it you can [feel] it."[46] To understand how tones are made is valuable, he then explains, because "if you remember as you are playing what a marvelous thing a single tone is you will be more careful of each tone you play and will listen, listen to each one."

For most of 1921 Cowell played few recitals and composed only unadventurous music. This was partly because he was preparing earlier compositions for publication and writing his first article (assisted by Robert Duffus, a longtime friend of Ellen Veblen). Cowell's "Harmonic Development in Music" was a bona fide theoretical treatise with Seeger-inspired ideas, Seward-assisted prose, and not a single reference to Seeger or Seward. It was long enough to be serialized in three successive issues of *The Freeman*, a new Irish journal devoted to politics, philosophy, and art. (Similar articles about modern music theory had appeared in other "generalist" journals such as the *Monist*, which in 1917 had published Ernst Bacon's comprehensive treatise on tone combinations, later issued as a small book, *Our Musical Idiom.*)[47] The *Freeman*'s editor prefaced the first installment of "Harmonic Development in Music" with a note that the article would give "scientific justification for the explorations which our contemporary musical pioneers are making." Without such justification, the editor said, those pioneers were doomed to suffer "the stigma of mere levity and anarchic license."[48]

In this article Cowell contended, as Seeger and others had, that the harmonic development of music consisted of the gradual acceptance of each successive interval in the overtone series. In each century of Western musical history, composers introduced new overtone relationships to the hearing of their listeners. (For example, Cowell credited Palestrina, Monteverdi, and Bach with introducing the fifth and sixth, seventh, and eighth and ninth partials, respectively, into the harmonic vocabulary.) Cowell actually provided a chart showing which composers popularized which overtone ratios—somewhat confusingly, it should be added, since not only does he not really account for the intonational differences between the overtone series and equal temperament, he also skips over the intervals in the series that do not fit his theory.

According to Cowell, the final steps in this acceptance of higher overtones had been taken by Wagner, then Schoenberg, then Ornstein. Henceforth, composers could go no further than the fifteenth to sixteenth partial relationship—the half step—because the next interval (i.e., from sixteenth to seventeenth partials) would be microtonal, smaller than the half step available on contemporary instruments. Nevertheless, he added, "There is no reason to doubt that this step, which is quite in the historic line of musical growth, will eventually be taken," leading to a new design for keyboards and a new notational system.[49]

Until equal temperament is abandoned, Cowell argued, "harmonic progress" will take only two directions: *tone clusters,* of course—the stacking up of the now acceptable half steps—and *polyharmony,* the superimposing of triads (both terms published for the first time in this article). His argument for the latter was the same as that in "New Musical Resources": since each individual tone actually produces a rich "chord" (the overtone series), the ear was already hearing a kind of polyharmony whenever two (or more) tones sounded at once. He then proposed that conventional accompaniments to simple melodies could be modernized by simply using polychords or clusters in the place of triads and seventh chords.

Cowell predicted that music would also progress down "other avenues," notably rhythm, meter, and tempo. More complicated relationships in these domains would also be necessitated by the gradual acceptance of intervallic relationships: "The common factor of music is vibration, into which tone as well as time, meter and tempo may all be resolved." He concluded the article with an observation about the usefulness of such musical speculations. "As an art and as a science the work of exploration has just begun; and this, for a jaded world, is perhaps a sufficient moral."[50]

While serving as a modestly impressive debut article for a twenty-four-year-old, it did not penetrate deeply the "jaded world" into which it was sent. It had appeared not in a music magazine but in a short-lived generalist journal. It was far too technical to be appreciated by most readers, for whom "modern" music probably meant ragtime and jazz, not the severe Seegeresque experiments to which Cowell alluded in his prose. Seeger later explained the kind of culture in which such an article had appeared: "In America [in the 1920s], talking about music was done in the newspapers and by teachers who taught you harmony and counterpoint, and on rare occasions, history of music out of a textbook."[51] For anyone privileged to have had the latter, Cowell's article may have been a godsend. To the rest it was probably an irrelevancy.

Nevertheless, to the people of Carmel it was a demonstration not only of Cowell's scientific mind, but of his versatility—especially in that he was now a writer, perhaps the most venerable of all artistic trades in the minds of Carmelians. The *Freeman* article was "very clearly and scientifically propounded," the *Carmel Pine Cone* said. But while "his ability as a composer has long been recognized, that he is also a powerful writer is a source of much gratification to those interested in his career." Within weeks the newspaper declared that Cowell's article was "exciting wide comment among musicians and music students," especially for its new terms "polyharmony" and "tone cluster."[52]

The year 1922 brought both triumph and disaster for Cowell. That year Cowell's friend and fellow Halcyon devotee Dane Rudhyar wrote about him glowingly in the premiere American musicological journal, the *Musical Quarterly.* Rudhyar linked Cowell with Ornstein, identifying both composers as the two men who had "imperilled [the] existence" of "the musical unit, the note," which, until then, had stood "undefiled." Why? Because both used tone clusters, albeit as "tentative efforts . . . still very empirical in character."[53] Also that year Associated Music published no fewer than nineteen of Cowell's compositions, ten of which featured clusters: *Dynamic Motion,* its Five Encores, *The Harp of Life,* and a set called *Three Irish Myths* (containing *Tides of Manaunaun, Voice of Lir,* and *The Hero Sun*). These were all staples of his recital repertoire. Fittingly, all of the sheet music to these pieces contained back-page ads both for Ornstein's music and for a recently published biography of Ornstein. In announcing the publication of these pieces, Cowell's hometown newspaper briefly recounted his life, noting that in New York he had met Leo Ornstein.[54] With the publication of Cowell's cluster pieces, other pianists began playing them. During 1922 at least three pianists featured Cowell works on their recitals— Richard Buhlig, Margaret Nikolovic, and Winifred Hooke. Within five years, Cowell would claim that over one hundred pianists were playing his music.[55]

In 1922 Cowell published his second article, an arcane piece for the journal of the Temple of the People. In "Tonal Therapy," Cowell describes experiments at Halcyon in which colored light is used to cure diseases. He considers whether a musical tone might also neutralize a disease and suggests that, because of its ability to sustain a tone, a violin would work better for experimentation than a piano. Cowell then reports such an experiment conducted by Dr. and Mrs. Dower. Noting that the results were "surprisingly good" if inconclusive, Cowell explains how the tones E and B will probably have a "curative effect" on cancer and syphilis, as will B♭ and E♭ on tuberculosis and C and G on strep throat. Finally, Cowell expresses enthusiasm for this "wonderful field for research," hoping furthermore that "energetic composers may [write] . . . special music to be used in healing, in which the proper tones will predominate" (see appendix 3 for citation and full text).

During 1920–21 Cowell had become increasingly serious in his devotion to Edna Smith; sometime in 1921 they had become engaged. Although she appears intermittently in the records of his life before then, it is unclear how their relationship grew to the level it did. Henry recalled that he had longed for years to find the "companionship of any girl that I considered decent."[56] Apparently, with common interests and experiences binding them together, Edna became that girl. The growing fallowness and conservatism of his compositional life during the first years of the Roaring Twenties may, in fact, be the consequence of a blossoming of his love life, which probably led him away from the abstract and ideal world in which he had always before preferred to live.

As 1922 opened, Henry and Edna were on the verge of marriage. They planned it for just after Cowell would return to New York from a spring 1922 trip to California, where he was scheduled to play some recitals, including one at Mills College the first week of April. On April 16, apparently while staying at Halcyon, Cowell received the news that Edna had been killed in a gruesome accident. Edna and her sister Genevieve had stopped their car to pick wildflowers beside a railroad track. When they drove across the track, a train broadsided them, smashing the car to bits and throwing their mangled bodies fifty yards from the collision. Edna was still clutching the door handle in her hand. The coroner's jury found the state negligent for not having erected a safer railroad warning system at the crossing and awarded Smith's wealthy family an undisclosed sum.

Although he went on composing and giving recitals, seemingly oblivious to what had happened, Cowell went into months of what he later described as "numbness and misery" and began a series of relationships with younger men—frankly sexual relationships that would later come back to haunt him.[57] But when Edna's family gave some of her inheritance and settlement money to Henry's education fund—thousands of dollars—he considered it his "sacred duty to spend every dollar of that fund."[58] He realized he could now fulfill the plans that he and Seeger had made: in 1916, Seeger recalled, he and Cowell jointly had "spent no small amount of time in planning assaults, in the form of concerts, upon New York, Paris, and Berlin, in which tone clusters and string plucking . . . figured largely."[59] Now, finally having not only the repertoire but the means to accomplish this, Cowell planned a European tour.

It was a bold, typically bohemian enterprise. As Cowell himself had once considered doing, many young American composers of his generation had gone to Paris, Vienna, or Berlin to learn European techniques. But Cowell now went to teach the Europeans *his* techniques. It was a propitious time to do so. Since the end of the Great War new, adventurous music had begun again to flourish in Europe. In November 1918, in the wake of the armistice, Arnold Schoenberg had founded the Society for Private Performances in Vienna, a forum for modernist composers. In 1921 the first Festival for the Promotion of Contemporary Music was held in Donaueschingen. In 1922 Salzburg offered its first Festival of Contemporary Music, at the close of which the International Society for Contemporary Music was formed. Meanwhile, in New York City, expatriate composer Edgard Varèse formed the International Composers Guild (1921) and the League of Composers (1923), both of which gave concerts featuring the progressive work of young European composers. Cowell's 1923 tour of Europe—not unlike Ornstein's earlier tours of the continent—was a personal response to the growing dynasty of European new music, his first insurgence in a campaign for the respectability of "ultra-modern" *American* music around the world.

It was for this 1923 tour, his first "assault" on the international musical establishment, that he wrote a new piece entitled simply *Piece for Piano with Strings.* It was a tone cluster piece, like many of his others, except that Cowell played or modified some clusters with a new musical resource never suggested in his book: playing with his hand directly on the piano strings, strumming, plucking, thumping, and damping them.[60] Cowell, ever the cataloger and neologist, eventually coined a new name for the "new instrument" comprised by these techniques: the "string piano."

§   §   §

The sounds of the string piano had been explored for generations before Cowell invented the term. Early nineteenth-century piano manufacturers, for example, had dreamt up an assortment of keyboard attachments to mimic Turkish music: a "cymbals" effect produced by hitting brass strips against the lower strings; a "drum" effect produced by hitting the back of the soundboard; a "bassoon" effect produced by pressing parchment-covered wood against the strings. Other piano makers devised pedals that triggered bars to touch the piano strings lightly and make harmonics. Dozens of patents for all these sorts of effects were issued before 1850.[61] Even without such devices, some pianists played directly on the strings for humorous effect. The virtuoso Olga Samaroff claimed to have played on the strings with brushes and cloth as early as 1887 and continued doing so at parties well into the twentieth century.[62] An obscure entertainer named Otto Lemberg was said to have played directly on the strings around 1890.[63] Adrian Wettach—better known as "Grock" the clown—sometimes played inside the piano as part of his act in the 1910s.[64] The first "serious" composer to write for piano strings was probably Percy Grainger: at the close of the third movement of his *In a Nutshell* suite (1916), he directs the pianist to play on several bass strings with a yarn-covered mallet (example 18).

Like many children, Cowell may have played on the piano strings out of simple curiosity, especially since, before the piano, he had played zither and vio-

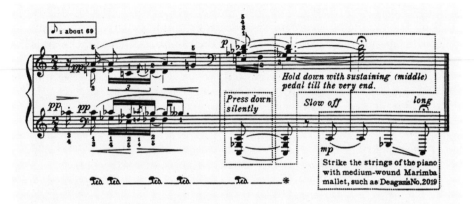

Example 18. Percy Grainger, *In a Nutshell* (piano version), ending

lin.[65] He clearly contemplated such things at Halcyon (and even perhaps at Berkeley). But his first piece to notate the technique was the *Piece for Piano with Strings.*

The piece begins with echoes of the mystic cluster pieces, then turns to the futurist virtuosity of *Dynamic Motion* and its Five Encores—splashy, athematic, abundant with motoric pulsations and textural filigree. After fifty measures, Cowell softly sweeps the fingers across two octaves of bass strings, damps some strings with his hand, slaps a flank of strings, and plucks a one-measure melody. The opening virtuosity resumes, followed by a quiet reprise of the piano string-sweeps and damping to close the piece.

It is not clear how often Cowell played this piece on the tour. But predictably, both it and his tone cluster pieces drew mixed reactions.[66] Anna Strunsky Walling recalls that at his Carnegie Hall debut (the beginning of the tour) the hall was empty except for the first three or four rows, which were occupied exclusively by Cowell's friends. Although there was no hostility, Walling's mother began to giggle as Cowell reached into the piano, later explaining that there was something "embarrassing about the whole procedure."[67] Cowell claims that at his Leipzig concert two factions in the audiences began shouting, one haranguing Cowell, the other telling the first group to be quiet. A brawl broke out on stage, during which Cowell continued playing, even though people were throwing programs and books at him.[68] In France the editors of *Le Courier Musical* were impressed enough with the string piano piece to publish it within two months of Cowell's Paris debut.[69] When Cowell returned to New York, some pianists called his string playing "musical immorality."[70] A few local critics, however, managed to keep an open mind. One chided audience members who had laughed: "There is no more reason why he should not . . . strike [the piano strings] than why a fiddler should abstain from plucking the fiddle strings in pizzicato."[71] Another praised Cowell's string piano piece as a sequel to Grainger's *Nutshell* suite and rebuked those who scoffed: "The people who called for strait-jackets had better be calling for ears, for themselves."[72]

Overall, many open-minded musicians saw Cowell's unusual techniques as a means of compensating for the deficiencies in his compositional technique. This point of view was well stated by the Czech pianist Ludvik Kundera: "Cowell as a composer," he wrote, "was a complete disappointment," because Cowell relied on the quality of each "new technique" to determine the success or failure of the piece in which it appeared. "His innermost expression is, however, very simple, usually one-part melody, accompanied and apparently thickened by noises of some kind, either clusters of all diatonic or chromatic tones on the piano, or analogous clusters on his 'string piano.' . . . The source of all Cowell's inventions is his interest in the color of the sound."[73] It is true: Cowell exalted the newness of his ideas above the development of his ideas. Because the European tradition of musical organicism ran deep, this emphasis on mere novelty probably troubled European listeners more than it did Americans.

When Cowell returned home to Menlo Park in June 1924, he played his European recital program in San Francisco, where at least one critic defended his string piano ideas on the same basis that other critics had already defended his clusters—as an intellectual claim staked on childlike play, a methodical approach to a juvenile impulse. "It may be said that there is nothing new in these tricks," C. W. Brown wrote for the *San Francisco Chronicle*. "Many a child has beguiled the tedium of the practice hour by doing these very things. . . . The novelty, however, lies in their serious use toward an artistic end, in the endeavor to utilize every resource of the instrument."[74] With a sense of self-confidence perhaps bolstered by critical praise, Cowell began writing pieces in which *every note* was attacked or modified by the hands on the strings. The first two of these pieces, probably written that year, displayed two different approaches to the piano strings—one crosswise, the other lengthwise. The first piece, *Aeolian Harp,* clearly takes the ancient idea of harps being played by the wind as a word play on the use of a piano's strings as a harp, one of the most popular of American piano makers being the Aeolian Company. In *Aeolian Harp* Cowell used the piano like a zither. The player stood at the keyboard, plucking solo notes and strumming chords while controlling the harmony at the keyboard. Designed to be played on upright pianos, *Aeolian Harp* was novel in technique but old-fashioned in harmonic idiom.

His other string piano piece of 1924, *The Sword of Oblivion,* was in several respects far more radical. Inspired by an image in John Varian's Irish mythology, this grand piano piece requires the player to rub and scrape the coils of the bass strings at varying rates of speed so as to produce high-pitched glissandi—the sounds of swords being unsheathed, perhaps (example 19). In the middle section of the piece, the pianist must play slow repeated notes on the keyboard while pressing down and releasing their respective strings so as to vary the pitch a half step. Virtually nothing of conventional musical substance happens in this section; rather, the thunks and thuds simply generate reverberations that imply vast space—oblivion. Despite (or because of) its radical approach to the piano, *The Sword of Oblivion* was neither published nor, it appears, performed. *Aeolian Harp,* on the other hand, became one of Cowell's most widely performed works.

In 1925 Cowell coined the name "string piano," announcing in the pages of *Musical America* that he had discovered a wonderful new instrument that "has the incalculable advantage of being already in nearly everyone's drawing-room."[75] He began compiling a systematic list of every possible way to elicit sounds from the strings, braces, soundboard, and lid—strumming, tapping, scraping, and hitting them with fingertips, fingernails, palms, and various objects, including knives, thimbles, pencils, and darning eggs. Most of the effects he produced, he said, "do not suggest other instruments. Some of them do, but none can be exactly reproduced on any other instrument." After listing 165 such effects, however, he abandoned the list as hopelessly impractical. The huge breadth of possibilities discouraged him from devising any new notational symbols. Instead, for each string piano piece he would follow the notational prototype of *Piece for Piano with Strings,* combining traditional staff notation with footnotes that told the player how to manipulate the strings.

In 1925 he also received requests to write new string piano pieces for three other pianists, all of them California women. His response was a string piano duet titled *Duet for St. Cecelia* and a three-movement work that Cowell originally called his "string concerto," later renamed *A Composition for String Piano with Ensemble.* The latter piece, which contained an arrangement of the *Duet for St. Cecelia* as its second movement, was premiered in Los Angeles in January 1926 by Adolph Tandler and his Little Symphony, with Winifred Hooke at the piano.[76] Each movement mingled the string piano with a different combination of instruments: the first movement, three woodwinds, horn, and strings; the second movement, a solo violin; and the third movement, a string quartet. A month after its premiere, Cowell played the piece with a pickup group in New York; it was never performed again. Cowell rewrote the first

Example 19. *The Sword of Oblivion* (complete) (Reprinted by permission of the David and Sylvia Teitelbaum Fund, as successors to Henry and Sidney Cowell)

movement, removing all of the inside-the-piano effects, and used it as the first movement of his Piano Concerto (1928).

Besides these works for others, Cowell in 1925 wrote another solo string piano piece for himself to play. John Varian had recently asked him to set his poem *The Ban Shee* to music, using a piano and high-pitched soprano.[77] Cowell agreed to do so, then decided to drop Varian's text and simply evoke the actual cries of the legendary Irish spirit by using what Seeger had called "inarticulate pitch"—sliding tones that could evoke primitivistic "wailing."[78] Combining the crosswise and lengthwise techniques of *Aeolian Harp* and *Sword of Oblivion* and putting them at the service of supernatural imagery, Cowell produced his most eloquent string piano piece. To play it, however, required two players—himself, standing in the crook of the piano, and an assistant who sat and worked the pedals.[79]

These string piano pieces, and the others that followed them during the 1920s, displayed some of Cowell's most resounding "new musical resources." But those resources had never appeared in his manuscript of that name. By the same token, many of the "resources" mentioned in the book—techniques, to be more precise—were seldom or never actually taken up in Cowell's music. But through the book and the compositions written around it, Cowell transcended the nagging criticism that he didn't develop his musical ideas. The real legacy of the rhythm pieces, cluster pieces, and the string piano was the very notion that idea itself was more important than process. The worth of a piece of music (and therefore of its composer) rested more on the freshness of a technique than the development of it. Insofar as "New Musical Resources" aspired to be a kind of Unified Field Theory of music, it did so only in the way it reset one's gauge of musical value. Not surprisingly, the resetting went in Cowell's favor.

5

The Bohemian Legacy

By the mid-1920s Henry Cowell was beginning to enter the mainstream, or at least that modest tributary of progressive art that ran through twentieth-century America. He had done something his parents had never been able to do—make a living from his art. Yet Cowell faced a hazard that most American bohemians did: the conflict between individualism and alienation. This conflict was described as early as the 1820s by Alexis de Tocqueville. The inhabitants of the New World, de Tocqueville wrote, are individualists who "acquire the habit of always considering themselves as standing alone." The democratic spirit, he wrote, separates the American from his neighbors and contemporaries. Yet, by the same token, it "throws him back forever upon himself alone"—isolated, marginalized, shunned.[1] This proves especially troubling for an artist: being merely an individualist can divide one from the culture that one hopes to lead.

With his clusters and string piano Cowell had distanced himself from both precursors and peers. Around the world he had achieved a kind of freakish notoriety. But mere uniqueness came relatively cheaply, leaving him with little more than a scrapbook full of awestruck reviews. What remained was to show the world that he was part of a tradition that would make his work more than merely aberrant. Having defied the ruling traditions in Western music he had to make a new tradition that could enshrine his compositions for posterity. Beginning in the mid-1920s, Cowell built that tradition, the American musical avant-garde. The result was that, as Peter Yates said, Cowell "contributed more than any other one person to uniting the more radical composers of America into the belief that there was a future for them."[2]

To do that Cowell had to shift his emphasis. Composing and performing had to give way to lecturing, organizing, publishing, authoring, and teaching. The premises of all these activities were, in true bohemian fashion, paradoxical: Cowell was patriotic yet multicultural, utilitarian yet visionary, arcane yet anti-elitist.

If there is a core idea behind all of his work in the post-bohemian years, it may be found in his most celebrated remark, first recorded in 1955 and quoted frequently since: "I want to live in the *whole world* of music!"[3] That remark clearly bespoke the bohemianism he had imbibed as a child, with its glorification of boundary crossing, its refusal to be constrained by conventional limits, its resistance to being pinned down to any one ideology or practice other than freedom. It was that very attitude that drove him to escape from the solitude and recluseness of his mother into the glare of public life. In a series of far-flung enterprises from the mid-1920s on, he showed his determination to live in that "whole world" of music by not just writing and playing new music, but teaching it, studying it, and promoting it.

The most obvious early manifestation of that determination was to flee the humdrum status of being merely a local genius, a hometown musical hero, in search of world fame. Following the example of his mother and the counsel of Seeger, he spent the 1920s criss-crossing the country in his jalopy, playing for anyone anywhere who would book him into a recital hall, gymnasium, library, or theater. Sustained by the money from Edna Smith's family, and resolved to break free of his heartsickness over her death by leaving the boundaries of the United States, he made tours to Europe in 1923, 1926, 1929, and 1931, traveling further into the continent each time. With every tour, he was rebuffed by most critics and audiences—a badge of honor to a bohemian—yet celebrated by a small group who saw him as a daring harbinger of futurist techniques.

It was on his 1929 tour that he crossed one final boundary into a part of the world heretofore taboo for American musicians. On his third international tour Cowell played in London, where he was heard by a Russian consul charged with finding new artistic attractions.[4] The consul arranged for Cowell to come to the Soviet Union for five weeks. What Cowell found there both repulsed and tantalized him. On the one hand, the Bolshevik musical culture was far too conservative and monochromatic for his radical mindset; the reception given him by the government's Cultural Relations Society was cold (they cancelled his scheduled concert). Other societal conditions unnerved him: the closeness of living quarters, the fervency of Lenin worship, the vexatious bureaucracy, the squeezing out of private enterprise, and the marriage laws, which seemed to force many young couples into loveless, inescapable unions in order to find and keep their housing. But Cowell, not traveling with a group and more or less unsupervised by government hosts, observed the mundane life and real character of the Soviet people. In doing so, he was amazed at their generosity, cooperative attitude, and lingering free-spiritedness: the refusal of porters to accept tips, the equality of men's and women's wages, the constant offers to share food and lodging with him, the crowds of men and women bathing nude and uninhibited in the Moscow river, and the hunger of common people for scientific experiment and cultural progress.[5] He had observed firsthand what seemed the best fruits of the socialism espoused by his parents and the Bolshevism praised by John Varian.

What inspired Cowell perhaps the most was the almost insatiable appetite of local conservatory students to hear his strange new music, an appetite about which he wrote in gleeful detail:

> After I played my first number for them, there rose from the hall an indescribable roaring and bellowing, like Niagara Falls and a touch-down at a football game combined. Yells, shouts, clapping, and stamping of feet jumbled into one mighty din. . . . The noise showed no sign of abating, so I raised my hand, and when there was quiet, I began to play the second number on the program. Upon which, the noise began again, and rose to such a wild pitch that I was forced to stop. The students sent a delegate onto the stage . . . to ask if I would please be good enough to play the first composition over. I did so. The same sort of roaring followed, and I again tried unsuccessfully to start the second piece on the program. They sent up the delegate again to ask if I could please consider playing the first piece a third time. [Upon playing the next piece] its reception was the same, and after I had played it four times in succession I was permitted to go on and play the third piece. The third piece, as it happened, contains some very unusual methods of playing the piano, and it had created such excitement that I had to play it through no less than seven times![6]

When he tried to have an intermission, at five o'clock in the afternoon, the students pleaded with him not to. They could have the hall only until 8:15. Cowell dutifully played until then, repeating every number not fewer than three times. For the first occasion in his career, Cowell had served up his strangest music and received hearty calls for encores, "more unbounded enthusiasm on the part of the audience than I have ever received anywhere."[7] The Soviets had given him a taste of a musical society apparently striving for the highest and best—as he saw it—one where newness was prized and strangeness celebrated. The final triumph for Cowell came when the Soviet government agreed to publish two of his piano works, *Lilt of the Reel* and the ferocious cluster piece *Tiger*.

From that visit on he praised the Russian people for their love of "ultramodern" music. He also found himself drawn to the qualities of socialism that allowed its adherents to escape the crippling poverty he had endured as a youth (and to some extent still did). He, like many American artists of the 1930s, saw the Soviet Union as a place in which essential needs were met for all, allowing all to better their taste in art and, freed from the terrors of unemployment or social casting, to explore new ideas freely.

On his final European tour, Cowell reclaimed a part of his youth he had long neglected. Exotic musics had enchanted him as a boy in Chinatown. Now, he found, he could systematically explore and assimilate them through technology—the phonograph. In 1931 he received a Guggenheim Foundation Fellowship to travel to Berlin to study non-Western musics through field recordings at the *Staatsbibliothek,* which had an enormous collection of phonograph discs. This trip was the beginning of what became a passion for record collecting, a hobby that fulfilled the promises of his Halcyon days: it combined the art of music—in this case the exotic music of alien traditions—with the progressivism of modern technology. In the ensuing years Cowell amassed thousands of 78 rpm recordings of multicultural musics, many of which remain to this day in a closet at the New School for Social Research.[8]

Yet, for all his cosmopolitanism, his deep need to roam the planet and assimilate the world's music, Cowell had a deep streak of Americanism. The army had undoubtedly solidified the patriotic part of his soul. Now the entrepreneurial and authorial activities he undertook from the mid-1920s on became his own personal war on Europe.

American composers had tried for decades to find a national musical identity and declare their independence from the European tradition. As Arthur Farwell wrote in 1903, "the promise of our national musical art lies in that work of our composers which is sufficiently un-german. . . . It is only by exalting the common inspirations of American life that we can become great musically."[9] In searching for melodic themes that were distinctly "American," most composers simply adapted Negro spirituals or ersatz Indian melodies. What they did with those themes, it should be noted, remained European in method and intent. As Charles Hamm suggests, the real question for early twentieth-century American composers became: what should one strive for in real "American-ness"?[10]

Cowell understood the adjective "American" as a definer of ideology more than of style. "American" meant pioneering, novel, in some measure ungovernable, and resistant to foreign domination. It was music that was *free,* unfettered by dogma, free even to accept or reject European models. Music of the New World not only had to be "newer" than that of the Old World, it had to be eclectic, distinctive only in its refusal to have a distinctive sound. From the mid-1920s through the early 1930s this idea of American music became the force behind Cowell's attempt to raze the musical establishment and erect a new one.

Part of that razing was propagandistic. Cowell had seen in Europe the class structure of new music: while European modernists such as Schoenberg and Stravinsky were known in America, American modernists were unknown in Europe, unless they, like he and Ornstein, were also performers. Europe continued to maintain the prestige that allowed it to dominate Americans' perception of cultural progress. With that prestige on their side, European composers had banded together into new music guilds to promote one another's music through performances and articles, instilling a kind of pride in being "avant-garde," on the front end of artistic evolution. But in his characteristically self-assured way, Cowell felt that he and his composer colleagues were equally avant-garde. American composers did not need better compositional craft so much as better public relations.

With that in mind, Cowell wrote dozens of magazine articles that argued for American musical parity and even supremacy. He began with "America Takes a Front Rank in Year's Modernist Output" (1925), which attacks Europeans' "idea we cannot produce fine composers." Carl Ruggles and Leo Ornstein, he argued, were better composers than Schoenberg and Stravinsky.[11] In 1927 he started a two-year deluge of articles on Varèse, Chavez, Slonimsky, Ives, Weiss, Rudhyar, Harris, Ornstein, and others, in magazines ranging from general journals (such as the *New Freeman* and *New Republic*) to arts journals (*Aesthete* and *Argonaut*) to music journals (*Modern Music* and *Pro-Musica Quarterly*) to foreign-language journals (*Melos* in Germany and *Musicalia* in Mexico). Despite the variety of intended audiences and editorial requirements of these journals, Cowell's prose always maintained the celebratory, sometimes hyperbolic tone of a press release for American music. He praises Varèse for his rhythmic variety—on the first page alone of *Hyperprism,* he notes, "there are thirty-two different rhythmical manners of filling a measure."[12] He lauds Slonimsky for his "simple but highly fruitful" idea of creating music "built up exclusively out of literal concords."[13] In such articles Cowell almost never writes about the *musicality* of the composers or the quality of their compositions per se, except in an occasional generality, such as applauding the "never-ending sparkling flow" in Chavez's music.[14] But he does consistently gauge a composer's worth by the logic or sheer newness of his methods. The composers that he championed, Cowell said, "are together forming a gigantic American musical culture," which by virtue of its diversity "is becoming one of the most interesting the world has known."[15]

In 1933 Cowell collected many of these articles, wrote new ones, and got other composers to write about one another for a book published by the intellectual cradle of his youth, Stanford University. The preface to that book, *American Composers on American Music: A Symposium,* showed that Cowell now thought himself the arbiter of true Americanism in music. To be included in the book, he explained, a composer "had to be someone with a definite point of view, preferably an individual one. This led to inviting many progressive and 'modern' composers to give statements, as they often have a refreshing new outlook." To allow the contributors to dwell on more conventional types of music would not only be "dry," but would have "no relation to the direction now being taken by American music."[16]

The direction being taken, of course, was the only direction that Cowell understood: his own, and that of his friends. He himself provided nine of the nineteen essays about individual composers, and the rest often seemed like mutual back-scratching: Weiss wrote about Riegger, Riegger about Weiss; Cowell wrote about Slonimsky, Slonimsky about Cowell; Seeger wrote about his wife, Ruth; and so on. Aside from the individual essays, part of the book was devoted to "general tendencies," featuring essays by Gershwin on the jazz influence in modern American music, Dane Rudhyar on the oriental influence, William Grant Still on the role of African-American composers, and Charles Ives on the future of music itself.

Cowell coupled his Americanist rhetoric with entrepreneurship. Heartened by the International Composers Guild's promotion of new music, yet discouraged by its European domination, Cowell formed an alternative group that would balance its repertoire more equally between European and American composers. The New Music Society of California, as its 1925 cream-colored prospectus announced, was a West Coast affiliate of the International Composers Guild dedicated to performances of "ultra-modern" compositions. Cowell's list of ultra-modern composers was telling: Stravinsky, Schoenberg, Ruggles, and Rudhyar—the latter a fellow member of the Temple of the People, whom Cowell at the time considered the only American composer besides Ruggles to write "really important music."[17] Now, in announcing the New Music Society, Cowell placed those two American composers on the same plane as the acknowledged European masters, a calculated assertion of America's cultural equality.[18]

While the New Music Society mounted performances, Cowell started a publication program. Although there were some American journals whose contributors wrote about the music he cared for (notably *Modern Music*), Cowell felt that the United States needed a periodical like *Le Courier Musical,* which actually published complete new compositions (including his own *Piece for Piano with Strings*). One day in 1927, while returning home from a camping trip with his father and stepmother, Cowell suggested starting a journal that would *only* publish scores, the "frankly experimental" and otherwise unpublishable scores of himself and his friends. He quickly raised $1,200 to start it ($900 of that was to hire secretaries to type subscription solicitations at ten cents a letter). He sent out thousands of letters, and got an astonishing 594 subscribers (at $2 apiece) for what he called the *New Music Quarterly*. Charles Ives, who called the journal "a circulating music library via a magazine of unsaleable scores," ordered two subscriptions, hinting he might order more. When the first issue appeared in the fall of 1927, it contained only an engraved score of Carl Ruggles's *Men and Mountains*. About half of the subscribers cancelled. Ives ordered twenty-five more subscriptions.[19]

Cowell's tiny empire of New Music survived partly because it was portable. Sidney Cowell later explained that "New Music consisted of a box of cards and letterheads."[20] In this way it could endure the crush of hard times. But it survived also because, over the objections of Seeger and Ruggles, Cowell had invited Ives to sit on the board of the New Music Society. In Cowell's eyes, Ives was a pathfinder whose music would prevail because, in Cowell's optimistic words, "Public favor comes to those great enough to be independent."[21] But more important to the survival of the New Music enterprises, Ives had made a huge fortune in the insurance business and would earn much more during the great bull market of 1928–29. Ives essentially bankrolled the *New Music Quarterly* with occasional donations and dozens of subscriptions. In turn, the *New Music Quarterly* became the first principal publisher of Ives's music, with Ives always picking up the tab. Cementing the relationship, Ives wrote Cowell into his will.[22]

Counting on Ives's support, Cowell concocted yet another noble, commercially doomed project, a New Music Quarterly Recordings series. He argued the need for this series of recordings on patriotic grounds. To issue recordings of American composers' work would make it "very dignified for us to take our rightful place in a world series including Europeans of all lands," he explained, "a thing that has never been accorded us before." The prospectus for this series was far more nationalistic than even that for the *Quarterly* had been. In a mere three sentences, for example, Cowell not only uses the word "American" four times, but, in effect, tries to sell the recordings on the premise of liberty and justice for all: "There has been an increasing demand for opportunities of hearing the works by contemporary American composers. A number of general societies perform a certain percentage of American works; and in the larger centers, there are special organizations [that] include American works on their programs. While programs of American works are presented in the music centers, these programs are available only to a small percent of those interested in hearing them."[23] By summer 1934 three discs had appeared, one with Cowell's now standard pairing of Ives and Ruggles. As these new products appeared, Cowell finally felt comfortable enough with his perennial sponsor to stop calling him "Mr. Ives" and address him in a letter as "Dear Charlie," signing it "Love, Henry."[24]

Cowell was finally able to harmonize his championing of America and his love of the Soviet Union in yet another enterprise. Like many American artists in the late 1920s and early 1930s, Cowell had been charmed by Communism, the comraderie it provided, and the egalitarian ideals it seemed to espouse. Cowell's compositional hero Carl Ruggles had joined the Communist Party and in 1926 was part of the founding editorial board of the Communist newspaper *New Masses*. One of the most vociferous columnists for that paper was "Carl Sands"—a pseudonym for none other than Charles Seeger.[25]

Sometime in 1931 or 1932—accounts vary—Seeger, Cowell, and Jacob Schaefer founded a seminar in the technique of writing workers' songs. Seeger later recalled that one winter night in New York City, Cowell came into the Seegers' apartment and said, "You know, Charlie, you were worried about the connection of music and society back there in Berkeley; there's a little group of good musicians who are moved by the Depression and are trying to make music that can go right out onto the streets and be used in protests and at union meetings. I think you might be interested in it." Seeger replied that he was, attended a meeting of the group and spoke to them, telling them that Marx himself was a proletarian pawn of the intellectual bourgeousie. This inflamed the doctrinaire Marxists in the group, but Seeger decided to keep coming despite—or because of—the hostile reception.[26]

This group, which began to call itself the Composers Collective of New York City, met on occasional late afternoons in dingy lofts with upright pianos, all rented by the Communist Party through its musical arm, the Pierre Degeyter Club. Seated around the piano, they discussed the musical needs of common workers and played newly composed "proletarian songs" for one another. In time they published two books of workers' songs and held contests to encourage the writing of more of them. To make their songs readily singable by almost anyone, most of the group's affiliates—which included young Jewish composers such as Marc Blitzstein, Aaron Copland, and Elie Siegmeister—had to backtrack, reversing their pursuit of modernism and embracing stark simplicity. They felt the necessity to do so, because, as they later wrote, the collective had been "called upon in the few years of its existence to provide music of every description for the ever-growing needs of the people's music movement in this country."[27]

Although Cowell is always credited as one of the founders of this group, it remains unclear how involved he remained with the collective as the 1930s wore on. He was, after all, still consumed by all his other projects—the New Music Society, *New Music Quarterly,* and New Music Recordings, not to mention teaching classes, composing, touring, concertizing, and so forth, all of which continued unabated during the life of the Composers Collective. Cowell is not mentioned as being in attendance in any of the available minutes of the group. Although he wrote six workers' songs, he apparently published only one of them, and that under a pseudonym. And he repudiated the Soviet Union when the Russian papers published a cartoon of him that attacked his financial motives.[28] Yet he did show his sympathies for the collective's aims in two articles: "Kept Music" and "'Useful' Music."

The first, which appeared in *Panorama* in 1934, bore a title that he admitted up front was a kind of bait: "What are titles for, but to capture the interest of the potentially bored, and force them to read something that they are not interested in?" From that confrontational beginning Cowell attacked conductors, Broadway, big business, and "society women" who cultivated their "pet composers." These women, he wrote, subverted composers' progressive instincts through the seductions of money and boardroom politics, taming true composition into mere "social music."

> What is this social music? It must be well-written technically with a smooth and polished style, with deftness in handling of tone colors, and real knowledge of subtleties of nuance. It must not be very old-fashioned, but voluptuously romantic,—post-Wagnerian, with dashes of Debussy and Stravinsky for flavoring. It must be slightly exotic, must be emotional and waft delicately through the sex-centers, arousing sex emotions pleasurably, but not in an unseemly way. It must create a slightly drugged mood—cast a spell. It must not be intellectual, nor induce thought. It must incite no radical feelings. It must be just modern enough so that it can be called frightfully original, but it must have no experimental modern qualities—the "modernism" must be just a suggestion, and taken from the above-mentioned known models—Stravinsky or Debussy. It must be a style pleasing to those who like Wagner, Tschaikowsky, Grieg, Humperdinck, Puccini, and Debussy.[29]

Although there are other forces that drive modern music into such a state, he wrote that these society women are "the most successful and prominent of those who influence the trend of contemporary musical style into a kept style."

The irony of this misogynistic tract, of course, was that Cowell had been from the beginning not the victim but the darling of avant-garde-leaning "society women" (such as Veblen), who had showered their money on just such bohemians as himself.

" 'Useful' Music" appeared in *New Masses* in the fall of 1935. In this article Cowell again begins abrasively, describing the common tendency of a modern listener to "limit his musical experience to the pleasures of a mild jag, vaguely sexual, thoroughly sentimental." This attraction toward inconsequential music is "a very unhealthy form of dissipation." It make music a sedative, anesthetizing the listener to the "vital developments" in truly modern music. But rather than enumerating those developments, Cowell dwells on what should be the true use of music. That use should be either to unify a group that would be otherwise be "less emotionally bound together" or to provoke people into action. He describes in detail how a man singing a tune united a group of picket-toting strikers and an onlooking crowd. They bonded together in a "a solid phalanx," scaring away both the police and the scabs they were escorting. The article ends tersely: "Music had been put to use."[30]

Cowell was able to promulgate these views through his new professorial post. In 1919 a group of prestigious freethinkers (including Thorstein Veblen) who believed their academic freedom had been abridged at other universities founded a college in New York, calling it the "New School for Social Research," or simply, "the New School." Holding lectures and seminars in rented brownstones, the school at first catered to adults who wanted to discuss political and economic issues. In 1921 Alvin Johnson became the director and broadened the curriculum to embrace the arts and humanities. In 1930, in order to accommodate the students who were flocking to it, the New School constructed a new building in Greenwich Village. There it became a center of contemporary arts, hiring part-time and full-time teachers ranging from Martha Graham to Frank Lloyd Wright to Charles Seeger and, not surprisingly, to Henry Cowell.[31]

It was a perfect situation for both Cowell and the New School. Henry could not legitimately teach anything but unfamiliar, progressive new music and the school didn't want any other kind of music to be taught. Not required to engage himself with thorny issues in music history or theory, he could base his whole curriculum on personal experiences with new music. In that regard, he could easily play the role of expert. The school gave him authority and he gave the school authority.

Cowell taught his first course at the New School in the spring term of 1930. Entitled "A World Survey of Contemporary Music," this course consisted entirely of four ninety-minute sessions, all held on Friday nights. The succession of topics was a précis for Cowell's musical worldview. He began with a discussion of the "paradoxical" situation in Russia, how well organized its composers were, though caught in the thicket of Communist conservativism. He then critiqued neo-classicism in western Europe (although he did praise the "new vocal style" arising on that continent). Next came a treatment of oriental musical principles, an exercise in comparative musicology. In the final lecture-demonstration, he unveiled how American composers were "breaking apron-strings" with Europe, bringing on "the inception of indigenous musical materials."[32]

In subsequent semesters he taught many of the same principles at greater length in various courses, studiously avoiding the actual duplication of any one course. Instead, he restlessly tried to vary the content just enough each semester to keep every course stimulating to him—and to his students, many of whom were novices at music and wanted to keep retaking from Henry Cowell. Although he changed course titles and descriptions, he kept the focus of all of them remarkably constant: "What the Twentieth Century Has Added to Music," "Appreciation of Modern Music," "Workshop in Modern Music," "Contemporary American Music," "Creative Music Today," "Creative Music in America," "Creative Music in the Americas," and so forth. Occasionally, he taught ethnic musics—which for him was simply another form of new music. As Edward Carwithen has written, Cowell simply wanted his students "to accept the most divergent of musical experiences, and to develop an openness for 'new' music," which is to say, any music unfamiliar to its hearer.

He also hoped to create controversy, as he wrote to Ives in 1933: "For my next series [of classes at the New School] I will have some very good fights. I am getting . . . all the enemies (and they all accepted!) to come down to the school and give their views on American music. Ten at the same forum, there will be some young blood to show up their point of view! I think the fur will fly. It should be a healthy exposé."[33]

Beginning on Wednesday nights in January 1933, Cowell gave a series of twelve lectures illustrated with the piano and, according to the New School catalog, "rare records." The first six lectures concerned the "historical position" of music, dealing with music as magic and ritual, music as it entered both the peasantry and the aristocracy, the church and the military, and so forth. The next six lectures were more polemical, as the class summaries suggest: topics include "citified middle class music," "the influence of wealthy patrons," "music . . . to be liked for the moment," and "how music as an art, as well as music as a language, may be beneficial." This last topic, according to the catalog, was "illustrated by a number of works of different tendencies, showing the influence of each tendency and where it leads."

Cowell's teaching career was a kind of fulfillment. For two decades his attachment to Seeger had been profound, matched only by his need to rival him. He had coopted many of Seeger's ideas for his music, written them up in his book manuscript, and, after listening to records in Europe, had even begun calling himself a "comparative musicologist," a term that Seeger had coined with reference to himself. Now as a full-fledged professor, Cowell had entered the legion of academics, but with a typically bohemian twist: he had no college degree.

While Cowell lived publicly many principles of his bohemian upbringing, he had a privately bohemian side as well, the intimate side of his life, which was as complex as it was hidden. Even in his youth in the San Francisco Bay Area, Cowell must have observed the sexual libertinism that went hand in hand with the artistic life. His mother's preachments notwithstanding, free love and homosexual relationships had been more open matters in the Bay Area than elsewhere. Same-sex relationships were also prevalent in the musical world in which he took part during his twenties and thirties. Through his New Music Society and Composers Collective, Cowell had published and promoted works by a number of composers who were quietly known to be gay.[34]

Cowell later recalled that his first explorations of his sexuality—the typically autoerotic kind—began when he was twelve and no longer slept in the same bed as his mother.[35] In 1914 his mother had squelched his first boy-girl relationship. Just after Clarissa died, Cowell recalls, he formed friendships with young men his own age, relationships in which they "fell into a mutually spontaneous habit of playing together with the hands" in a sexual way. During the army years, Cowell claims to have had no sexual relationships, and was indeed disgusted by his peers' frequent recourse to prostitutes. About the time he and Edna Smith got engaged, he had forsaken his homosexual ties. But when she died he resumed them.

A relationship in 1922 at Halcyon with a man about four years younger than he brought him under suspicion. When the relationship became known to the younger man's family, both men received counseling from the temple's Guardian-in-Chief, Dr. Dower, and the police were called. Cowell was extensively questioned and, threatened with arrest and trial, he promised to the district attorney not to engage in any more homosexual liaisons. The matter was dropped.[36]

On his 1925 tour to Germany, Cowell met Else Schmolke, a matronly woman who loved the arts and adored Henry. Thenceforth, when Cowell toured in Germany, he lived with Else, who was, he later explained, the first woman with whom he had intimate relations. In between his visits, she wrote him occasional letters (in German), full of romantic longing. On his 1932 trip to Europe Henry tried to arrange for her to come to America so that she could marry him. But the Nazi government forbade her to do so. Cowell turned to the American government for help. His now sixty-year-old half-brother, Clarence, had a friend in the Senate. Henry and Clarence went to Washington to see if the friend could intervene and get Schmolke out of Germany. But he could not and the relationship between Else and Henry ended.[37]

Once again Cowell revived his old gay relationships, but now with a difference. His initial relationships had been with young men about his own age. The second wave of homosexual relationships in his life appears to have been with young men slightly younger than he. By the 1930s, Cowell now being in his thirties, he apparently entered into sexual relationships only with minors—boys between the ages of twelve and seventeen. For a full three years he had what he would call "improper" relations with many of the local working-class young men who liked to swim in the pond behind his house or go camping with him. He had mutually masturbatory and orally sexual encounters with these young men, taking intimate snapshots along the way. All of this, understandably, he kept painfully quiet. He had crossed the line from bohemian libertinism into something he knew was criminal.

His sexual encounters with young men became a separate compartment of his life, a hidden underside to his cheery public exterior. He later explained that intimacy with young men "never occurred to me when I was working, playing, lecturing, but when I was idle, I just couldn't help myself."[38] It was as though his mystic cluster pieces were now being acted out in his life: a plain and tuneful tonal melody on the surface, with a dark, cloudy mass repeated underneath. This hidden side, too, bespoke a bohemian penchant for recluseness, arcaneness, and life beyond the mainstream.

§   §   §

In many regards one might say that Cowell was living the bohemian dream on which he had been raised. He had built a small but secure aesthetic kingdom, one governed by education and enterprise, aloofness from the mainstream, and boundary crossing at every level. But in the 1930s, for at least four reasons, the dream collapsed.

The first reason was the continuing refusal of large audiences to take his music seriously. Among most listeners Cowell's novelty-driven experimental music had never been able to transcend its sideshow atmosphere. On his tour of eastern Europe in the summer of 1926 he had bewildered the critics, who called his music "more or less successful vaudeville" and asked "Why [is] it considered progress to make a piano sound like a zither?"[39] "On the whole, an amusing evening," a London critic wrote, "but we prefer Grock."[40] Homer Henley described aptly the pyrotechnics that European audiences witnessed during the 1926 tour: "What they saw was a player who laid his palms flat-wise over blocky areas of keys, striking them all at once; who beat the keys with clenched fists in apparent transports of hysteria; who rolled thunderous surges of immense sound from the entire length of the keyboard with his forearms; who leaped upon the quivering nerve-ganglia of the piano's inner structure and loosed the eerie wailings of banshees, and the tenous crystal threads of fairy voices singing tiny, chiming chants at immense distances."[41]

In promoting "ultra-modern" American music in Europe, Cowell was thwarted by the rise of fascism generally and Hitler specifically, forces that disdained American music on nationalistic grounds and furthermore considered all modernism in the arts *Kultur Bolshevik*. The German government had limited the broadcasting of foreign works to 17 percent of the music played. When Cowell went to one radio station to ask that more American works be played, the station responded by dropping its quota of foreign music to 5 percent.[42]

But by then Cowell was complaining that even the American public was treating his clusters as "merely . . . a gymnastic method of piano playing"[43] and a "freak way of gaining notoriety."[44] Part of the problem was that so many observers referred to his clusters as "elbow music." Newspapers used the term, even in headlines;[45] even Cowell's close friends, including the Varians, used the term.[46] Of course, what these observers probably referred to was his forearm technique, in which the left elbow defined the lower boundary or the right elbow the upper boundary. At least one observer did report that "in a complicated rush of notes, hard pressed for an extra hand, [Cowell] strikes two or three with his elbow";[47] and several of Cowell's pieces seemed to allow for such a gesture. But Cowell insisted that performers of his music not use the elbow, in order to avoid the risk of "accent[ing] one of the tones and separat[ing] it from the others." He added, "I never use my elbow, despite rumors to the contrary."[48]

Yet, while he publicly scorned keyboard gymnastics, Cowell was less discreet in private. Jules Eichorn recalled vividly Cowell playing in a way that suggested he was as well versed in the pianisms of minstrelsy and vaudeville as he was in his cluster music. At a small recital at Ansel Adams's studio, Cowell "said he would like to play an excerpt from *Tannhäuser* but that he needed a whisk broom. Mystified, but complying, Ansel produced the article he wanted. Then Cowell began to play . . . forcefully with his left hand while holding the whisk broom in his right hand. Then with a dusting of the keys motion, he imitated the cascading sound of the treble part. . . . The effect was electrifying! It sounded like a full orchestra, which heightened the effect that Cowell wanted and at the same time it was poking fun at Wagner's music. . . . To top it off, Henry then performed Chopin's 'black-key etude,' op. 10, no. 5, in the same manner, only using an orange in his right hand instead of a whisk broom. This object he oscillated rapidly back and forth to produce the desired melodic effect."[49] These mannerisms, it should be noted, were rather common tricks of the trade. (Slonimsky even recalls using them at the St. Petersburg Conservatory in the 1910s.)[50] They could not help but make Cowell's clusters seem like just another gimmick.

One of the many cluster curiosities of the 1920s was Cowell's first music recorded for player piano. The Pleyela Company of France had a long history of preparing piano rolls from the playing of master pianists (Paderewski, Rubinstein, and dozens of others). Cowell was deeply honored when in 1923 the company asked to make some rolls of his playing, although it wasn't "sure whether [the rolls] would take too much wind pressure."[51] He chose five cluster pieces (*Tides* and four of the Five Encores to *Dynamic Motion*). At least some of the listeners who bothered to purchase them apparently thought the rolls defective because huge blocks of keys kept going down together. Cowell visited a piano store that sold player pianos and rolls and asked to hear something by Henry Cowell, not disclosing his identity. When the clusters began to sound, the salesman apologized that the player must be broken. He tried another roll with, of course, the same results. Before the distraught salesman called a repairman, Cowell revealed his name and explained tone clusters.[52]

More than clusters his string piano had become an object of humor. In 1926 Cowell played *The Banshee* at Aeolian Hall in New York, a recital space at the Aeolian Company's headquarters, more or less dedicated to showing off the latest in new musical novelties. When Cowell explained how many ways of playing the piano he had discovered, the well-known classical pianist Olga Samaroff made fun of Cowell in a sarcastic newspaper column. "I have been experimenting with the 'string piano,' without suspecting the magnitude of what I was doing, since I was five years old, and I am sure of the melancholy fact that I am older than Mr. Cowell. I have played upon it with clothes brushes, dust cloths and hairpins. I have a specially developed technique with a dinner napkin. . . . I gnash my teeth to think how I have misunderstood myself and my art." When in 1924 a kitten sprang into her piano while the pianist was practicing Schumann, she continued, she should have known that this was "the discovery of a 166th variety of sound obtainable" from the piano. With too many objects on the piano to allow her to lift the lid, Samaroff tried scaring the kitten out by banging freely on the keyboard. "If I had had a grain of sense I would have stopped to write down my composition and my discovery. I should have developed a proper nomenclature for the various rhythms and tonal details. I should have invested heavily in kittens, hired a hall, engaged Mr. Gilman to write the necessary program notes and now I should have stood where I undoubtedly belong, in the very front rank of futuristic creative geniuses."[53]

Such dismissive responses to Cowell's music only intensified when in 1928 he produced a three-movement work for string piano and chamber orchestra for Nicolas Slonimsky to conduct. In the third movement, "The Leprechaun," Cowell exploited most of the piano's anatomy, playing on the strings, the lid, and the frame with various implements, including rubber-headed drumsticks, a guitar pick, a pencil, and a darning egg. Despite Cowell's usual pre-performance speech asking the audience to "listen . . . without prejudice," the *Boston Globe* reported that Cowell's "weird sounds" provoked not only in the audience but even in the orchestra itself "fits of imperfectly suppressed mirth."[54]

Perhaps to dispel the aura of gimmickry that now clouded his musical experiments, Cowell began in 1928 to shop his manuscript for "New Musical Resources" to publishers. Alfred Knopf accepted it on an almost cruel basis: if Cowell could get a subsidy for five hundred copies and exempt the first thousand copies from royalties the publisher would print it. He did, and in 1930 Knopf published a run of exactly one thousand.

New Musical Resources as printed showed how important Cowell had come to consider his book and his own place in music history. He lengthened the introduction, asserting more vigorously the unique worth of the book and the personal necessity of writing it. "The aim of any technique," he wrote as the book opened, "is to perfect the means of expression." In this book, he says, he hoped to explain to himself why the techniques he "felt impelled to use" and "instinctively felt to be legitimate" did in fact have "scientific and logical foundation."[55] At the same time, throughout the book, he expunged many traces of those composers and theorists who had used his terms and ideas before he had: he removed his references and thanks to Charles Seeger; he deleted a reference to Schoenberg's prior mention of the idea of polyharmony; a citation to the acoustician Hermann Helmholtz disappeared; and he omitted all reference to Schoenberg and Ornstein in connection with tone clusters. On the other hand, he lengthened the book in various substantial ways, most notably by inserting new chapters on tone color, dynamics, and form, all based on his premise that every aspect of the music should derive from the overtone series.

A second reason for the end of Cowell's bohemian dream was the death of his closest friends and mentors. If Cowell wanted to live in the whole world of *music,* it was because that world was the only world in which he truly could live: his bohemian indoctrination, his poor health, his social and sexual awkwardness all conspired to deny him a place in "regular" society. But certain friends and mentors—Ellen Veblen, John Varian, and Samuel Seward—had become his lifelines, his surrogate society, his soul mates. Within the span of six years, all three of them died.

In 1926 Ellen Veblen died, leaving her body to science and her cabin at Halcyon to Henry, the executor of her estate. By then he was so bound up in entrepreneurial activities and touring that he left the cabin and all of her possessions boarded up, a solemn monument to her life of mysticism. Within a few years thieves allegedly broke in and stole her letters from Thorstein, which ended up being quoted in a prize-winning biography of the economist.[56]

Her contribution to Cowell's life had been incalculable, if for no other reason than that she had brought him to Carmel. Without Veblen's intervention, the aging and increasingly reticent Clarissa Dixon would probably have been content to keep her son isolated from the outside world indefinitely, protecting him, instructing him, keeping notes on his daily behavior, conversing with him endlessly, even sleeping in the same bed with him. But when Veblen virtually adopted Cowell and moved him to Carmel, she brought him into a tightly knit community that would educate, value, and reward his precocious bohemianism. It would also teach him the necessity of building his own musical communities later in life.

Five years after Veblen died, John Varian also passed away and Henry, having lost the two great "illuminations" of his mystical life, soon sold Ellen's cabin and abandoned Halcyon. Thereafter, no references to Henry Cowell appear in the *Temple Artisan,* nor does Cowell mention Halcyon or Varian and how they shaped his thinking, other than a grudging acknowledgment late in life that his Halcyon years were "a fruitful and interesting time," one that he remembered vividly.[57] As Cowell's reputation for musical inventiveness increased, his acknowledgment of Halcyon's role in that inventiveness decreased. In two different resumés compiled around the time of Varian's death, Halcyon is mentioned only once, as one of many "other places" in which Cowell had given lectures. Henry also would identify as his own "Original ideas" concepts such as the "Physical relation between tone and rhythm," "Polytempo" and the "Rhythmicon," never mentioning his collaborations with Russell Varian (let alone Charles Seeger). Cowell even omitted his *Temple Artisan* article "Tonal Therapy" from his list of publications.[58]

Neverthless, the legacy of Halcyon in Cowell's life and art remained potent. The Varian family and the Temple of the People provided a seedbed in which the ideas planted by Seeger could flower. But Halcyon also gave Cowell a vast body of poetry and myth that would inspire much of his best-known music. He would not again find so rich a body of imagery from which to tone-paint, so deep a doctrine to nourish his imagination, or so openminded a community to sanction his will to experiment.

In 1932 Sam Seward died suddenly. Shocked, Cowell reflected on the professor's impact on his life: "I feel that he was responsible for my being educated, and that it is highly probable that without his aid, I would never have been able to have a public career, nor to have developed culturally."[59] Not only did Seward help Cowell organize and polish his theoretical musings—many of them drawn directly from Seeger—he virtually redeemed Cowell from the intellectual isolation in which his upbringing had left him. By inaugurating the fund for his schooling, Seward let Cowell encounter an artistic world far beyond the circumference of local bohemian circles. He gave Cowell a gateway through which to enter what became a very cosmopolitan path of avant-gardism, far exceeding the free-spirited but parochial boundaries of the San Francisco Bay Area.

A third reason Cowell's bohemian dream collapsed was the onset of the Great Depression, which, as the 1930s opened, was beginning its long, icy grip on the nation. Millions of American workers began to lose their jobs and homes. Businesses boarded up their windows and shacks built of wood and metal scraps—homes that would make Cowell's tiny well-built cabin seem a mansion—began to multiply in the outskirts of the cities. Children went begging (or stealing) and schools closed or cut their hours. The physical toll of the massive economic dearth could be seen in the faces of the men and women who populated the lengthening streetcorner soup lines. The psychological toll was harder to gauge, but it was clear that the optimism required to indulge in arcane art was being sapped.

With the onset of the Depression, Cowell grew utterly dependent on Ives, upon whom, he wrote in 1931, "the financial burden of ALL the new musical activities in America" rested; "there IS no one else," he added, calling the situation "monstrous."[60] In the early 1930s Cowell slipped into a virtual quid pro quo pattern of dealings with Ives: time and again he would importune Ives for money to float the *Quarterly,* Ives would respond, and Cowell would publish either more of Ives's music or an article celebrating Ives as a pioneering American composer. Cowell now began to elevate Ives to the stature of Ruggles—a thorn in Ruggles's side, since he believed that "no wealthy man can produce anything worthwhile in art" and deeply resented Cowell's newfound attention to Ives.[61] But Ives, like Ruggles, Henry wrote, composed pieces with "strong native tendencies," works that denoted minimal foreign influence.[62]

By 1935, despite Ives's continual transfusions of cash into the *New Music Quarterly*—he was paying one-third of the bills—the journal was on its last leg. The recording series was doing about as well. (Cowell sardonically remarked to the composer John Becker in April that "Every once in awhile I get word that our records have been played somewhere!")[63] That same year, as Cowell struggled to keep the quarterly and the recording series propped up, Stanford notified him that his summer teaching job was about to end. His New Music Society concerts could barely break even and his ability to make money playing his own recitals was well nigh past. Such music as he had to offer seemed all but irrelevant to anyone who had fallen on hard times. And although Cowell had enlisted enough prospective buyers to sell out two printings of *New Musical Resources,* in 1935 Knopf remaindered the third printing of the book. By then, despite his zeal for work, Henry Cowell again found himself much as he was when a teenager living with his mother, and much the same as many men on the verge of middle age now were: increasingly poor, dependent, lonely, threatened with idleness, searching for employment and companionship.

The fourth and final blow to Cowell's bohemian dream, the one that irrevocably destroyed it, came in 1936. At 11:00 P.M. on 21 May, three policemen knocked on the door of Cowell's cabin in Menlo Park. They were met by three teenage boys, who were waiting for Cowell to return; six of their friends, they said, had taken Cowell's car to San Francisco to go skating. The police waited about two hours for Cowell to arrive. When he did (accompanied by a female companion), they served him with a warrant charging that he had had oral sex with one of the boys. Cowell denied the charge. Then, during questioning, he began to confess not only to this charge but to other sexual encounters he had had with the boys, even producing for the officers lewd snapshots he had taken. A year later, a friend assessed Cowell's state of mind at the arrest: "I believe Henry was glad to have it end, at almost any price."[64]

From his jail cell he told reporters that he would not fight the charge and would spare the young men the publicity of a trial. Within a week he had written a frank confession and plea for leniency, partly because, he said, he was not exclusively homosexual but was in fact in love with a woman he hoped to marry. These arguments failed to persuade the district attorney's office to drop the charge.[65]

On some sheets of New Music Quarterly Recordings letterhead, Cowell penciled a document to his father and Harry's third wife, Olive. Under the heading "Some Ideas Concerning My Case," Cowell said there was little point in hiring a lawyer and no point in trying to repudiate his confession: the district attorney already had all the evidence and there were lots of boys ready and willing to testify against him. He wished no bond—"I am happy here," he wrote—and wanted to avoid any appearance of resistance, because "I am very anxious to avoid any line of Action which might lead to inquiry about illegal acts committed out of this county and for which I might therefore be brought to trial elsewhere." He pled that his "radical friends" not organize in his behalf: "that would be a disaster."[66]

But Harry and Olive did hire an attorney, who began his defense strategy with a plea of not guilty at the preliminary hearing and a promise that his client would seek hospitalization. By the time the Superior Court trial date arrived, a month after the arrest, Cowell had persuaded his attorney to change the plea to guilty and ask for probation.[67] A disgruntled former member of the Temple of the People read about Cowell's arrest in the newspaper and contacted the district attorney's office to reveal that Cowell had been questioned and warned about his homosexual acts in 1922. That revelation destroyed Cowell's chances for leniency.

At Cowell's sentencing hearing, Dr. Ernst Wolff, a psychologist who had been hired by the Cowell family, explained in detail the history of Cowell's life, the intermittence of his sexual behavior with young men, and his conclusion that Cowell was not a "true homosexual" but was bisexual. (He even prepared a time-line chart of Cowell's sexual past, noting when and how his heterosexual tendencies had been frustrated: Clarissa's opposition to his teenage relationships, the death of Edna Smith, and the denial of Fräulein Schmolke's emigration.) Dr. Wolff and a second witness, Dr. E. W. Mullen, the medical superintendent of Agnew State Hospital, both testified that Cowell had been shocked out of any further homosexual activity by being arrested. Both doctors were sure he could make a "heterosexual adjustment" and that to send him to prison would simply aggravate his homosexual side. But the district attorneys repeatedly argued that Cowell not be taken at his word to desist in such behavior, because he had already promised to reform when caught at Halcyon years earlier. Upon cross-examining Mullen, assistant district attorney Louis Dematteis asked: "Should it have occurred, Doctor, that back in 1922, when a similar upset occurred, that he was carefully questioned, that the matter was very diligently brought to his attention, and that it was only through his promises not to continue that any prosecutions were forestalled, would not that have brought it to his attention as sharply as it has been brought now, and should not that have caused a discontinuance, if that will assist him in the termination of these things?"[68]

In the pursuit of leniency, Cowell could not have chosen a worse time to confess to a sex crime. Moralists throughout the nation were waging a crusade against leniency for sex offenders. Cowell's international fame had brought unprecedented coverage to the case, even by the Hearst newspapers, in which sex crimes among less prominent people were almost daily fare. Swayed by the need to make an example of the repeat sex offender Henry Cowell, Judge Maxwell McNutt denied probation and sentenced the composer to San Quentin for the standard term of one to fifteen years.

That July afternoon, after being sentenced, Cowell made a final statement for the record at the district attorney's office (see appendix 4). Upon reviewing his life history, Cowell invoked two aspects of his thinking that had been ingrained in him by his mother—the need for scientific explanations and the right to self-definition. He explained that at Halcyon in 1922, "The people that brought it to my attention treated the matter as something more or less religious, and their idea was that if I would get religion that it would be all right, and, consequently, the gross physical aspects of the whole thing were never discussed, and, frankly, I feel that . . . the physical basis of the acts should first be cleared up before the mental or spiritual or emotional things could be straightened out." He went on to explain that, since his problem now had been approached in the proper light, "I am absolutely confident, in my own mind, that such a thing would never occur again with me. I base that, of course, on greater knowledge of myself than anybody on the outside could possibly get at."[69]

Cowell's friends reacted variously to his plight. Either spurred by personal indignation or intimidated by public sentiment, some turned against him. Carl Ruggles briefly broke ties with him; Ernst Bacon did likewise, as he later said, "to my considerable shame."[70] Most anguishing to Cowell was Ives's response, which was something between horror and loathing. At first, upon hearing the news, Harmony Ives tried to keep it from her husband. But, as she wrote to Charlotte Ruggles, "I told Charlie & he & I feel just as you do. A thing more abhorrent to Charlie's nature couldn't be found. . . . He will never willingly, see Henry again—he *can't*. . . . he will never get used to it." She then quoted her husband's reaction: "I thought [Henry] was a man but he's nothing but a g——d—— sap!"[71]

Other friends remained loyal to Cowell, some by refusing to accept details of why he was sent to prison.[72] A rumor circulated that it was Cowell's leftist leanings and praise of the Soviet Union that had incited the authorities to frame the composer.[73] Schoenberg was troubled by the whole matter but took it philosophically: "One will understand how distressed I was when I learned he was arrested and convicted. . . . I could not believe that [he] could be capable of such violations. But when I had to realize it was true, I understood what the great interpreter of human soul and passions, William Shakespeare, said: 'There are other things in heaven and earth / Than are dreamt of in your philosophy.'"[74]

On 8 July 1936 Cowell entered San Quentin, the largest prison in a penal system that recently had been rated the second worst in the nation.[75] Conditions were severe under the newly appointed warden, Court Smith. Cells were badly overcrowded, the dungeon was still in use, beatings continued, food and water bred disease, medical care was poor, and visits and letter writing were stiffly regulated. Other deprivations would particularly affect Cowell. Radios were forbidden and neither musical scores nor journals could be brought or sent in (except direct from publishers). He would have almost no access to a piano and, with neither desk nor table in his cell, could compose only on score paper laid on a book.[76] He had to work the spools all day in the prison jute mill, constantly endangering his hands. After his shift in the mill, he complained, he was too exhausted to do serious creative work.[77] Perhaps worst of all, he had to endure being labeled a "288'r," the term inmates used derisively for sex offenders (after Section 288 of the California Penal Code).

Prison, Henry genially said, was "not unlike the army years I remember"—bland and restrictive, yet orderly and disciplined.[78] But the analogy was hollow. His incarceration had clearly stabbed at the heart of the bohemian ideals he had hoped to live. It was the ultimate refutation of freedom, the hardening of every boundary imaginable, and the exposure to ridicule of all that he had tried to keep secret.

Olive Cowell worked hard to get him released, presenting to the board of pardons no fewer than eighty-seven testimonials by prominent citizens on Henry's behalf.[79] In this she was helped by the man who years earlier had been the first to pronounce Cowell a genius, Lewis Terman. Fortuitously, Terman had lately shifted his scholarly focus from the study of genius to the study of sexual variance. Terman found in Cowell at least four of the five psycho-social factors that he believed led to homosexuality: excessive maternal affection, an absent father, a lack of involvement in "masculine" activities, an "overemphasis" on spirituality, and a lack of vigilance in protecting the child against seducers.[80] Despite the testimonials and a plea for compassion made by Terman, the board of pardons fixed Cowell's sentence at the maximum of fifteen years. This should have destroyed whatever career Cowell had left. But what Cowell did next demonstrated to the world how the self-reliance and entrepreneurship he had spent his life cultivating could turn his circumstances into a haven for the life of the mind.

After the fixing of his sentence, Cowell was transferred from the jute mill and assigned to work with John Hendricks, the bandmaster in the San Quentin Education Department.[81] Once more, Cowell was immersed in music. In the following months he embarked on what amounted to a new musical career, rehearsing the band, teaching musicianship to about two hundred students a day, correcting papers and correspondence course lessons, composing, arranging, and copying music for both prison and outside ensembles. He wrote journal articles, practiced solos on the flute, violin, and shakuhachi, and completed a sixty-five-chapter book manuscript, on which he had been working since he entered San Quentin.[82]

The manuscript, entitled "The Nature of Melody," was more or less a supplement to *New Musical Resources.* As in *New Musical Resources,* Cowell again implies that the measure of quality in music is to be found in its trueness to a system. But unlike that earlier book, this one proposed no "new" resources, but only systematic ways of gauging the quality of any melody, old or new. Cowell explained that in writing melodies "a dire lack of scientific guidance calls for an accepted formula, to avoid haphazard methods being tried out any longer." Tracing the origins of melody from speech, Cowell lays out the fundamental elements of the art based on the three essential "neumes" (a step up, a step down, and a repeated note). He then explains the active and passive tones to be found in the major scale, likening them to the elements of grammar: inactive tones are nouns, active are verbs. After next explaining the structure of various Western and non-Western scales, Cowell outlines a method for constructing and developing musical motives, how to "modulate" from one motive to another, how to make compound melodies, and so forth. At the end of the treatise he assures that the reader is now prepared for the study of counterpoint.[83] It was the last step in Cowell's attempt to reduce all musical elements to scientific formulae, and, again, it borrowed heavily from the previous work of Charles Seeger.[84] But without the aspect of novelty that *New Musical Resources* possessed (or the undamaged reputation of its author), the book not surprisingly failed to attract any of the publishers to whom Cowell's friends showed it. More than anything a testament of Cowell's indefatigability amidst trials, the book remains unpublished.

In his San Quentin band concerts Cowell programmed a mixture of popular and serious (though seldom "modernistic") music. Although a subsequent warden feared that the programming of serious music damaged inmate morale,[85] some prisoners developed a strong taste for the repertoire. As Cowell explained it in a letter to Ernst Bacon, "There are some [prisoners] who do not enjoy 'classical' music . . . but among those who do, there is a preference for a rather severe program, and we do not dare to put on what they consider compromises, they resent this."[86]

Cowell kept composing, often in a pan-ethnic style that became, in a place of varied ethnicities, a logical choice. He wrote, for example, a band suite entitled *How They Take It,* which alluded to different ethnic styles in order to represent the diverse prison population. The titles of other pieces from the prison years make Cowell's interest in such styles more explicit: the *Oriental Dances* (1936), *Back Country Set* (for piano, 1937), *Celtic Set* (for band, 1938), *The Exuberant Mexican* (1939), and the band piece *Shoonthree* (a Gaelic word for the music of sleep, 1939).[87]

Occasionally Cowell returned in his prison pieces to earlier techniques. *Rhythmicana* (1938), for example, carries on the ratio-based rhythmic experiments of pieces like the *Quartet Euphometric* and *Fabric*. But Cowell also invented new procedures while in prison. The one that would become the most influential grew out of a collaboration with the choreographer Martha Graham. When the two spoke of doing a sarabande, Cowell remembered,

> I said, "Well, would this sarabande then be in eight measure phrases"—which is what you have if you have it in its own right. She said, "Yes, but I'd like very much to be able to change this and prolong it or curtail it here and there if I could. How could this be?"
>
> So then I developed an idea which normally would be eight measures long and would therefore have a certain melody and contour and a certain way of ending, but I arranged it so that it could end sooner or could be expanded to end later. Then I wrote down all of these various versions of the melody, so this was a flexible rhythm, because she could then take any one of them, so that the normally eight-measure phrase could be curtailed into as few as five, or expanded to as many as fifteen.[88]

Cowell also wrote another dance piece in prison, *Ritual of Wonder,* which provided thirty-seven separate bars of piano music, all in a variety of meters and textures, with the following instructions: "Single measures with which to construct passages. They may be used in any order of succession, transposed, sequenced, inverted, retrograded, used in part, the two hands inverted one to the other, etc." Such seemingly tossed-off ideas inaugurated what Cowell would later call "elastic form," a precursor to the kinds of indeterminacy practiced by many experimental composers after him.[89]

Cowell's prospects brightened as he got new medical evaluations painting him as a good prospect for a "heterosexual adjustment." The most notable of these came from the dean of American research into sexuality, Adolf Meyer. Henry also got a job offer from Percy Grainger, who wanted him to be his musical secretary. More important than both the medical evaluation and the job offer was the election of Culbert Olson, a New Deal Democrat, as governor of California in 1938. Olson was determined to revamp the prison system, deemphasizing punishment and promoting rehabilitation as the purpose of prison.

Cowell proved himself an indispensible case study in just what Olson hoped to promote. In 1940 only about a third of American prisons had music programs of any sort.[90] But by then Cowell had created in San Quentin a thriving school of music. As of June 1939, Cowell had had 1,549 registrations in music classes, 343 registrations in elementary corresondence courses, and 59 more in advanced courses. He was teaching twenty-two hours a week, supervising other classes three more hours, holding two hours of teachers' meetings, rehearsing the band five hours, and playing the flute with them an additional seven and a half hours.[91] As if his official work were not enough, he formed a small prison orchestra, about which he wrote to John Becker: "We can only rehearse very easy things, but it is a real step. I have been writing some things for this group, and it has stimulated some of my best composition students to do likewise."[92] He inaugurated a series of chamber recitals in which he played duets—some newly composed by him—with Raul Pereira, a former orchestra leader and virtuoso violinist who had been sent to San Quentin for writing bad checks.[93] During his free time, between dinner and lights out, Cowell continued to write and to arrange for performances of his music outside prison. In a letter to Grainger he summarized his achievements in San Quentin, which included writing the book on melody and eleven journal articles as well as composing more than fifty musical works. With understated pride he noted that "some of it seems to have turned out well."[94]

His exemplary good behavior reduced his sentence to under ten years, and in June 1940, with less than half of that time served, his family's and friends' lobbying bore fruit: Cowell won his parole and moved to Grainger's house in White Plains, New York.[95] Parole restrictions hampered his ability to travel, but he still kept remarkably busy: in the first four months of 1941 he conducted the New York Civic Symphony Orchestra twice, acted as commentator for a WNYC broadcast of American music, played at least two recitals for civic groups, judged a composition contest for the New York State Federation of Music Clubs, oversaw more than a dozen major performances of his own works, composed seven new ones, arranged another, and wrote five articles. As it turned out, he was also permitted to teach; during these same four months he taught two courses at the New School and gave special lectures for Columbia University and the Progressive Education Association.[96] Meanwhile, he pursued psychoanalysis with Dr. Joseph Wortis, visiting him about once a week for the first year of his parole. By the end of that year, the war effort opened a way for Cowell to work for the government on a project that would lead eventually to his pardon.[97]

In December 1940, while in Washington, D.C., Cowell had learned of a new federal program to be known as "cultural defense." A joint venture of Morton Royse, a professor working for the Department of Justice, and Nelson Rockefeller, the Coordinator of Inter-American Affairs, cultural defense was designed to combat widespread Nazi propaganda to the effect that artists in the United States disdained Latin American culture. By arranging for the exchange of scores among North and South American composers, Rockefeller and Royse hoped to refute the Nazi claims and hence quell their successes in the hemisphere. At this time the head of Latin-American Music Relations for the Pan-American Union was none other than Charles Seeger, who suggested that Royse consider hiring Cowell for this work. Overlooking Cowell's prison record, Royse deemed him an ideal emissary for the collecting and routing of scores.[98] On 3 July 1941 the San Quentin Prison Board restored Cowell's civil rights, enabling him to be employed by the government.[99] In September he surprised many people, and pleased not a few, by marrying a former student and onetime assistant of Seeger, an ethnomusicologist and divorcée six years his junior named Sidney Hawkins Robertson, whom he had known since 1917.

Sidney in some ways resembled Edna Smith. She was the child of rich parents who indulged her precociousness with lessons in all the fine arts. She graduated from Stanford in Romance languages and philology in 1924, the same year that she married Kenneth Robertson, a philosophy major. In 1934, after briefly teaching ethnic music at the Peninsula School for Creative Education in Henry's hometown of Menlo Park, she divorced Kenneth and turned to charitable work. As Edna had done two decades earlier, Sidney decided that she had been leading too "self-indulgent" a life and searched for good causes in which to immerse herself. She soon moved to New York to work with Jewish immigrants in the realm of "social music." In 1936 she took a job with Seeger, who was then at the Special Skills Division of the Resettlement Administration in Washington, D.C. Of those days she recalled that Seeger's "many-sided brilliance was exciting, endearing, and absolutely maddening if you were trying to get anything done."[100] She made field recordings of American ethnic musics, a task that suited her to organize the first state-based field recording project in California. This became the WPA Northern California Folk Music Project, housed in an office in San Francisco from 1938 through 1940—the year that she became engaged to Henry Cowell.

The engagement seemed to all a sign that Cowell was on the road to rehabilitation. Henry wrote to Harmony Ives about it: "I wish to tell you and Mr. Ives of my forthcoming marriage to Sidney Robertson, to take place very soon. . . . I am sure you will be happy for me over this event, to which I look forward with such intensity. [Sidney] is a musician, plays the piano well, and has collected folk-songs throughout the country. She is very successful in being on friendly terms with country people, and wins them over completely. She is thirty-seven years old, of old American stock, with a bit of New Orleans French blood."[101] In turn, Harmony responded with words from Charlie: he had now resumed speaking to his old friend Henry.

Most Latin American music published in the United States during the next two years was edited and submitted for publication by Cowell, who used the office of the Pan-American Union to carry out the cultural defense project.[102] At the same time, he oversaw the Music Distribution Project at the New School for Social Research, which disseminated the music of U.S. composers to Latin America under a grant from Rockefeller's office.[103] Only one thing hindered him in this work: as a parolee he could not travel outside the country. For that he would need executive clemency.

Culbert Olson was then trying to retain his governorship against the challenge of the conservative Republican Earl Warren, who campaigned largely on a law-and-order platform. Warren attacked Olson's parole policy, showing that Olson's administration paroled at a rate almost five times that under the former governor. Warren also observed, just two weeks before the 1942 election, that almost five hundred of the parolees were sex offenders.[104] On 4 November, Warren defeated Olson by fifteen points. Eight days later Cowell applied for a pardon from the lame-duck governor. He stated his reasoning thus: "The work I am doing is considered important in the war effort and makes the fullest use of my experience and ability, so I am requesting this pardon in order that my contribution need not be curtailed unnecessarily."[105] On 1 December Sidney Cowell added her plea for clemency, explaining that "This was a case which might have been handled medically from the beginning, but . . . it was handled otherwise. Now, however, Mr. Cowell's rapidly expanding professional activities and our happy marriage seem to me to offer every proof that his rehabilitation is complete."[106]

Sidney hand-carried her letter to the governor's office. The same day, the governor's secretary sent a memo to the pardon board, asking its members to consider the case because "this applicant has an opportunity to enter government work in connection with our Latin-American relations."[107] By its 10 December meeting the board had prepared a file on Cowell full of doctors' evaluations and letters of support from law enforcement officials and prominent musicians. Surprisingly, the board rejected his application. Citing "the nature of the crime to which [the] applicant plead guilty, sex perversion," the board urged that he complete his term "and then permit some period of time to elapse thereafter enabling [him] to demonstrate complete rehabilitation."[108]

The same day that the board gave its finding to the governor, Charles Seeger wrote a letter to Olson impressing upon him the importance of Cowell's work in the music exchange program and adding that "he may be nominated at almost any time for a more conspicuous position. Under present conditions this could not be done." With three weeks left in office, Olson overrode the pardon board and granted Cowell unconditional clemency. In doing so he cited a now favorable recommendation from Judge McNutt, Seeger's letter, the character references of friends, and the evaluations of doctors that "this applicant has been cured of the physical urge which impelled commission of the crime for which he was convicted."[109] In 1943, with a full and unconditional pardon in hand, Cowell became senior music editor of the overseas branch of the Office of War Information.

§ § §

Cowell's imprisonment did to his career what he had tried to do to the musical establishment: tear it down and rebuild it in a completely different image. Some of the renovation was stylistic. The restricted access to a piano forced Cowell to write for the instrument in ways that depended less on his playing technique and more on abstract musical structure.[110] At the same time, his frequent access to wind and string players, especially during his last year and a half in San Quentin, allowed him to refine his ear for orchestral sonority. And to live with men of all classes, nationalities, and races enhanced his sense of music's ideal diversity.

Other changes were psychological. His quest for parole drove him into an artistic circumspection that dissuaded him from some of the radical projects he may have envisioned. For example, while in prison he wanted to write more leftist music. But his new reluctance to do so is noticeable in a letter to Marc Blitzstein: "I do most earnestly wish that I might undertake the writing of similar things [as Blitzstein's] but of course, I am hampered by the situation as far as the texts go."[111] Conlon Nancarrow also observed that "politically" the newly freed Cowell "kept his mouth completely shut."[112] The damage to his reputation in California uprooted him from the West Coast bohemianism that had nurtured his early experiments. He more or less had to renounce his citizenship in the dreamy-eyed state to which his parents had once fled for refuge from conventionalism. He landed in the once-despised New York for most of the rest of his life, moving with Sidney into a house outside of Woodstock, a home resembling his old one in Menlo Park, with farmers for neighbors, a one-room schoolhouse nearby, and Methodist psalm-singing wafting through the summer night air.[113]

Cowell's reputation among some of his ultra-modern composer friends suffered from his being identified as homosexual. Although many of the composers in his circle lived gay private lives, they would not speak of it openly. Meanwhile, the two composers Cowell most admired were openly hostile to any alleged feminization of music, whether by the likes of Brahms (that "big sissy," as Ruggles called him)[114] or Wagner (whom Ives called a "soft-bodied sensualist . . . pussy").[115] Indeed, ultra-modern music was uniformly associated with a kind of machismo; it was music that, as Irving Weill wrote in 1929, was distinguished by its "virility."[116] Cowell's own piano music was sometimes venerated for its manliness. Slonimsky admiringly cited the "masculine harp tone" produced by Cowell's plucking of piano strings.[117] Another writer described the aftermath of Cowell's performance of tone clusters in this way: "When he finishes, the piano trembles as if it had been violated."[118] But Cowell's imprisonment signaled to many of his peers a denial of manhood, a passage into effeminacy. Homosexuality was "male-inversion" in the scientific literature, a man's maladjustment to his gender. Cowell and his psychologists explained that he had been feminized by his upbringing, with its dearth of competitive sports and the constant presence of his mother. Not surprisingly, many of Cowell's composer friends suddenly broke ties with him, Ives being only the most extreme of a group. In their biography of Ives, Henry and Sidney would later write with considerable restraint that Ives insisted devotion to art not be "incompatible with a rugged masculinity and all the heroic pioneer virtues."[119] Henry's early life had satisfied Ives's ideals. But his homosexuality had breached them, and for that, Cowell seemed doomed henceforth to the penance of freedom.

If it was only in the world of music that Cowell seemed comfortable and content, even there he became estranged. The late 1930s and early 1940s had brought on a dramatic shift in the place of bona fide new music in society. Cowell, who had written fervently regarding the need for "useful" music, now asked, "Is music of use in time of bitter war? Can it 'carry on'? In what form, and how?"[120] America's entry into World War II had virtually compelled young American composers to simplify their music or face extinction at the hands of an indifferent public. Because of that, a certain rustic Americana began to replace the hard-nosed leftism of earlier times.[121] As the end of the war approached, the formerly avant-garde League of Composers was commissioning frankly patriotic works and *Modern Music* was about to end because of massive wartime paper shortages. Experimental music was simply not being performed and could not even be heard on new records because the government had banned commercial use of shellac, halting virtually all record-making in the United States.

Once the war ended, "ultra-modern" music was a luxury in which more people could indulge. Even composers like Ives found new, broader audiences and bounteous critical attention. (In 1947 he won the Pulitzer Prize in music, heretofore the privilege of a far less radical breed of musician.) By the late 1940s, the next generation of composers—some of whom Cowell had championed and even taught—took more radical approaches to composition than Cowell had even contemplated. If the mercurial and onetime social outcast Henry Cowell wanted to live in the whole world of music, it may have been because he no longer had a private musical niche to call his own. "I was bristlingly modernistic when I was quite young," he would write, "but I have become much simpler since."[122]

The reasons behind this simplification were painfully clear. Cowell's incarceration had isolated him, destroyed his entrepreneurial public life, and severed him from the daily access to fresh ideas he had once enjoyed. Olive Cowell observed that although her stepson had overcome the pain of his incarceration, "he never accepted it . . . it did something to him—it did something to his music."[123] The imprisonment had also made him the object of scorn in front of prospective audiences. Charles Seeger, explained it well: after prison Cowell "was just determined on one thing, that if he was going to make a comeback in the field of American music, he wasn't going to prejudice it with [anything] that wasn't perfectly safe."[124] His subsequent vow to inhabit the whole world of music was partly a vow to retreat from the radicalism that he was no longer in touch with, no longer adept at, and which to pursue could be dangerous. Whereas Cowell had once tried to be on the cutting edge of new music, after prison he chose to be on the blunt end of it.

As things turned out, it was a bad time to simplify. By the end of the 1940s a small but hardcore musical audience was emerging, one with a ravenous taste for the avant-garde. The shift in taste for musical severity could be seen on one night in 1949: Cowell gave a lecture reminiscing about the radical music of the 1920s to enthusiastic applause, while in a nearby hall Harold Shapero's newly written neo-Romantic Sonata in F Minor was being hissed.[125] Among fellow composers, Cowell's best known and most admired music was that of the 1910s–1930s, his radical, experimental works. Even though he had by this time written hundreds of pieces in old-fashioned styles, those works failed to attract the same degree of attention that his cluster and other novelty pieces had. Yet now, with a growing young audience for experimentalism, Cowell declined to further his experiments.

From June 1940, the month he was released from prison, until his death in December 1965, Cowell produced over 350 compositions. A fair number of these are simple pieces for children, short occasional works (e.g., fanfares or birthday presents for Sidney), or mere fragments. But many others are ambitious works for orchestra, chorus, or chamber ensembles of various kinds, including an oratorio (*The Creator,* 1963) and a three-act opera (*O'Higgins of Chile,* 1949, never fully scored or performed). These late, post-imprisonment works offer ample testimony that Cowell no longer cared for experimentation in the way he had formerly conducted it. Previously, Cowell had altered style from work to work; now he switched within the same work, discarding stylistic orthodoxy (whether modernist or archaic) in favor of a pan-ethnic, multivernacular vision of music that became a kind of kaleidoscope of sonic dialects. Moreover, the post-prison music tends to feature simple forms—often Americanist designs such as jigs, reels, and hymn and fuging tunes—forms that embrace conventional melodic and accompanimental textures and exceedingly regular phrase syntax, all occasionally interrupted by Cowell's earlier "ultramodern" materials, that is, clusters and free dissonance. But such techniques were neither experimental nor technically advanced during and after the 1940s. As David Nicholls has written, "In the forties and fifties, the main battle for center stage in American musical life was being fought between proponents of serialism, indeterminacy, and traditional tonality. Compared with the mainly Eurocentric flavors of these three *grand vins,* Cowell's trans-ethnically inspired music must have seemed rather small beer."[126]

Charles Seeger had time and again been Cowell's savior and champion, rescuing him from musical illiteracy, an impoverishment of ideas, social isolation, and even incarceration. But Seeger gradually became Cowell's worst critic. In Seeger's eyes, although Cowell churned out pieces for a quarter-century after leaving prison, "Henry never pretended that he was a composer. He didn't look upon himself as a composer. He was a man who simply couldn't be happy unless he was composing and he composed all the time—every spare moment that he had, he'd write notes. . . . He fell in love with the writing of notes." To Seeger, musical value and durability faded from Cowell's ambitions: "He had to write music because he wanted to write music and the writing of it became the center of his activity. . . . I could see less and less of the love of music and more and more of the excitement in writing, just for the sake of writing."[127]

But Seeger overstates how much indeed *writing notes* was the center of Cowell's activity. Cowell inhabited the musical world not just compositionally, but tutorially, authorially, and entrepreneurially as well. After prison, Cowell pursued his career as a professor by taking on heavy loads at the New School (until his stroke in 1964), Columbia (1950–55), Peabody (1952–56), Eastman (1962–

63), and other institutions. Consider the courses for which he was responsible in the single academic year of 1951–52:[128]

New School	Peabody	Columbia
World Music	Form and Analysis	Opera Literature
Modern Music	History of Music	Symph. Literature
Living Composers	Music Literature 1, 2, 3, 4	20th-Century Music
Pre Elem. Mus. Theory	Music Literature 5, 6, 7, 8	
Elem Mus. Theory	Music of the 20th Century	
Intro to Mus. Theory	Principles of Teaching	
Advanced Mus. Theory	Principles of Composition	
Orchestration/Works		

At the same time as he was manning this severe slate of teaching, Cowell was prolifically writing and publishing prose. He went from being a scattershot freelance writer for any journal that would accept a manuscript to becoming the in-house critic for that bastion of the American musical establishment, the *Musical Quarterly.* From 1948 through 1957 he wrote thirty installments of the quarterly's "Current Chronicle," which reviewed recent performances of contemporary compositions. This column became one of the basic sources for droves of American musicians who wanted to know what was happening in modern music, without actually going to hear it or play it. Henry also took on, with Sidney, the task of authoring a standard biography on Charles Ives. The book he produced in 1955 has the ring of atonement to it: after causing the greatest pain to the person who had been his hero and financial savior, the least Cowell could do in return was lionize "Dear Charlie." He did so to a degree far beyond what he would offer to the other men in his life that he at one time or another had called the "greatest living" or "only really important" composers in his acquaintance (Schoenberg, Ruggles, Rudhyar, et al.). "I consider Ives the same as a father," Cowell once wrote. And the book proved it.

Meanwhile, just before the book came out, his real father died. In January 1954, at the age of eighty-eight, Harry Cowell passed away in relative obscurity, remembered as a retired tennis instructor, a onetime friend of men like Jack London and George Sterling, and as the father of a son who was unnamed in his obituary but identified only as a lecturer at Columbia University and the Peabody Institute. In death, Harry at last discarded that monicker and reclaimed his real name: the obituary told of the passing of one Henry Clayton B. Cowell.[129] During the three small memorial services held at his and Olive's home, son Henry played *The Harp of Life* and *The Banshee* to a somber crowd. He remarked to Olive: "I can not feel sorrow; I can only see Harry's shining face."[130]

Seven months later, Henry Cowell at last had a birth certificate made for himself—he had never had one—verifying the information of his birth by citing articles about him in two music encyclopedias. On the certificate he listed his father's name as "Harry Clayton Blackwood Cowell." It was to his genealogy what rolling back the dates was to his music: he was the first of his kind, not Henry Cowell Jr. but the original, the only bona fide Henry Cowell.

Two years later, there arose another consequence of his youthful bohemianism. In May 1956, the FBI began a series of inquiries into Cowell's potentially "subversive" activities. Probably prompted by Cowell's praise of the Soviets, his employment at the New School, and his long friendship with Communists or former Communists (e.g., Seeger), the FBI used methods such as "pretext phone calls" to his home to inquire about his employment, his wife's activities, and so forth. But the bureau was quickly stymied in its search and concluded that it found "no identifiable subversive derogatory information with respect to the subject or his wife."[131] His circumspection had paid off. And with that final assurance, Cowell was prepared to enter the last phase of his public life.

Four years before his death, Henry Cowell became President Kennedy's unofficial ambassador of American music, representing the United States at music conferences around the world. In 1962 he also became the vice president of the National Institute of Arts and Letters. And in that year, *American Composers on American Music* was reprinted, eliciting fulsome praise by critics across the nation. Cowell, once the unbathed bohemian, closet Communist, and sexual predator, had not only entered the mainstream but had more or less walked across it, becoming nothing less than the patron saint of his country's music. Of this unforeseeable outcome he remarked in 1962, "I seem to have placed my bets well."[132]

The principal "bet," of course, was on himself. It was a wager born of the self-assurance inculcated by his parents, validated by intelligence testing, bankrolled by his neighbors, and nurtured by teachers. The self-confidence that brimmed in him, even through the prison years and beyond, allowed him to keep writing in notes and words, fearlessly and even recklessly letting some bit of his upbringing resound in each page of manuscript. One senses continually in his words and music the cosmopolitanism of the Pacific Coast tempered by a zealous nationalism, or the belief in arcane wisdom and mystic faith jostled together with an implicit faith in the super-rational, the rebellious avant-gardism of his parents' circle of friends and the two "Charlies" in his life tied to a desire to confirm and extend venerable traditions, and so on. There was no need to harmonize the clusters of ideas one found in his music or prose. Any notion could be set against any other so long as it was stated and restated with importunity. Ideas needed only to be juxtaposed, never resolved—just as one could find the most disparate pieces sitting side by side in Cowell's collected opus, or indeed hear in a single piece some simple, plebeian tune set on top of a dense haze of sound.

Just so, in what is perhaps his greatest triumph, Cowell was able to create the enduring yet irresolute legend of Henry Cowell, American composer. It was a legend in which the dissonance between truth and image could linger forever unresolved. The Henry Cowell he presented to the world was not the progressivist whose ideas were firmly planted in California's mystic soil, but a free spirit, *sui generis,* uninfluenced, capable of imagining new musical resources with no prompting outside of himself, writing cluster pieces years before anyone else did. This Henry Cowell was not exploitative, whether of Ives or teenage boys, but was rather without guile and altruistic in all of his relationships. This Cowell was not a dabbler in tone color and motoric rhythms, but a symphonist, an heir in the great dynasty of venerated composers, not bound by the refusal to develop and revise but able, in fact, to transcend such requirements by being "ultra-modern" and living in the whole world of music. This Cowell was not the bohemian boy who never grew up, but a professor, a pioneer, a scholar, and a patriot.

As time wears on, it becomes clear that the greatest and most imponderable legacy of Henry Cowell is the very puzzle of himself that he left: who he was, how he worked, what he thought and, most of all, felt. Behind such lingering mysteries, the only thing certain about him is how he wished to be remembered. In the end, both genius and genie, he showed himself clever and powerful enough to grant that wish to himself.

Appendix 1

Paul Rosenfeld's 1924 Review
of Henry Cowell's Work

Felicitations on the discovery of a method cannot be denied Henry Cowell; and in an age of small technical innovations he cuts a not unrespectable figure. Those tone-clusters of his, sounds produced on the pianoforte with the side of the hand, the fist and the lower arm, extend the scope of the instrument, and offer some new possibilities to composition. Concordances of many close-lying notes have been used by Leo Ornstein since ever he wrote his Dwarf Suite; and Percy Grainger calls for tones struck from the strings inside the box of the piano in one of the Nutshell movements; but it has been left for the young Californian to demonstrate completely the quality of sound to be produced on concert grands by the deliberate application to the keyboard of muscles other than those of the fingertips, and by the application of the fingers to wires themselves. New lovely rolling sounds occur in all of the pieces of Cowell which employ the new method of tone-production: Dynamic Motion, Antinomy, and The Voice of Lir in particular. The Piece for Piano with Strings has a fine dead quality of resonance not to be produced on any harpsichord. And it seems probable that writers for the pianoforte will profit by his experiments and enlarge the expressivity of the instrument. It is even possible that Cowell's method may find itself applied to the music of the past; that passages of Beethoven sonatas will be treated by it, and brought to greater effectiveness. The limitation of the applicability is very strict, nevertheless. Because of the nature of the muscles used in producing the tone-clusters, it is probable that these will lend themselves to effective usage only under the conditions of very moderate *tempi*. The controlling muscles are relatively cumbrous. It was evident that Cowell could only manage them under retarded conditions of time.

Meanwhile, the discovery of a method constitutes Cowell's chief claim on renown. His musical inventiveness is less developed than his technical. Those of his pieces which do not employ the clusters—and To Olive is the best of these—exhibit a musical helplessness and suffer from monotonous repetitions of small phrases. Those which do employ them when they are not pathetically MacDowellesque run dangerously close to constituting literal transcriptions of nature. Naturalism is the general characteristic of the work of people whose primary interest is the development of a new method or a new instrument. Still, Cowell is not devoid of musical gifts. The people who called for straight-jackets had better be calling for ears, for themselves.

Paul Rosenfeld
The Dial 76 (April 1924): 389–90

Appendix 2

Frederick Whitney's Description of the Meeting of Henry Cowell and John Varian

How the Poet and the Composer Met

Bards and Troubadours sang their verse; but nowhere else in literature has anything of such importance occurred as the coming together of J. O. V., the lyric-epic poet, and Henry Cowell, the modern composer. For it was none other than Mr. Varian's visions in verse of the creation of the Cosmos, drawn out of Irish mythology, that made possible the one great addition to musical expression which this age has produced; the "cluster tone" by Henry Cowell; and the production of music the grandeur of which is as yet unappreciated except by the few. In fact, these two men stand at a unique position in their respective but correlated lines of art.

But more of this elsewhere. One day at the door of a rose-clambered cottage in Palo Alto there came a knock, and from inside there answered Mr. Varian's cheery, "come in!" And a boy about fourteen, short of stature and with a tousel of hair and a shy manner, entered. Mr. Varian looked at him and knew him, for he had heard of this boy composer who lived in a tiny cottage up back of Menlo with an invalid mother; sold lily bulbs for a few scant dollars and wrote music. The boy took a chair at Mr. Varian's bidding, stuck his heels over a rung, laid a MS roll across his knees, and, looking up at Mr. Varian with an introductory smile, said, "I have written a sonata to Russell."

Now, Russell is Mr. Varian's eldest son, and if you had known him at that time, and him being the subject of a sonata, yours would have been an ample supply of the same introductory smile. He, about twelve years of age, was then freckled along with his red hair and primitive celtic features; had grown much of his present six-feet-oneness and was in the midst of being quite awkward about it, and having a soul wholly unborn to the romance of musical composition. He came in at the call of his dad from the yard where he was in the midst of making a flying machine out of a cigar box and some rubber bands, and he proceeded forthwith to expound the wonders of his invention right over the unsuspecting MS. If you had seen you would have smiled, but—one look taken more deeply and the smile would have died. For that boy, standing there with the other boy and the poet father was a sign and a symbol; a part of the new Cosmos to be born. There was distinction in all three[.]

And I doubt not that in that very moment the poet and the composer looked at one another in soul recognition across the ages, and the Gods approved. The poet asked the composer to play his piece, which he did; and, so far as anyone knows, that was the end of the sonata, for it seems to have been lost. But the singer had met his poet and the poet his singer, coming together thus in this quaint way, with its touch of unconscious Irish humor, on a momentuous day. A day of portentious and prophetic skies whereunder the rhythmic thunders of creation were to break forth in new-formed music and distinctive song.

At a later time one Canto of Mr. Varian's story of creation was produced at Halcyon as a musical drama, being set to music by members of the occult group of which Mr. Varian was a member. The second production, given at the same place, was set to music by Mr. Cowell. In it occurs the well-known and instantly successful Prelude, "The Tides of Mananaun [*sic*],' which is the first of a series of marvelous music themes drawn from Mr. Varian's epics and sung in cluster tones.

Troubadour 3 (July 1931): 6–7

Appendix 3

Henry Cowell's 1922 Article

for the Temple of the People

Tonal Therapy

Some interesting experiments in the therapeutic value of tone have been conducted recently in Halcyon with the aid of Dr. Abrams' electronical devices with which, we hope, ARTISAN readers are already familiar. But even though Dr. Abrams' remarkable machines of electronic reactions are understood, it will be well for an understanding of the tonal experiments, to go over part of the ways of operating the machines.

In order to determine whether a patient has a certain disease, a specimen of his blood is placed in a metal container which is connected with an instrument regulating the current of electricity and from this instrument to the subject, a healthy person from whom a reaction can be obtained if the disease is present. It has been found that each major disease: syphilis, T.B., cancer, etc., has a correspondence in a certain ohmage of electricity, and when the instrument is regulated to the number representing this current, if the patient is diseased, certain reactions can be made evident from the subject, which do not occur if the patient is not afflicted. First, an area of the abdomen, different in different diseases, will give a dull thud when percussed, instead of a resonant sound; second, a rod passed over this area will stick, and move on only under compulsion.

It has been found that if a colored light, a different color for each disease, is thrown upon the blood container, the reactions from the subject are neutralized, and he reacts as though there were no disease present in the patient. And it is further found that owing evidently to some negative relation of the color to the electrical current corresponding to the disease, this color when applied to the patient has curative properties.

The question immediately suggests itself, is there not also a musical tone which will be neutralizing to the disease? And if so, will it not be more potent than colored light? For while the light can only be thrown on the outside of the skin, and then usually only on a certain spot, a tone can penetrate, and will vibrate through the entire body. Inquiry revealed that Dr. Abrams had conducted experiments along this line, but without any great amount of success, with a piano. Now, a tone struck on a piano is not sustained, but begins to die out almost at once; also, the piano cannot easily be placed in direct contact with the blood container. So Dr. and Mrs. Dower decided to hold another experiment in Halcyon. For this a violin was used, since the vibration can be sustained upon it, and the neck was placed directly on the table with the blood specimen in the Dynamizer. Great interest was shown, and Halcyon turned out to witness the results.

The results were surprisingly good, and although not conclusive, open up a remarkable field for investigation.

Dr. Dower used for the experiment blood specimens tested by Dr. Abrams, and known to contain certain diseases. Dr. Dower first established the reactions of the rod sticking on the subject, then the violinist played long sustained tones, going up through every tone in the chromatic scale. The doctor continued to move the rod over the sticking area. When the tone B was sounded, the rod did not stick. And when the octave and double octave of B were sounded, there was no reaction obtained with the rod. The tone E also negated the reation. These tones, then, when sounded in any octave, though the higher octaves seemed more potent, were negative to the disease, which was cancer in this case, and will probably prove to have a curative effect upon it.

But why two tones? Why E and B? Why, because these two tones a fifth apart, have the closed vibration relation to each other possible to two different tones, and B is the first overtone of E, after the octave. And in other diseases it was found that two tones related a fifth apart would both succeed in removing the sticking reaction from the rod.

The following results were obtained from experiments with other diseases: T.B., B♭ and E♭; syphilis, E and B; Strep, C and G. The tone C in altissimo, next highest on the piano, was found to have a general negative effect.

Dr. Abrams was much interested in the experiments and conducted some similar ones in San Francisco afterwards, which to a large extent checked up with those at Halcyon, and it is understood that he is having built an instrument to apply tonal treatment.

There remains a great deal to be done in making sure of the right tones, and checking up, and in working out the reason of some of the musical relationships; but a wonderful field for research is opened for Physicians, Musicians, and Scientists. It has been known that music has therapeutic value, but if we are able to identify a certain tone with a certain disease, matters will be placed on a much sounder basis; and it is to be hoped that energetic composers may find the idea of writing special music to be used in healing, in which the proper tones will predominate. The overtones are a series of natural super-vibrations from any single musical tone.

Temple Artisan 22 (April–May 1922): 97–99

Appendix 4

Henry Cowell's Statement in His Defense

Statement of the Defendant
Taken in the Office of the District Attorney
July 6, 1936
2:00 P.M.

Present: Deputy District Attorney, Louis B. Dematteis, Probation Officer Francis Robinson, Duncan Oneal, Esq., the defendant, Henry Cowell, and the court reporter, W. H. Girvin.

MR. DEMATTEIS: Mr. Cowell, it is customary when a court passes judgement to the State's Prison, to take certain information for the benefit of the Prison Board, so I would like to ask you a few questions along those lines, solely for that purpose.

THE DEFENDANT: Yes, sir.

Q. And, of course, your true name is Henry Cowell?

A. Yes, I have a middle name, Dixon, which I do not however usually use.

Q. Your middle name is Dixon?

A. Dixon, yes, sir, but that name is not used by me except on documents where it is obligatory.

Q. So you have practically, in your adult life, used the name of "Henry Cowell"?

A. Yes.

Q. And, as I understand it, you were born in Menlo Park?

A. I was.

Q. And what was the date and year of your birth?

A. March 11th, 1897.

Q. And you lived in Menlo Park most of your life?

A. Well, I have Menlo Park as headquarters, but every year since about 1920 I have lived part of the year either abroad or in New York City, so that I have Menlo Park as a permanent residence but was very frequently away either in New York City or abroad.

Q. About what age were you when you first left home for any lengthy period?

A. About, well, at the time of the earthquake, when was that, 1906, I made an extended trip to the East with my mother.

Q. Your mother was with you at that time?

A. Yes, as an adult my first extended trip was at the time of the army when I was stationed in the East.

Q. That was in 1917 or 1918.

A. Yes.

Q. Now, is your mother still living?

A. No, she died in 1918 or 1919.

Q. Your father is still living, is he not?

A. Yes, sir, present today.

Q. What is his name?

A. His name is Harry Cowell.

Q. And where does he reside?

A. 171 San Marcos Avenue, San Francisco.

Q. Have you any brothers?

A. I had a half-brother.

Q. What is his name?

A. Clarence Davidson.

Q. And how old is he?

A. He is 25 years older than I.

Q. That would be 64, you are 39?

A. Yes.

Q. Where does he reside?

A. Des Moines, Iowa.

Q. Have you any sisters?

A. No.

Q. Any half-sisters?

A. No.

Q. So you have no brothers or sisters of full blood?

A. No.

Q. Now, you attended grammar school here in Menlo Park, did you?

A. I went for one week to Los Lomitas Grammar School, which is in the vicinity of the City of Menlo Park.

Q. Where did you receive your elementary training?

A. I did not receive any elementary training.

Q. Did you attend any school at all?

A. Would you like me—I would like to explain it, it sounds rather odd. I was ill a good deal of the time and we moved very frequently, with the result that I had about one week in Los Lomitas School in Menlo Park before the time of the earthquake in 1906. After that we visited at my mother's relations in Kansas and Oklahoma at periods too short for me to enter school, and then went to Des Moines, Iowa, to her son, where I entered public school in the third grade, but although I was nominally there for one year, I actually had five protracted sicknesses, so that I was actually in school perhaps two weeks, and following that I never entered any elementary school again, or any high school.

Q. Where did you receive your musical training?

A. I received most of my musical training at the University of California, and then after that at the Institute of Musical Art in New York and also the Institute of Applied Music in New York.

Q. Now, with reference to your general education and training, you acquired that by some means?

A. I acquired that mostly through my mother who had been a school teacher in her youth, and I had private instruction from her, and I was a very constant reader on educational subjects all during the period of my childhood.

Q. And your mother acted in the capacity, in addition to being a mother, as more or less of a private tutor?

A. Yes, she did.

Q. And your basic education was attained from her, and then your musical work was done at the University of California and the other universities that you mentioned?

A. Correct, I had corollary material for my musical education at the University of California and at other places consisting of certain subjects, the physics of sound, mathematics, and general history and cultures of different peoples.

Q. About how long, putting it together, would you say that you attended California there?

A. I attended California three and a half years. I was just to complete the period of four years when I entered the Army.

Q. And you were in the Army how long?

A. I believe it was about 18 months, that is close, a rough guess, but it is within 16 to 19 months, something of that kind.

Q. Did you go overseas?

A. No.

Q. You remained here in the United States?

A. Yes, I was going to say that following being a cook for a certain period I became an assistant bandmaster and finally a bandmaster.

Q. You were bandmaster when you were discharged?

A. Yes, sir.

Q. Now, your work has been confined particularly to musical work?

A. Yes, my profession and interest lie exclusively in the field of music, although they manifested themselves in different ways, that is, I feel that I am primarily a composer of music, but being a composer of serious music, and not supplying any means of livelihood, I became a professor of music in different institutions and have taught music, both privately and in institutions mostly later as a means of livelihood, and also have made extensive concert tours, I have made five concert tours through Europe, and probably have toured the United States every year, as I say, since 1920, as a concert artist.

Q. And you, of course, have not learned any trade?

A. No.

Q. Have you ever been convicted of any crime before?

A. No.

Q. Do you use intoxicating liquors?

A. I use them but not to an excess, I have never been intoxicated.

Q. That is, your use would be a very mild use?

A. Very mild, yes, sir, I would say.

Q. Occasional?

A. Yes, sir.

Q. And do you use narcotics in any form?

A. No.

Q. Is anyone dependent upon you?

A. No.

Q. You have never been married?

A. No.

Q. Have you ever had any accident, that has severely injured you physically?

A. Let me see, an accident, no, I think not, no accident.

Q. You spoke about some illnesses, there in your early years?

A. Yes.

Q. What was the nature of those, were they quite serious illnesses?

A. They were not particularly serious. At the time that I spoke, the illnesses that I mentioned were typical children's diseases, scarlet fever, chickenpox, measles and influenza, which all came during the same year. The most serious physical trouble that I have ever had, as far as I know, was a malignant carbuncle, I have a scar as large as that (indicating), here on my back, and I was in the County Hospital in this county for a period of about two months following an operation on it.

Q. Other than that you had no protracted serious illnesses?

A. No, I have not.

Q. And what is your religion?

A. It would be, I suppose, Protestant, I assume, because it is not Catholic, Christian in general, I am not affiliated with any church at the present time.

Q. Now, what nativity is your father?

A. My father, at the present time, is an instructor of tennis in the San Francisco State Teachers' College.

Q. I asked you what nativity?

A. I thought you said activity. He was born in Ireland.

Q. And your mother?

A. She was born in Iowa.

Q. And as far as your association with people is concerned, you have been normal in that respect, that is, you had quite a number of associates, have you not?

A. Yes, sir, I have had, I know a very large circle of friends.

Q. You have had no difficulty in getting along with your associates?

A. No.

Q. Have you any explanation or anything you wish to state as to the cause of this crime?

A. Well, I think that, without any question, that the testimony of the Doctors today, covered the point, as far as—I think that is true. I am absolutely confident, in my own mind, that such a thing would never occur again with me. I base that, of course, on greater knowledge of myself inside than anybody on the outside could possibly get at. I can realize, very readily, that one does not want to make any mistakes in that way. There was something which, it seemed to me, was not made perfectly clear by the testimony today on either side, which I would like perhaps to tell you, and that is, that the occasions that you mentioned when similar things, although they did not lead to the same—to a crime of this magnitude—but when similar things occurred, which you brought out today, that, following that period, I went to Europe where I met this woman, and incidentally, I brought a letter from her in case you doubted her existence, which I received since I was here, that I led with her a normal life, that is, I suppose any extra-marital relations might not be considered legally normal, but they were normal sexually, they were not homosexual, over a period of years, and that this recent trouble was brought on by the knowledge that I was not able to bring her over here as my wife, although I made every attempt to do so. I went with my half-brother, as a matter of fact, to Washington, where he knew a Senator, and we tried to find whether there would not be some way in which she might have been brought to this country as my wife, and found that it could not be arranged, that she could not come except in the quota which at the time would have taken eight years. And, as far as the awareness of the act was concerned, on account of the bringing to light of it formally, I must say, very frankly, that it was not sufficiently brought to mind to me so that I had a realization of what it meant at all in the same way that I have at the present time. The people that brought it to my attention treated the matter as something more or less religious, and their idea was that if I would get religion that it would be all right, and, consequently, the gross physical aspects of the whole thing were never discussed, and, frankly, I feel that that was absolutely a necessary basis for the enlightenment and carrying out of my case, that the physical basis of the acts should first be cleared up before the mental or spiritual or emotional things could be straightened out, and this was never gotten down to in any way that it was brought to my attention at that time. That is my own basis for feeling that this thing has absolutely cleared up at the present time. Is that the sort of statement you mean that I make to you?

MR. DEMATTEIS: Yes, I think that clarifies it about to the extent it can be clarified. I think that is all for the purpose of this statement.

Appendix 5

Titles

At this point in a "life and works" treatment of a composer one might expect to find a list of the composer's works, a chronology of his or her music, or perhaps a catalog of the genres in which he or she composed. But here I will forgo that enterprise. To begin with, Henry Cowell's already cataloged compositions number over 950—at least in the now definitive and commonly accepted book by William Lichtenwanger, *The Music of Henry Cowell.* It would be redundant and quite disproportionate for me to restate Lichtenwanger's list, even if only the portion deriving from Cowell's pre-incarceration years, the time period on which this book focuses. Lichtenwanger himself devotes more than 147 densely filled pages just to the years from 1897 to 1936.

Nevertheless, an issue worth visiting is that of Cowell's prolificness itself. How many works did he actually write? The question is not as simple as it may seem.

Consider two matters. First, among the 520 pieces listed by Lichtenwanger as being composed by Cowell before he went to jail, there are over 150—well over a fourth of them—for which a name exists but no score has been found. Although some non-extant scores certainly may have been lost or given away (and may resurface), many other pieces listed by Lichtenwanger may be nothing more than names used on recital programs, mentioned in newspaper reviews of his performances, or conveyed in letters by Cowell, his mother, or others. Given Cowell's assiduous habit of saving virtually every scrap of paper that documented his musical history, it seems doubtful that even a small fraction of these "missing" works were discarded or simply lost. More likely is that Cowell gave preliminary or alternate titles of works that later came to be known by other names. Indeed, a number of Cowell's manuscripts have multiple titles on them, showing that he considered more than one title for a given work before settling on a final one. Given all the evidence, many of the "missing" works are probably extant ones under different names.

Second, hundreds of the "pieces" listed by Lichtenwanger are extremely short, some as short as five measures. Certainly the early works, anniversary pieces, letters to Veblen, etudes, or etude-like effusions qualify as little more than jottings. Consider Lichtenwanger nos. 89–98: of these ten pieces one does not survive and the other nine range in length from 9 mm. to 29 mm. (average length is less than 19 mm.). Clearly not all of Cowell's cataloged compositions can be considered real "works" in the conventional sense. Many are simply fragments, which most composers would not even have listed in their compositional legacy, because doing so might actually dilute that legacy. Cowell, however, had been a cataloger, a maker of lists, since he was a boy. The collector's mentality was so pervasive in him that he appointed an aesthetic cubbyhole for every effort, no matter how minuscule or ephemeral. More to the point, he (rightly) saw himself as competing for squatter's rights in the landscape of musical history. If he could not do so on the basis of aesthetic profundity perhaps he could do so by sheer prodigiousness. In that regard, Lichtenwanger's voluminous catalog invokes the spirit of the music's maker.

One should also note that Lichtenwanger's numerical list of works can be misleading about the relative heft of the works to which numbers are assigned. He assigns one full number (no. 4), for example, to two five-measure solo lines scrawled on the back of another six-measure piece. At the same time he assigns one number (no. 353) to the complete set of "Ings," really a series of pieces written from 1917 to 1955 and totaling hundreds of measures. So when considering the 966 numbered "works" in the catalog, one must realize not only how daunting was the task Lichtenwanger undertook but also how hard to gauge the bottom-line results of that task can be.

With those caveats in mind, however, there remains a vast body of work to consider. During the early, more "bohemian" years, almost all of Cowell's works were solo piano works, small chamber works, or songs for voice and piano. All of those works relied on an eclecticism of utterance that in itself expressed Cowell's bohemianism, his sense of boundary-crossing for its own sake. But one finds in the titles of the works—whether or not works exist behind some of those titles— further manifestations of his bohemian predilections. That is what I would like to dwell on for the remainder of this appendix.

§ § §

By far the largest genre in Cowell's pre-incarceration compositions is the solo piano piece—nearly 300 of them written before 1936. Most of these are old-fashioned dances or functional pieces: mostly waltzes (13) and marches (6), but also mazurkas, polonaises, tangos, minuets, rags, and jigs. A few are simply billed as "dances," sometimes with a supernatural modifier attached: "Fairy's," "Brownie's," "Sprite's," and so forth. Another large body of piano works includes compositions given generic titles—sonatas (4), sonata movements (8), preludes (7), etudes (10), and a few identified only by tempo markings. Many of these generic pieces, not surprisingly, are student works, composed while Cowell was taking classes at Berkeley and elsewhere. The nondescript titles perhaps show him striving for a sense of legitimacy, of trueness to the Western classical tradition. Related to such titles are those that specifically allude to other styles and composers (e.g., Chopin, Grieg, Schumann). Most such pieces have not survived.

More interesting, of course, are the evocative, picturesque, novelty-oriented, or fanciful titles that Cowell gave to dozens of his piano works. The most common of these, not surprisingly, were the piano works that allude to Irish legend and myth, pieces mostly traceable to John Varian's cosmology. Consider this list:

Tides of Manaunaun
Red Flame of Midyar
The Hero Sun
The Voice of Lir
The Sword of Oblivion
The Vision of Oma
The Vron of Sorrows
The Fire of the Cauldron
The Harp of Life
March of the Feet of the Eldana
The Trumpet of Angus Og
March of the Fomer
The Banshee
The Battle of Midyar
Domnu, Mother of Waters
The Sleep Music of the Dagna
The Fairy Bells
The Leprechaun
The Fairy Answer

It is obvious from this list that Cowell reveled in the imagery of Varian's Irish mythology. And indeed these pieces seem rooted in that imagery: a simple idea of a "sword" or a "vision" or "tides" gave Cowell a palpable sonic concept that he could work out in a brief, single-minded work. The imagery also provided an otherworldly tone that seemed to inspire him (just as his very first bit of juvenilia had been inspired by Longfellow's "Golden Legend"). Something in the bohemian mind was always drawn to the mysterious, the arcane and spiritual.

By the same token, that kind of mind—especially in its Californian manifestations—gloried in the tangible world of nature as much as in the supernatural. In
nature Cowell, the youthful botanist and entomologist, found abundant images
to prick his imagination (just as the imaginations of romanticists and impression-
ists had been before his). Consider especially Cowell's attraction to watery, often
sea-based titles:

Rippling Waters
The Cauldron [a Carmel-area ocean site]
Sea Picture
The Three Streams
The Ocean
Sea Ride
Singing Waters

Likewise, he adopted titles related to mists and clouds—

It's Snowing
Clouds Cirrus
Cumulus Clouds
The Winter Rain
The Cloudlet
Mist Music
The Snows of Fuji Yama

—or to night and wind—

The Weird Night
The Night Sound
Moonlight Forest
The Winds
When the Wind Chases You

By comparison, among his naturalistic titles Cowell used only three animal references
(*Snake Piece, Mastodon, Tiger*) and two plant titles (*The Lotus* and *Little Daisy*).

Cowell also titled a number of works after sheer states of mind. Not surprisingly, perhaps, since Cowell was always considered an optimist, these tend away
from negative states of mind and toward positive ones. Indeed, these titles display
a spectrum of excitatory, even manic, moods: *Exultation, Exuberance, Euphoria,
Scintillation, Frenzy.*

At the same time, Cowell occasionally titled works after common objects, especially paper ones (*Advertisement, Timetable, Telegram*). That same sense of offhand-
edness led him to affix titles that were mere colloquial effusions, suggesting the bo-

hemian penchant for the improvisatory, the spontaneous and unlabored. There is, indeed, a touch of Dadaism in titles such as *What's This?*, *It Isn't It,* and *How Come?*

One final category that should be mentioned is that of the "Ings"—Cowell's set of characteristic pieces that all had gerunds for titles, all suggesting states of motion:

Floating
Frisking
Fleeting
Scooting
Wafting
Seething
Whisking
Sneaking
Swaying
Trickling
Whirling
Rocking

Clearly this was one of the most direct ways possible to attach a kind of Hanslickian affect to a piece of music, a piece representing nothing more nor less than "sound in motion." With the "ing" titles to provoke his imagination, Cowell could spin out pieces that, for their single-mindedness of technique and uniformity of texture, became, in effect, etudes.

In considering Cowell's other instrumental works from this period—less than one-sixth as many as his solo piano works—one finds a very narrow range of titles. Almost all of them are generic titles (sonata, quartet, andante, and so forth). The principal exceptions appear among his handful of orchestral works, where one finds two titles that echo his mystically titled piano works: *The Birth of Motion* and *Atlantis.*

Cowell wrote about half as many songs as solo piano pieces during his pre-prison years. Among them one finds no generic titles, of course, no vocal equivalent of "dance," "sonata," or the like. The titles are those of the poems being set, most of them written either by his mother, by members of her circle, or by other California-based writers (especially Robert Louis Stevenson). Several of the texts concern children and family; several others, politics (mostly from the World War I period); and many a smattering of other themes, mostly sentimental (romance, home, and so forth). But, not surprisingly, most of the texts that Cowell set revolve around natural and supernatural themes.

As with his solo piano pieces, most of the nature songs are about water in some form or another:

The Waves
Sonnet on the Sea's Voice
My Sea
At the Seaside
Among the Rushes
The Fish's Toes
Where Go the Boats
Jealousy: Land and Sea
The Morning Pool
Rain

Many others concern the sky and birds:

Moonlight
Sunset
The Sun's Travels
The Stars and the Sun
The Meadow Lark
To a Skylark
Birds
The Black Vulture

The supernatural titles, which are slightly less frequent than the natural, often come from John Varian texts: *God of the Future, The Daga's Song, Manaunaun's Birthing,* and at least six others. Five more songs that evoke the Carmel-style mysticism of Cowell's youth are to texts by Clark Ashton Smith (e.g., *White Death* and *The Dream Bridge*).

Corresponding to his flight from bohemianism after prison, however, Cowell's compositional titles grew more and more generic. The natural and supernatural titles virtually disappeared (except for reworkings of earlier pieces), while nondescript appellations abounded—not so much the kind he had used before (e.g., sonata, dance), but now symphonies (21 of them), hymns and fuging tunes (18, adapted from the genre found in early American tunebooks), and dozens of occasional pieces written for Sidney. Although ethnic references appeared in a number of titles (*Persian Set, Homage to Iran, Ongaku,* etc.), Cowell still favored titles that asserted his music as thoroughly American—"American," that is, not in his old sense of "pathbreaking," but in the new sense of "pragmatic." In his post-prison quest for redemption—and, as is customary with increasing age—Cowell moved quietly almost from defiance to deference, putting himself forward not as an ecstatic California bohemian but as his nation's elder statesman of music, a purveyor of, by now, time-tested and reliable craftsmanship. The later titles reflect that metamorphosis.

Notes

Introduction

1. The quotations are from Henry Cowell and Sidney Cowell, *Charles Ives and His Music* (New York: Oxford University Press, 1955), 9, 12, and 3, respectively.

2. See the comments in Kyle Gann, *The Music of Conlon Nancarrow* (Cambridge: Cambridge University Press, 1995), 1.

3. Charles Hamm, *Music in the New World* (New York: Norton, 1983), 594; Eric Salzman, *Music in the Twentieth Century: An Introduction,* 2d ed. (Englewood Cliffs, N.J.: Prentice-Hall, 1974), 137.

4. Henry Cowell to Nicolas Slonimsky, 15 December 1936, excerpted in Nicolas Slonimsky, *Perfect Pitch: A Life Story* (New York: Oxford University Press, 1988), 165.

5. Peter Yates to Peyton Houston, 29 June 1941, Letters of Peter Yates to Peyton Houston, 1931–76, Mandeville Department of Special Collections, University of California at San Diego.

6. The source of this quotation asked me not to cite him/her by name—suggesting the continuing sensitivity of this topic.

7. See Joscelyn Godwin, "The Music of Henry Cowell" (Ph.D. diss. Cornell University, 1969).

8. Sidney made the remark in a telephone conversation with Steven Johnson, 15 February 1990, transcript in author's possession. Publicly Sidney complained that the dissertation contained too many excerpts of Henry's unpublished work. Privately, however, she challenged Godwin's credentials, saying that he had critiqued her husband's work without a firm knowledge of American experimentalism, and therefore was simply unqualified to publish his conclusions.

9. All three of these titles were published in Brooklyn by the Institute for Studies in American Music, in 1986, 1977, and 1982, respectively.

10. Sterling, as quoted in Franklin Walker, *The Seacoast of Bohemia* (Santa Barbara: Peregrine Smith, 1973), 10.

11. Sidney Robertson Cowell, interview by Rita L. Mead, 12 December 1974, typescript, 3 vols., Institute for Studies in American Music, Brooklyn College of the City University of New York, 1:2.

12. Nicolas Slonimsky, "Henry Cowell," in *American Composers on American Music: A Symposium*, ed. Henry Cowell (Stanford: Stanford University Press, 1933), 63.

13. See Richard Taruskin, "Stravinsky and the Traditions," *Opus* 3 (June 1987): 10–17; Maynard Solomon, "Charles Ives: Some Questions of Veracity," *Journal of the American Musicological Society* 40 (Fall 1987): 443–70; Michael Hicks, "John Cage's Studies with Schoenberg," *American Music* 8 (Summer 1990): 125–40.

14. In locating many of these sources, I have relied heavily on Martha Manion, *Writings about Henry Cowell: An Annotated Bibliography* (Brooklyn: Institute for Studies in American Music, 1982), and William Lichtenwanger, *The Music of Henry Cowell: A Descriptive Catalog* (Brooklyn: Institute for Studies in American Music, 1986).

15. Robert Gittings, *The Nature of Biography* (Seattle: University of Washington Press, 1978), 35. The syndrome of which Gittings writes follows a typical pattern: the widow first attempts to write an official biography and then, failing that, hinders anyone who would examine the artist through a lens other than hers, especially if the lens focuses on private matters.

16. The history of access to the collection (and Sidney Cowell's managing of it) is authoritatively detailed in George Boziwick, "Henry Cowell at the New York Public Library: A Whole World of Music," *Notes: Quarterly Journal of the Music Library Association* 57 (September 2000): 46–58.

17. Slonimsky, "Henry Cowell," 57; Barbara Burks et al., *The Promise of Youth: Follow-Up Studies of a Thousand Gifted Children* (Stanford: Stanford University Press, 1930), 324.

18. "Reminiscences of Henry Cowell" (16 October 1962), 16, in the Columbia University Oral History Research Office Collection.

19. Hugo Weisgall, "The Music of Henry Cowell," *Musical Quarterly* 45 (1959): 485.

20. Cesar Saerchinger, "Berlin Becoming Acquainted with American Art," *Musical Courier*, 30 December 1923.

Chapter 1: Easily Explained by Heredity

1. Clarissa Dixon, "Woman and Nature," *Westminster Review* 169 (March 1908): 289.

2. Hugh Quigley, *The Irish Race in California and on the Pacific Coast* (San Francisco: A. Roman, 1878), 283–84.

3. The ideas treated in this paragraph are discussed in depth in R. A. Burchall, *The San Francisco Irish, 1848–1880* (Manchester, Eng.: Manchester University Press, 1979).

4. Michael Williams, *The Book of the High Romance: A Spiritual Autobiography* (New York: Macmillan, 1921), 209–10.

5. Kevin Starr, *Americans and the California Dream, 1850–1915* (New York: Oxford University Press, 1973), 241.

6. *San Francisco Evening Bulletin,* 29 January 1899, excerpted in California WPA Writers' Program work *History of Music in San Francisco, Volume VII: An Anthology of Music Criticism* (1942; rpt. New York: AMS, 1972), 211–12. Several of the volumes in the WPA series were helpful to my understanding of San Francisco's musical culture in the nineteenth century.

7. From Ashton Stevens's account of an interview with the composer Edward Mac-Dowell, *San Francisco Examiner,* 11 January 1903, excerpted in *History of Music in San Francisco,* 227.

8. The information in this paragraph derives from several sources, including the Irish Civil Registration Records, Clonmore parish, 6 February 1866 and 27 July 1867, microfilm of holograph in the Family History Library of the Church of Jesus Christ of Latter-day Saints, Salt Lake City, Utah; John O'Hart, *Irish Pedigrees; or, The Origin and Stem of the Irish Nation,* 2 vols. (New York: P. Murphy and Son, 1915), 1:393–95; and *Thom's Irish Who's Who* (Dublin: Alexander Thom, 1923), 49.

9. Quoted in *Poetry: A Magazine of Verse* 27 (February 1926): 290.

10. As reported in Godwin, "Music of Henry Cowell," 1–2.

11. Olive Cowell, "Facts about Harry Cowell," photocopy of one-page typescript in archives of Menlo Park [California] Historical Society. According to Olive, when Harry moved into the city he had about four hundred dollars: "He got hold of an Irish landlady for a room, hung up his pants near a transom, and found the money gone the next morning. He was bereft. The Irish landlady got him a job on [the trolley line] if he would learn the streets of San Francisco. And to his dying day he could reel off the names of the streets in San Francisco" (Olive Thompson Cowell, interview by Rita L. Mead, 8 November 1975, typescript in Institute for Studies in American Music, Brooklyn College of the City University of New York, 10). Eventually he got a job as a printer with the James H. Barry Company, setting type for every sort of book in its eclectic catalog (see the notation in *Langley's San Francisco City Directory* for 1896, which gives Harry's address at the Barry Company).

12. As spoken by a character in Harry Cowell, "The Road to Romance," *Overland Monthly* 59 (February 1912): 131.

13. The "winged ape" quotation comes from George Sterling to Jack London, 29 October 1915 (original location unknown), supplied to me by David E. Schultz in an e-mail, 15 June 1998. The "babble and cackle" quote comes from *The Daybooks of Edward Weston, Vol. II, California,* ed. Nancy Newhall (New York: Horizon, 1966), 97.

14. This motto is referred to in Olive Cowell to Anna Strunsky Walling, 23 January 1944, in Anna Strunsky Walling Papers, Manuscripts and Archives, Yale University Library.

15. Olive Cowell to Anna Strunsky Walling, undated letter in Walling Papers.

16. Sidney Robertson Cowell, telephone conversation with Steven Johnson, 15 February 1990.

17. Consider "Mal de Mer(e)," *Overland Monthly* 57 (February 1911): 169; and "Swallow Flight," *Overland Monthly* 61 (March 1913): 290. Alfred Perceval Graves, *Irish Lit-*

erary and Musical Studies (1914; rpt. Freeport, N.Y.: Books for Libraries Press, 1976), 128–42, treats the heritage of Celtic nature poetry.

18. See "December Is Here," *The Independent* 65 (17 December 1908): 1488; "First-lings," *Overland Monthly* 59 (May 1912): 428; "Spring Renascent," *Overland Monthly* 61 (May 1913): 470; "Winter Folk's Song," *Overland Monthly* 62 (October 1913): 401; "An April Eve," *Overland Monthly* 63 (April 1914): 359.

19. See his "Irregular Ballade of Dead Lady-Loves," "Polyandry," "On and Off," and "A Vision," in, respectively, *Overland Monthly* 53 (March 1909): 225; 57 (February 1911): 157; 57 (March 1911): 273; and 65 (June 1915): 573. My selection of these sources echoes that of Steven Johnson in "The Influence of California Bohemianism on Henry Cow-ell's Early Development," paper read at the Rocky Mountain Chapter of the American Musicological Society, 4 March 1990.

20. See "Arraignment," "In Minor Key," and "The 'Vasty Inn,'" in, respectively, *Overland Monthly* 58 (September 1911): 241; 66 (December 1915): 541; 64 (September 1914): 258.

21. *Overland Monthly* 64 (December 1914): 615.

22. *Overland Monthly* 56 (August 1910): 195.

23. "On the Massacre of Jews in Russia," *Overland Monthly* 52 (August 1908): 174.

24. In, respectively, *Overland Monthly* 55 (May 1910): 505; 64 (November 1914): 474; 66 (September 1915): 234–35.

25. "An Alleged State Duty," *American Journal of Politics* 3 (November 1893): 457. The quotations in the following paragraph are from pages 457 and 464 of this article.

26. On Hennepin, see Spencer Ellsworth, *Records of the Olden Time; or Forty Years on the Prairie* (Lacon, Ill.: Home Journal Steam Printing Establishment, 1880), 155–56.

27. This quotation and the one that follows are from "Clarissa Dixon Passes Away," *Palo Alto Times,* 16 May 1916.

28. Anna Strunsky Walling, in one of several brief, unsorted drafts about the life of Henry Cowell (hereafter collectively titled "Henry Cowell"), in Walling Papers.

29. Olive Cowell, interview, 10.

30. This information comes from Walling, "Henry Cowell."

31. "A Fatal Doubt," *Overland Monthly* 22 (November 1893): 474.

32. Olive Cowell (interview) says that the local avant-garde was scandalized when Harry and Clara began living together out of wedlock. According to Godwin, "Music of Henry Cowell," the two married in Oakland in February 1893. But no marriage certificate was filed and no wedding announcement appeared in the local newspapers.

33. Eleanor Pearson Bartlett, in *The First Year at Stanford: Sketches of Pioneer Days at Leland Stanford Junior University* (Stanford: The English Club, 1905), 25–26.

34. For a flavor of this see the speeches published in *The Leland Stanford Junior University, Exercises of the Opening Day, October 1, 1891* (Palo Alto: Stanford University, 1891).

35. On the early history of Menlo Park, see Roy W. Cloud, *History of San Mateo County, California,* 2 vols. (Chicago: S. J. Clarke, 1928), 1:201–9.

36. Olive Cowell, interview, 13; see also the mention of the Cowells' place among the early settlers of Menlo Park, in Margaret Moore, "'Youngsters over 50' Gather to Exchange Talk about Old Times in Menlo Park," *Menlo Park Recorder,* 11 October 1951, 6.

37. Walling, "Henry Cowell."

38. The date given on Cowell's "Delayed Certificate of Birth," filed 1 September 1954, was verified by (a) two music encyclopedias that show his birthdate, and (b) Edward Harkins, a neighbor who was fourteen years old in 1897.

39. The chart is found in John H. Paton to Harry and Clarissa Cowell, 11 April 1897, Cowell Collection, Music Division, New York Public Library for the Performing Arts.

40. For this quotation and the rest of the information in this paragraph, see Clarissa Dixon, "Material for Biography," typescript of holograph in Cowell Collection, 3.

41. Ibid., 2.

42. Walling, "Henry Cowell."

43. *St. Nicholas* 27 (Oct 1900): 1109. The offer of payment is found in a letter from the magazine to Clara, 16 January 1900, Cowell Collection.

44. Unless noted otherwise, all of the quotations in this paragraph are from Walling, "Henry Cowell."

45. Dixon, "Material for Biography," 64.

46. "Reminiscences of Henry Cowell" (16 October 1962), 2–3.

47. Henry Cowell interview, as aired on a tribute broadcast for Cowell (produced by Ev Grimes and Steve Cellum), National Public Radio, 24 October 1976.

48. Walling, "Henry Cowell."

49. Dixon, "Material for Biography," 59–61.

50. The most extensive published account of this is in "Henry Cowell," *Globe and Commercial Advertiser* (New York), 31 January 1920. See also Dixon, "Material for Biography," 61.

51. This and most of the information in this paragraph comes from Dixon, "Material for Biography," 62–66.

52. Some of the information in this paragraph initially came to me from Oliver Daniel, "Henry Cowell," *Stereo Review* 33 (December 1974): 72–82. Although, as Sidney Cowell has informally pointed out, this article contains many small errors in the way of spellings or dates, it also contains much unique information about Cowell's youth and upbringing. From all of the corroborating evidence I have seen, this article is actually the *most* accurate among all of the articles treating Cowell's youth.

53. Dixon, "Material for Biography," 67.

54. "Reminiscences of Henry Cowell" (17 December 1962), 67.

55. Walling, "Henry Cowell."

56. See the reference to "Mrs. Cowell's lectures" in a letter to Anna Strunsky [Walling], 6 January 1901, in *The Letters of Jack London, Volume One: 1896–1905,* ed. Earle Labor et al. (Stanford: Stanford University Press, 1988), 235.

57. Arnold Genthe and John Kuo Wei, *Genthe's Photographs of San Francisco's Old Chinatown* (New York: Dover, 1984), 19.

58. Henry Cowell, interview by John Edmunds for National Public Radio [date unknown—probably early 1960s], Yale University Library.

59. The quotations are from Henry Cowell, "Some Autobiographical Notes by Henry Cowell, No. 59182," typescript in Adolf Meyer Papers, Alan Mason Chesney Medical Archives, Johns Hopkins University. Olive Cowell, "Facts about Henry Cowell," confirms that Clara had refused sexual relations anymore; in a marginal note on Olive's typescript, Sidney Cowell contests this, blaming Harry for abandoning Clara first in his pursuit of Henrietta Grothwell (see below).

60. So he calls it in "Irregular Ballade."

61. Harry Cowell [under the nom-de-plume of H. C. Blackwood Cowell], "The Non-Survival of the Most Moral," *American Journal of Politics* 4 (1894): 630.

62. Olive Cowell, interview, 9, purports to be quoting this from a letter.

63. Clara Dixon Cowell, "The Free School System," *American Journal of Politics* 3 (1893): 405.

64. Dixon, "Material for Biography," 42.

65. Harry Cowell [as H. C. Blackwood Cowell], "School Ethics," *Popular Science Monthly* 46 (January 1895): 365.

66. Dixon, "Materials for Biography," 42.

67. Angela Kiefer, Oral History, 20 December 1973, typescript in Menlo Park Historical Society Library.

68. Cowell, "Some Autobiographical Notes."

69. Dixon, "Material for Biography," 43.

70. Cowell, "Some Autobiographical Notes."

71. Lewis M. Terman, *The Intelligence of School Children* (Boston: Houghton Mifflin, 1919), 249.

72. Henry Cowell, "The Process of Musical Creation," *American Journal of Psychology* 37 (1926): 235.

73. "Reminiscences of Henry Cowell" (16 October 1962), 12.

74. Harry Cowell, "San Francisco under Stress," *Poet Lore* 17 (September 1906): 74.

75. Harry Cowell, "San Francisco," *Overland Monthly* 52 (July 1908): 25.

76. A description of this appears in "Mid-Peninsula Reminiscences: An Interview with Blanche Walker Coats, A Lifetime Resident of the Central Peninsula," interview conducted by Sarah L. Bush, 1976, typescript in Menlo Park Historical Society Library, 7–8.

77. Henry Cowell to Harry Cowell, 21 May 1906, Cowell Collection.

78. Henry Cowell to Harry Cowell, 3 June 1906, mimeographed typescript of excerpts in Cowell Collection; Dixon, "Material for Biography," 69–70.

79. Dixon, "Material for Biography," 46.

80. Ibid., 48.

81. Ibid., 49.

82. Ibid., 41.

83. Ibid., 68.

84. "Reminiscences of Henry Cowell" (16 October 1962), 12.

85. As described in Lichtenwanger, *Music of Henry Cowell*, 1.

86. The quotations in this paragraph are from Dixon, "Woman and Nature," 284, 289. The acceptance letter for this article, dated 15 June 1901, is in the Cowell Collection.

87. Clarissa Dixon to Harry Cowell, 28 August 1907, carbon of typescript in Cowell Collection; see also Daniel, "Henry Cowell," 74.

88. Allen Churchill, *The Improper Bohemians: A Re-creation of Greenwich Village in Its Heyday* (New York: E. P. Dutton, 1959), 26. See also Peter Casill, *New York Memories of Yesteryear: Life and Times at the Turn of the Century 1890–1910* (New York: Expositor Press, 1964), 188–90.

89. Quoted in Churchill, *Improper Bohemians*, 25.

90. Henry Cowell to Harry Cowell, n.d. [1907], carbon of typescript in Cowell Collection; Dixon to Cowell, 28 August 1907.

91. Dixon, "Material for Biography," 69; "Reminiscences of Henry Cowell" (17 December 1962), 62. The quotation is from Henry Cowell to Harry Cowell, n.d. [1907].

92. Dixon to Cowell, 28 August 1907; see also Dixon, "Material for Biography," 41.

93. Dixon to Cowell, 28 August 1907.

94. Dixon, "Material for Biography," 69; Henry Cowell to Harry Cowell, 25 September 1907 and 11 October 1907, both in Cowell Collection.

95. Cowell, "Process of Musical Creation," 235–36.

96. *New York Times Saturday Review,* 6 March 1909, 132.

97. Clarissa Dixon, *Janet and Her Dear Phebe* (New York: Frederick A. Stokes, 1909), 4.

98. Ibid., 8.

99. Ibid., 42

100. Ibid., 55–56.

101. Ibid., 62.

102. Ibid., 154.

103. Ibid., 184.

104. "Loves of Little Girls," *New York Times Saturday Review,* 13 March 1909, 142.

105. The contractual information and correspondence with Stokes is in the Cowell Collection.

106. Cowell, "Some Autobiographical Notes."

107. Ibid.

108. Marion Todd, "The Boy Who Heard the 'Music of the Spheres' Astounds Artists," *Brooklyn Daily Eagle,* 19 April 1925, 10.

109. Henry Cowell to Harry Cowell, 5 May 1909, Cowell Collection.

110. Daniel, "Henry Cowell," 74. Henry and Clara are listed as living at the Guilbert farm in the 1910 census of Trego County, Kansas.

111. Dixon, "Material for Biography," 50.

112. Ibid., 70; "Reminiscences of Henry Cowell" (16 October 1962), 6.

113. Henry Cowell to Harry Cowell, 25 July 1910, Cowell Collection.

114. All of this information about their return comes from Dixon, "Material for Biography," 71–72.

115. Henry Cowell to Harry Cowell, 23 January 1911, Cowell Collection.

116. Henry's Menlo Park self-employment is discussed in Dixon, "Material for Biography," 72–75. Clarence Weaver, "The Memories of Henry Cowell," typescript of tape recording made in September 1976, in Menlo Park Historical Society, 2, adds that Henry also sold bugs he had caught to Stanford entomologists.

117. "Young Composer's Works Being Published," *Palo Alto Times,* 3 July 1922.

Chapter 2: The Pulse of Chords Tremendous and Remote

1. Quoted in Philip P. Wiener, ed., *Dictionary of the History of Ideas: Studies of Selected Pivotal Ideas,* 5 vols. (New York: Scribner, 1973–74), s.v. "Genius."

2. Quoted in Raymond E. Fancher, *The Intelligence Men: Makers of the I.Q. Controversy* (New York: Norton, 1985), 138; this book is also the principal source on Terman's work as described in this chapter.

3. The quotation and the information in this sentence come from Weaver, "Memories of Henry Cowell," 3.

4. This, at any rate, is the account passed from Cowell's widow, Sidney, to Godwin, "Music of Henry Cowell," 6.

5. Terman, *Intelligence of School Children,* 248–49. Except as noted, all of the quotations in the next two paragraphs are from this source. In this source, it should be noted, Terman calls his subject only "Henry." In Burks et al., *The Promise of Youth,* 322–24, Terman identifies "Henry" as Henry Cowell.

6. These are among the measures Terman outlines for fifteen-year-olds in Lewis Terman and H. G. Childs, "A Tentative Revision and Extension of the Binet-Simon Measuring Scale of Intelligence," *Journal of Educational Psychology* 3 (1912): 281.

7. L. M. Terman and M. H. Oden, *The Gifted Child Grows Up: Twenty-Five Years' Follow-up of a Superior Group* (Stanford: Stanford University Press, 1947), 323.

8. Terman, *Intelligence of School Children,* 246.

9. Robert L. Duffus and William M. Duffus, *The Innocents at Cedro: A Memoir of Thorstein Veblen and Some Others* (New York: Macmillan, 1944), 144. This is the source for most of what follows concerning Veblen. But see also David Riesman, *Thorstein Veblen: A Critical Interpretation* (New York: Scribner's, 1953), passim.

10. Riesman, *Thorstein Veblen,* 9.

11. Ellen Rolfe Veblen, *The Goosenbury Pilgrims: A Child's Drama* (Chicago: n.p., 1902), 104.

12. Dixon, "Material for Biography," 71.

13. Ibid.

14. Ibid., 75.

15. "The Boy Who Heard the 'Music of the Spheres,'" 10.

16. Dixon, "Material for Biography," 76.

17. Bartlett, *First Year at Stanford,* 26.

18. Weaver, "Memories of Henry Cowell," 1.

19. The information in this paragraph all comes from Dixon, "Material for Biography," 76–78.

20. Dixon, "Material for Biography," 78–79.

21. Henry Cowell to Harry Cowell, 12 January 1913, Cowell Collection.

22. This source is reproduced in Godwin, "Music of Henry Cowell," 403–23.

23. Mary Austin, "George Sterling at Carmel," *American Mercury* 11 (May 1927): 66–67, 72.

24. See Starr, *Americans and the California Dream,* 266–67.

25. Rosalind Sharpe Wall, *A Wild Coast and Lonely: Big Sur Pioneers* (San Carlos, Calif.: Wide World Publishing Tetra, 1989), 173.

26. The quotations from Gui de Angulo and Henry Miller are both found in Wall, *A Wild Coast,* 164 and 175, respectively.

27. The information in this paragraph comes from Starr, *Americans and the California Dream,* 270–71, 279; Walker, *Seacoast of Bohemia,* 15–17; and Austin, "George Sterling at Carmel."

28. George Sterling, *Sails and Mirage and Other Poems* (San Francisco: A. M. Robertson, 1921), 115.

29. Godwin, "Music of Henry Cowell," 22.

30. Lichtenwanger, *Music of Henry Cowell,* 11.

31. I determined the ages of the children from announcements of their birthday parties and related events over a period of years in the *Carmel Pine Cone.*

32. Cowell, "Some Autobiographical Notes."

33. The information about Edna Smith comes from miscellaneous notices in the *Carmel Pine Cone* that mention her name, occupation, and whereabouts; also Godwin, "Music of Henry Cowell," 7; and "Two Sisters in Auto Die at Rail Crossing," *New York Times,* 16 April 1922.

34. On the "Grand Manner," see Godwin, "Music of Henry Cowell," 21.

35. The harmonic adventure here seems to be the key (F♯ major) and the juxtaposition of chords unlinked by the functional progressions found in most of Cowell's earlier music. The second, contrasting character of Chapter I is that of an Irish folk tune, under which an F♯-C♯-F♯ drone sounds on each downbeat. After this, the first material returns, followed by a reprise of the second material—only now with the block chord revised into a *quartal* harmony (G♯-C♯-F♯).

36. Godwin, "Music of Henry Cowell," 20.

37. David Ewen, comp. and ed., *Composers of Today,* 2d ed. (New York: H. W. Wilson, 1936), 53.

38. Sidney Cowell, telephone conversation with Steven Johnson, 15 February 1990.

39. Terman, *Intelligence of School Children,* 248; see also Cowell, "Process of Musical Creation," 23.

40. Homer Henley, "Music: The Anatomy of Dissonance," *Argonaut,* 27 May 1932.

41. Henry Cowell, "Jazz Today," *Trend* 2 (October 1934): 164.

42. Todd, "The Boy Who Heard the 'Music of the Spheres,'" 10.

43. Henry Cowell to Clarissa Dixon, n.d., postmarked 5[?] July 1913, Cowell Collection.

44. The theater is described in Daisy F. Bostick and Dorothea Castelhun, *Carmel— At Work and Play* (Carmel, Calif.: Seven Arts, 1925), 68–69.

45. Walker, *Seacoast of Bohemia,* 79.

46. See "The Past Productions and Summary of Carmel's Historic Forest Playhouse," *Carmel Pine Cone,* 30 June 1921.

47. Albert Keiser, *The Indian in American Literature,* quoted in Walker, *Seacoast of Bohemia,* 110.

48. Austin's reminiscence appears in "People Talked About," *Carmel Pine Cone,* 29 August 1930, 9.

49. This and the other quotations and the biographical information in this paragraph are from the foreword to Takeshi Kanno, *Creation Dawn (A Vision Drama)* (Fruitvale, Calif.: Published by the Author, 1913), 1–4.

50. The quotations in this paragraph are from Kanno, *Creation Dawn,* 5–6, 11, 34, 36.

51. The quotations from Austin are in "People Talked About," 9; Clarissa's statements are in Dixon, "Material for Biography."

52. "People Talked About," 9.

53. Dixon, "Material for Biography," 81.

54. Anna Cora Winchell, "Lad Shows Signs of Real Genius," *San Francisco Chronicle,* 6 March 1914, 5.

55. Anonymous letter to Clarissa Dixon, 9 December 1913, Cowell Collection.

56. The quotations are from Samuel S. Seward, *Narrative and Lyric Poems for Students* (New York: Henry Holt, 1909), v–vi; and idem, *Note-Taking* (Boston: Allyn and Bacon, 1910), iii.

57. "Seward Lauded by Clergyman," *Palo Alto Times,* 31 August 1932.

58. "Palo Alto Youth Shows Musical Ability," *Palo Alto Times,* 30 July 1914.

59. These remarks and all of the information and quotations in this paragraph are from Cary de Angulo to Clarissa Dixon, 16 January 1914, Cowell Collection.

60. "Youthful Wonder Has Charm of Genius," *Palo Alto Times,* 23 January 1914.

61. The Bates connnection is mentioned in Samuel Seward, "To Subscribers to the Henry Cowell Fund," dated 28 October 1914, photocopy in Cowell Collection.

62. "Short Items of Interest," *Pacific Coast Musical Review* 25 (7 March 1914), 7.

63. The program gives it as "Etude no. 2." By this time, however, Cowell had written many pieces called "etudes," most of which were only a few measures long. His CD lists as full blown pieces "Etude no. 1" and "Etude no. 3," but no "no. 2." It was usually his "Etude no. 1" that Cowell played on recitals of this period. This piece, subtitled "The Cauldron," attempted to depict a well-known site at Point Lobos, a treacherous maelstrom where currents clash with the rocks.

64. Winchell, "Lad Shows Signs of Real Genius," 5.

65. Redfern Mason, "Work of Merit at Concert of Local Society," *San Francisco Examiner,* 6 March 1914.

66. Henry Cowell to Clarissa Dixon, 11 March 1914, Cowell Collection.

67. Dixon, "Material for Biography," 81–82.

68. Clarissa Dixon to Henry Cowell, 2 April 1914, Cowell Collection.

69. Among the more blatant examples of redating compositions is in the booklet (prepared by Henry through Sidney) that accompanies the record entitled *The Piano Music of Henry Cowell* (Folkways FG33499), 4.

Chapter 3: Trusting His Muse to a Guiding Intellect

1. The information in the first half of this paragraph comes from Dixon, "Material for Biography," 84; Clarissa Dixon to Henry Cowell, 2 April 1914; Henry Cowell to Clarissa Dixon, 2 April 1914; Ellen Veblen to Clarissa Dixon, 30 March 1914; and miscellaneous promotional photos from this period, all in Cowell Collection.

2. Cowell quoted in Ellen Veblen to Clarissa Dixon, 22 March 1914. The reference to his appearing as Wagner is from Henry Cowell to Clarissa Dixon, 7 August 1914. The "interestingly crooked" statement is from Veblen to Henry Cowell, 26 May 1914. All of these are found in the Cowell Collection.

3. Included with Veblen's letter to Clarissa, 22 March 1914.

4. Olive Cowell to Anna Strunsky Walling, 6 February 1958, Walling Papers.

5. Godwin, "Music of Henry Cowell," 8.

6. There are several accounts of this episode; see especially Dixon, "Material for Biography," 84–85.

7. Walter Anthony, "In the World of Music: Opera Star Will Sing in Concert," *San Francisco Chronicle,* 26 July 1914, 28; reprinted in "Palo Alto Youth Shows Musical Ability."

8. Henry Cowell, "Why Modern Music?" *Women's City Club Magazine,* December 1931, 16. See also his "Creation and Imitation," *Fortnightly,* November 1931, 5–6.

9. See Clarissa's lengthy discussion of this work in Dixon, "Material for Biography," 87–89.

10. The principal source on Seeger's biography (on which I have relied) is Ann Pescatello, *Charles Seeger: A Life in American Music* (Pittsburgh: University of Pittsburgh Press, 1992).

11. Quoted in Pescatello, *Charles Seeger,* 53.

12. Quoted in Pescatello, *Charles Seeger,* 97.

13. Henry Cowell to Clarissa Dixon, postmarked 28 October 1913, Cowell Collection.

14. Rose A. Glavinovich, "Rough Places Confront Genius in Pursuit of Beckoning Star," *Oakland Tribune Magazine,* 31 August 1924, 10.

15. Todd, "The Boy Who Heard the 'Music of the Spheres.'"

16. Charles Seeger to Joscelyn Godwin, 13 December 1974, photocopy in author's possession.

17. As reported in Weisgall, "Music of Henry Cowell," 487.

18. Charles Seeger, "Henry Cowell," *Magazine of Art* 33 (May 1940): 288.

19. For a brief biography of Sabin, see Reuben R. Rinder, *Tribute to Wallace Arthur Sabin* (San Francisco: Loring Club, 1938), a pamphlet produced for Sabin's memorial service.

20. The basic biographical information here comes from "Last Rites Set for E. G. Stricklen," *Oakland Tribune*, 4 January 1950, 19.

21. Kirchner's reminiscence of Stricklen, from which these quotations are taken, appears in Irving Stone, ed., *There Was Light: Autobiography of a University, Berkeley: 1868–1968* (Garden City, N.Y.: Doubleday, 1970), 244–45.

22. Prout, who had developed this idea most fully, abandoned it in later editions of his theory texts, having concluded it had too many flaws. The overtone-based systems of theory cited in this paragraph are discussed in David M. Thompson, *A History of Harmonic Theory in the United States* (Kent, Ohio: Kent State University Press, 1980), 22–35 and 40–45.

23. The information in this and the following paragraphs comes from Charles Seeger and Edward Stricklen, *Harmonic Structure and Elementary Composition: An Outline of a Course in Practical Musical Invention* (Berkeley: n.p., 1916). This was Stricklen's revision of their earlier syllabus entitled "An Outline of a Course in Harmonic Structure and Simple Musical Invention." The quotations in both paragraphs are from the first four pages of the 1916 version.

24. See Lichtenwanger, *Music of Henry Cowell*, 44.

25. Dixon, "Material for Biography," 89.

26. Quoted in Dixon, "Material for Biography," 41.

27. Cowell, "Some Autobiographical Notes."

28. Seeger to Godwin, 13 December 1974.

29. This is the reminiscence of Edith Partridge Harkins, recounted in Moore, "'Youngsters over 50' Gather to Exchange Talk."

30. Dixon, "Material for Biography," 8.

31. Seeger to Godwin, 13 December 1974.

32. Cowell, "Some Autobiographical Notes." The 7 April 1914 letter he wrote her mentioning the dance is in the Cowell Collection.

33. "Musical Numbers Are Entertainment Features," *Palo Alto Times*, 4 August 1915.

34. Dixon, "Material for Biography," 89.

35. See the letter written by both Henry Cowell and Clarissa Dixon to Ellen Veblen, 16 December 1915, Cowell Collection. Sidney Cowell, in a handwritten note on the letter, says that this was Clarissa's first mastectomy. Indications in several earlier letters, however, have led me to believe that it was her second, the first being in June 1913.

36. Charles Seeger, *Studies in Musicology II: 1929–1979*, ed. Ann Pescatello (Berkeley: University of California Press, 1994), 201.

37. The quotations in this paragraph come from "Henry Cowell Plays at Castilleja School Tomorrow," "Local Music Genius Gives Recital Tonight," and "Cowell Concert a Music Treat," *Palo Alto Times*, 9, 10, and 11 February 1916, respectively.

38. This quotation and the poem that follows appear in "Clarissa Dixon Passes Away."

39. Compare the *Carmel Pine Cone* notices on de Angulo's house guests, 3 May 1916 (Edna Smith staying for the next two months at de Angulo's) and 31 May 1916 (Henry Cowell now visiting here at de Angulo's).

40. The information about Cowell's movements during May and June comes from brief notices in the *Carmel Pine Cone*, 31 May and 21 June 1916.

41. Henry Cowell to "Peter" (Amy Seward), 18 September 1932, photocopy in my posession.

42. From the speech recorded in Frank Damrosch, *Institute of Musical Art, 1905–1926* (New York: Juilliard School of Music, 1936), 53. Most of the essential information in this and the next paragraph derive from this source and the institute twelfth-year catalog (1916–17), in the Juilliard School Archives.

43. Henry Cowell to Russell Varian [December 1916], Papers of Russell and Sigurd Varian, SC 345, Stanford University Archives, Stanford, California.

44. Henry Cowell to Ellen Veblen, n.d., postmarked 27 October 1916, Cowell Collection.

45. See the comments in Ellen Veblen to Henry Cowell, 15 November 1916, Cowell Collection.

46. Henry Cowell to Ellen Veblen, n.d., postmarked 18 November 1916, Cowell Collection.

47. Probably the handiest source for an introduction to futurist musical aesthetics is the collection of documents in Nicolas Slonimsky, *Music since 1900,* 4th ed. (New York: Scribner's, 1971), 1294–1304.

48. Charles L. Buchanan, "Ornstein and Modern Music," *Musical Quarterly* 4 (April 1918): 178.

49. Review of 30 March 1914, as cited in Vivian Perlis, "The Futurist Music of Leo Ornstein," *Notes: Quarterly Journal of the Music Library Association* 31 (1974–75): 739.

50. Lawrence Gilman, "Drama and Music: Significant Happenings of the Month," *North American Review* 201 (April 1915): 596.

51. Buchanan, "Ornstein and Modern Music," 177.

52. Ornstein quoted in Terence J. O'Grady, "A Conversation with Leo Ornstein," *Perspectives of New Music* 23 (Fall–Winter 1984): 128.

53. "The Music of a Day," *New York Times,* 26 November 1916, 18.

54. Quoted in Carl Van Vechten, *Music and Bad Manners* (New York: Knopf, 1916), 238.

55. See Cowell's letters to Veblen, 18 November and 22 November 1916.

56. Henry Cowell to Ellen Veblen, n.d., postmarked 22 November 1916, Cowell Collection.

57. Lewis Terman, "Notes on Henry March 1 1917," photocopy of holograph in Cowell Collection. A meticulous record-keeper, Terman wrote this document immediately following a dinner with Cowell during which the young composer detailed for Terman his experiences in New York.

58. "Henry Cowell," 31 January 1920.

59. Terman, "Notes on Henry."

60. "Cowell Plays Own Music for Club," *San Francisco Call and Post,* 19 June 1919.

61. See, for example, the review by Louise Vermont, *The Greenwich Villager,* 15 April 1922: "At the finish of [*Dynamic Motion*] three women lay in a dead faint in the aisle and no less than ten men had refreshed themselves from the left hip."

62. Admittedly, Cowell's logbook is probably not complete. But it is hard to imagine that he would omit his more daring cluster pieces from the log, while including so many trivial (and often extremely brief) pieces.

63. What I call arpeggiations here, David Nicholls calls "addition clusters" when each note of the arpeggiation is sustained until all have sounded—see his *American Experimental Music, 1890–1940* (Cambridge: Cambridge University Press, 1990), 157. His terminology echoes that of Mauricio Kagel, "Tone-Clusters, Attacks, Transitions," trans. Leo Black, *Die Reihe V: Reports, analyses* (Bryn Mawr, Pa.: Theodore Presser, 1961), 43–44. Kagel's is so far the most exhaustive treatment of how clusters might be used, but it is not strictly based on how Cowell used them. Oddly, he defines clusters as "only those sounds which are at least a *major third* broad and filled out with major and/or minor seconds" (43, emphasis mine).

64. The manuscript to *Conservative Estimate* bears twenty-three such colloquial prospective titles (see Lichtenwanger, *Music of Henry Cowell,* 86–87). Incidentally, Cowell's best known piece in this idiom is *Tiger*—a primitivist title given to a work originally bearing the futurist title *Dash.* The change of title simply confirms the proposition that, in musical terms, futurism and primitivism are the same. The "futurist" Ornstein suggested as much when he said that he devised clusters to "project the dark brooding quality . . . in prehistoric man" (as quoted in Gilbert Chase, *America's Music: From the Pilgrims to the Present,* 2d ed. (New York: McGraw-Hill, 1966), 578).

65. Seeger to Godwin, 13 December 1974, discusses the type of pieces that Cowell brought during his lessons; see also Charles Seeger, interview by Rita L. Mead, 15 November 1974, typescript in the Institute for Studies in American Music, Brooklyn College of the City University of New York, 37, and Seeger, "Henry Cowell," 289.

66. Ellen Veblen to Henry Cowell, 23 November 1916, Cowell Collection.

67. Terman, "Notes on Henry."

68. Henry Cowell to Ellen Veblen, n.d., postmarked 22 November 1916.

69. Veblen to Cowell, 27 November 1916, Cowell Collection.

70. Ellen Veblen to Henry Cowell, 23 October 1916, Cowell Collection.

71. Veblen to Cowell, 8 November 1916, Cowell Collection; on Cowell's confrontation with Damrosch see Terman, "Notes on Henry," Seeger, "Henry Cowell," 322, and Madeleine Goss, *Modern Music-Makers: Contemporary American Composers* (New York: Dutton, 1952), 269–70.

72. For a general account of the theosophical movement, see Bruce F. Campbell, *Ancient Wisdom Revived: A History of the Theosophical Movement* (Berkeley: University of California Press, 1980). For a thorough exploration of Cowell's relationship to

theosophy and its California adherents, see Steven Johnson, "Henry Cowell, John Varian, and Halcyon," *American Music* 11 (Spring 1993): 1–27.

73. George Harrison, interview by Dorothy Varian, 11 May 1962, typescript in Varian Papers.

74. Sidney Cowell cites Henry to this effect in an undated letter to Dorothy Varian, Varian Papers.

75. Frederick Whitney, "How the Poet and the Composer Met," *Troubadour* 3 (July 1931): 6–7 (see appendix 2 for the complete article). For a confirmation of this story, see Harrison, interview.

76. Harrison, interview.

77. The information in this sentence comes from John Varian to "Sister Ann" (Anne Hadden), 18 July 1914, and Russell Varian to Henry Cowell, 18 December 1916, both letters in Varian Papers.

78. John Varian to Henry Cowell, n.d., Varian Papers.

79. Robert V. Hine, *California Utopianism: Contemplations of Eden* (San Francisco: Boyd and Fraser, 1981), 43–44.

80. See the assorted references to Cowell in the *Temple Artisan,* the official journal of the temple, 1919–21.

81. *Temple Artisan* 17 (November 1916): 91.

82. Eileen Harrison to Dorothy Varian, 11 May 1962, Varian Papers.

83. Undated letter (ca. 1916) from John Varian to Henry Cowell, Varian Papers.

84. Quoted in Rita Mead, *Henry Cowell's New Music, 1925–1936: The Society, the Music Editions, and the Recordings* (Ann Arbor: UMI Research Press, 1981), 21.

85. Henry Cowell to Russell Varian, December 1916, Varian Papers.

86. Henry Cowell to Ellen Veblen, n.d., postmarked 20 October 1916, Cowell Collection.

87. John Varian to Henry Cowell, n.d., Varian Papers.

88. John Varian to Henry Cowell, 18 November 1916, Varian Papers.

89. Johnson, "Henry Cowell, John Varian, and Halcyon," 17.

90. As described in Goss, *Modern Music-Makers,* 268.

91. "Oberammergau in America," unsigned typescript in Varian Papers.

92. *Daybooks of Edward Weston, Vol. II,* 184

93. Sidney Cowell to Dorothy Varian, 16 September 1980, Varian Papers.

94. John Varian to Henry Cowell, 19 March 1917, Varian Papers.

95. "Convention Week Aug 1917," Agnes Varian Diary, Varian Papers.

96. John Varian to Henry Cowell, 26 October 1916, Varian Papers.

97. See the notice in *Temple Artisan* 17 (November 1916): 87–88.

98. Steven Johnson's statement that Varian patented the harp in 1911 is incorrect (see Johnson, "Henry Cowell, John Varian, and Halcyon," 10). That harp had no keyboard.

99. John Varian to Henry Cowell, 19 March 1917, Varian Papers.

100. These descriptions of new instruments are in a looseleaf poetry notebook in the Varian Papers, just following the poem "Hero Souls" (May 1916).

101. John Varian to Henry Cowell, 25 January 1918, Varian Papers.

102. Russell Varian to Henry Cowell, 20 October 1923, Varian Papers.

103. Henry Cowell to Russell Varian, December 1916, Varian Papers. The quotations in the following paragraph are also from this source.

104. Russell Varian to Henry Cowell, December 1916, Varian Papers.

105. Seeger, "Henry Cowell," 288. Commenting on this statement, Seeger's biographer said, "Charlie was terribly generous with his ideas" and the word "swiped" was more or less "a gesture in friendship"; "he never ever said, 'that was my idea, somebody stole it from me'" (Ann Pescatello, telephone conversation with the author, 22 January 1997).

106. Henry Cowell, "Charles Louis Seeger, Jr.: An Appraisal of a Local Composer," *Fortnightly,* 15 January 1932, 5.

107. Said Cowell, "First, [Seeger] pointed out that if I proposed to use new and unusual musical material I would have to work out a systematic technique for them so things would hang together. And, second, he told me that if my innovations were to establish themselves, I would have to build up a real repertoire embodying them, myself, letting them develop as I thought about them to make a sound world of their own. I have thought in these terms about my music ever since." Interview with Hugo Weisgall, 1959, quoted in Pescatello, *Charles Seeger,* 67. See also Sidney Cowell's reminiscence of Seeger's legacy in "Charles Seeger (1886–1979)," *Musical Quarterly* 65 (April 1979): 305–6.

108. Sidney Cowell to Dorothy Varian, 12 February 1979, Varian Papers. For a broad survey of Cowell's relationship with the Varians, see Dorothy Varian, *The Inventor and the Pilot* (Palo Alto: Pacific Books, 1983), 40–41, 48–57.

109. This and the following quotation are found in Seeger, "Henry Cowell," 323.

Chapter 4: The Work of Exploration Has Just Begun

1. This information comes from "Local Musician to Enter Service," undated newspaper clipping in Cowell File, Palo Alto Public Library.

2. In any case, the fractions in thirds are curious approximations for the given partials' degree of "out-of-tune-ness" with equal temperament. To get the "⅓"- and "⅔"- related note values he attempted for the first time a new notational symbol, triangular noteheads.

3. Godwin, "Music of Henry Cowell," 136.

4. See Mrs. Dalton F. Schwarz, "A Young Woman's View of Camp Crane in 1917," *Proceedings of the Lehigh County Historical Society* 32 (1978): 191.

5. Ibid., 193.

6. Lawrence Flick Jr., "Our Ambulance Rendevous at Allentown," *Philadelphia Record,* 24 June 1917, reprinted in Schwarz, "A Young Woman's View," 188.

7. Henry Cowell to Harry Cowell, undated letter from Camp Crane, Allentown, in Cowell Collection.

8. This and the following quotations in the paragraph come from an undated letter in the Varian Papers, but one whose content clearly show it to be from 1918, after Henry had received his kitchen assignment.

9. Nevertheless, Sousa wrote a tune for the group, calling it the "USAAC March." See John R. Smucker Jr., *Commemorative History Published by the United States Army Ambulance Service Association in Celebration of the Fiftieth Anniversary of the Establishment of the USAAS and the Founding of Camp Crane, Allentown, Pennsylvania* (Allentown: Wm. G. Schlechter, 1967), 21–22.

10. Ibid., 22.

11. Daniel, "Henry Cowell," 76.

12. Henry Cowell to Russell Varian, 6 January 1919, Varian Papers.

13. John Varian to Henry Cowell, undated [ca. 1918], Varian Papers.

14. Cowell told this story on several occasions. I draw this version from Sergei Bertensson and Jay Leda, *Sergei Rachmaninoff: A Lifetime in Music* (New York: New York University Press, 1956), 219–20; also "Reminiscences of Henry Cowell" (17 December 1962), 64–65.

15. As cited in the preface to Henry Cowell, *New Musical Resources,* ed. Joscelyn Godwin (New York: Something Else Press, 1969), x.

16. For a detailed overview of this book, see Kyle Gann, "Subversive Prophet: Henry Cowell as Theorist and Critic," in David Nicholls, ed., *The Whole World of Music: A Henry Cowell Symposium* (Amsterdam: Harwood, 1997), 172–90.

17. For the description of the manuscript and how it varies from the published version I am utterly indebted to the fine scholarship of David Nicholls in his notes to Henry Cowell, *New Musical Resources* (Cambridge: Cambridge University Press, 1996), 153–69.

18. Edward Griffith Stricklen, *Outline of a Course in Chromatic Harmony and the Intermediate Types of Musical Invention* (Berkeley: n.p., 1916), 34.

19. See Henry Cowell, "New Terms for New Music," *Modern Music* 5 (May–June 1928): 26–27.

20. Other combinations are equally plausible; for example, 4/4, 5/4, and 6/4.

21. Henry Cowell, "The Impasse of Modern Music: Searching for New Avenues of Beauty," *Century* 114 (October 1927): 676.

22. Chase, *America's Music,* 578.

23. See, for example, the sketch to *Sound March,* which abounds with the vertical cigar shapes of his cluster notation, but with completely vague intervallic boundaries.

24. These dates are according to Lichtenwanger, *Music of Henry Cowell,* 58, 72.

25. Thomas Vincent Cator, "Henry Cowell Plays," *Carmel Pine Cone,* 16 August 1929, 6.

26. "Musical Measurements," *Los Angeles Times,* 1 September 1929.

27. Marc Blitzstein, "Forecast and Review," *Modern Music* 8 (May–June 1931): 35–36.

28. Nicholls properly concludes that in the Varian-related works, cluster technique is "essentially decorative," although I think he goes too far in claiming that it "adds

nothing of real importance to the musical substance" (*American Experimental Music*, 156). Godwin traces all of the mystic pieces to Cowell's early fascination with the "Grand Manner" (see Godwin, "Music of Henry Cowell," 133).

29. There may also be an implicit difference in tonalities between the two layers, as one sees in *Tides*, for example (see Godwin, "Music of Henry Cowell," 28–29).

30. From the epigraph to the published version of Cowell's *The Voice of Lir*.

31. This and others of Cowell's cluster-based pieces are analyzed in Steven Johnson, "'Worlds of Ideas': The Music of Henry Cowell," in Nicholls, *The Whole World of Music*, 18–23.

32. Slonimsky, "Henry Cowell," 62.

33. In the manuscript to *Dynamic Motion*, Cowell has an explanatory note that defines the cluster notation as angular; in the equivalent note to *Banba*, the cluster notation is unambiguously curved.

34. See the Halcyon-related manuscript entitled "Clusteriana No. 1: Analysis of Tone Cluster Examples in the Form of Movement of One Cluster," discussed in Lichtenwanger, *Music of Henry Cowell*, 319–20. This manuscript seems to contain examples of different kinds of clusters and their movements, similar to those that would appear as examples in *New Musical Resources* (as published by Knopf in 1930), where a typeset version of this notation appears throughout the "Tone Clusters" chapter.

A variant notation appears in Cowell's published cluster pieces from 1922 on: clusters whose duration is a quarter note or less consist of a thick vertical beam between noteheads. It is this variant that has become standard in considerations of Cowell's work. In *Music since 1900*, Slonimsky likens Cowell's notation to one created by Vladimir Rebikov, a "special columnar notation, indicating that the conglomeration of keys are [*sic*] to be encompassed with the edge of the palm of the hand"; the piece for which he devised it is named *Hymn to the Sun*, published 1912 (199). Later in the book, Slonimsky refers to this piece as *Hymn to Inca* and says that the notation is "identical" to Cowell's (1498). I have not been able to locate any version of this piece, however, and I doubt that it exists. For more on the notation and phenomenon of clusters, see Michael Hicks, "Cowell's Clusters," *Musical Quarterly* 77 (Fall 1993): 428–58.

35. Morris Dickstein, respondent to Lou Harrison, "Remembering Henry Cowell," Henry Cowell Centennial Symposium, Lincoln Center, New York, 14 March 1997.

36. "Henry Cowell," 31 January 1920.

37. Henry Cowell to Ellen Veblen, 28 February 1920, cited in Lichtenwanger, *Music of Henry Cowell*, 76.

38. As recounted in Henry Cowell to Ellen Veblen, 4 January 1920, Cowell Collection.

39. See Henry Cowell to Ellen Veblen, 18 February 1920, Cowell Collection.

40. "Another Leginska Evening," *Musical Courier*, 26 February 1920.

41. See Henry Cowell to Ellen Veblen, 28 February 1920, Cowell Collection.

42. See "Cowell Concert Is Important Date in Life of Composer," *Palo Alto Times*, 26 October 1920, which mentions that this will be Cowell's "first pretentious concert," with tickets at one dollar apiece.

43. Russell Varian to "Dear Folks," 12 November 1920, Varian Papers.

44. Redfern Mason, "Henry Cowell Gives Recital in Home Town," *San Francisco Examiner,* 8 November 1920.

45. This and the quotations in the following paragraph come from Henry Cowell, "Piano Instruction Course" (with cover letter), on file at the Temple of the People.

46. The text here actually reads "see," but given Cowell's typical parallel constructions and the context, it is clear that he intended the word "feel."

47. Ernst Lecher Bacon, *Our Musical Idiom* (Chicago: Open Court, 1917); original publication as an article in the *Monist* for October 1917.

48. Henry Cowell and R[obert]. L. Duffus, "Harmonic Development in Music," *Freeman* 3 (30 March 1921): 63.

49. The quotation is from Henry Cowell and R[obert]. L. Duffus, "Harmonic Development in Music," *Freeman* 3 (13 April 1921): 111. The history of harmonic development is treated mainly in the earlier two installments: 30 March 1921: 63–65, and 6 April 1921: 85–87.

50. Cowell and Duffus, "Harmonic Development in Music," 13 April 1921: 113.

51. Seeger, interview by David K. Dunaway in that author's "Charles Seeger and Carl Sands: The Composers' Collective Years," *Ethnomusicology* 24 (May 1980): 161.

52. The quotations are from "Music Matters," *Carmel Pine Cone,* 14 April 1921, and an untitled notice in the *Carmel Pine Cone,* 2 June 1921.

53. D[ane] Rudhyar, "The Relativity of Our Musical Conceptions," *Musical Quarterly* 8 (January 1922): 108–9.

54. "Young Composer's Works Being Published." The paper also gave what appears to be the first public announcement of his forthcoming book, which it said would be called "The Unexplored Resources in Musical Effects."

55. "Composer Demonstrates New Type of Music to Toledoans," *Toledo Sunday Times,* 17 April 1927.

56. Cowell, "Some Autobiographical Notes."

57. On Cowell's homosexual relationships in the wake of Smith's death, see the "Proceedings on Sentence," 6 July 1936 (court document of State of California vs. Henry Cowell no. 25753, copy in Meyer Papers). The "numbness and misery" quote is from Cowell, "Some Autobiographical Notes." For more on Edna Smith, the engagement, her death, and the financing of Cowell's tour, see Godwin, "Music of Henry Cowell," 7 and 11–12; Olive Cowell, interview, 15–16; "Two Sisters in Auto Die"; and "Easter's Auto Toll Now Totals Eight," *New York Times,* 18 April 1922.

58. Walling, "Henry Cowell."

59. Seeger, "Henry Cowell," 322.

60. The work was originally planned in two movements, and Cowell considered several titles: "Two Movements" (given on the manuscript), "Piece for Keyboard and Strings," and "Morceau pour piano avec cordes." He never finished the second movement, however, and the first was published in 1924 as "Pièce pour piano avec cordes." See Lichtenwanger, *Music of Henry Cowell,* 101.

61. On these matters see Rosamund E. M. Harding, *The Piano-Forte: Its History Traced to the Great Exhibition of 1851* (Cambridge: Cambridge University Press, 1933), 118–50; Arthur Loesser, *Men, Women, and Pianos: A Social History* (New York: Simon and Schuster, 1954), 172.

62. Olga Samaroff, "Music: Henry Cowell's String Piano," *New York Evening Post,* 3 February 1926, 9.

63. W. J. Henderson, "Henry Cowell Plucks Piano," *New York Sun,* 3 February 1926.

64. Grock discusses his musical antics in his *Life's a Lark,* trans. Madge Pemberton (New York: Benjamin Blom, 1969).

65. Cowell gives the date he began his experimentation as 1914 in "The Stringpiano," *Musical America,* 30 January 1926, 20. In 1957, however, Cowell was quoted as saying that "in the 1920s it struck me that a person could play inside the piano, on the strings, just as easily as he could play on the keys" ("Pianist with a Punch," *Detroit News,* 14 February 1957). The latter date compromises Cowell's historical primacy, but comfortably distances his idea from Seeger's influence.

66. For a survey of the reviews see Manion, *Writings about Henry Cowell,* 126–34.

67. Walling, "Henry Cowell."

68. "Reminiscences of Henry Cowell" (16 October 1962), 19; also Walling, "Henry Cowell."

69. See *Le Courier Musical,* 15 February 1924 [musical supplement], 4–7.

70. As quoted in Adrian Pelham, "Music: Stravinsky and Cowell Break the Ice of Tradition," *Theatre Magazine,* April 1924, 34.

71. Pitts Sanborn, "Henry Cowell, musical theorist," *New York Telegram and Evening Mail,* 5 February 1924.

72. Paul Rosenfeld, "Musical Chronicle," *The Dial* 76 (April 1924): 390.

73. From a journal entry, ca. 1926, translated and quoted by Eva Drlikova in "Henry Cowell, Leos Janacek, and Who Were the Others?" *Sonneck Society Bulletin* 15, no. 2 (Summer 1988): 58–59.

74. C. W. Brown, "Cowell Is Undisturbed by Criticism," *San Francisco Chronicle,* 29 June 1924.

75. The quotations in this paragraph are from "The Stringpiano," 20.

76. On this piece and its premiere see Lichtenwanger, *Music of Henry Cowell,* 106–7; and Manion, *Writings about Henry Cowell,* 157–58.

77. See the letters to and from Cowell [ca. 1924] that discuss "The Ban Shee," in the Varian Papers; also Johnson, "Henry Cowell, John Varian, and Halcyon," 12.

78. See Cowell, "The Impasse of Modern Music," 677.

79. As Steven Johnson observes, *The Banshee* (now one word) follows the same shape as many other Cowell pieces. It begins softly in tempo rubato, grows progressively louder as it gets faster, then finally ends quietly and slowly. Cowell further articulates that shape by manipulating his sound effects. The chords in the piece, for example, grow increasingly dense. The first phrase repeats a three-note diminished triad (E-G-B♭); the second presents a cluster version of the same chord (E-F-G-A-B♭). The third pas-

sage, the climax of the piece, sounds a chromatic cluster spanning a major sixth, and for the first time presents chords that move from one position to another. See Johnson, "'Worlds of Ideas,'" 26.

Chapter 5: The Bohemian Legacy

1. Alexis de Tocqueville, *Democracy in America,* trans. Henry Reeve, 2 vols. (New York: Colonial Press, 1900), 2:106.

2. Peter Yates, interview by Adelaide G. Tuster, January 1967, typescript in Oral History Program, University of California at Los Angeles, 60.

3. Quoted in Weisgall, "Music of Henry Cowell," 498.

4. This information comes from "Items about Concert Tour in Russia," *Temple Artisan* 29 (1929): 67.

5. Cowell talks about these experiences in his "Adventures in Soviet Russia," *San Franciscan* 5 (December 1930): 16–17.

6. Henry Cowell, "Playing Concerts in Moscow," *Musical Courier* 23 (May 1931): 6.

7. "Cowell Writes of Music in Russia," *Oakland Tribune,* 23 June 1929, 6S.

8. I personally viewed these in 1997, in the closet of the basement room where Cowell frequently taught at the New School.

9. Arthur Farwell, quoted in Hamm, *Music in the New World,* 417.

10. Hamm, *Music in the New World,* 424.

11. Ruggles's *Men and Mountains,* he argued, had a "freshness and openness" that was "distinctively American." Moreover, it had "a perfection of technic suggested by Schoenberg but, I think, never attained by him." By contrast, Schoenberg's *Pierrot Lunaire,* despite its "sophistication," contained "a feeling of approaching decay." Ornstein's Piano Concerto "is what Stravinsky's [piano concerto] should have been and was not." The latter's music manifests only nervous energy, with no originality in its craftsmanship: "The only counterpoint to be found anywhere in Stravinsky's works is of antiquated style." Henry Cowell, "America Takes a Front Rank in Year's Modernist Output," *Musical America,* 28 March 1925, 5.

12. Henry Cowell, "The Music of Edgar Varèse," *Modern Music* 5 (January–February 1928): 16.

13. Henry Cowell, "Analysis of an Unfamiliar Modern Composer," *Singing and Playing* 3 (August 1928): 26.

14. Henry Cowell, "Four Little-Known Modern Composers," *Aesthete* 1 (August 1928): 1.

15. Ibid., 20.

16. Cowell, *American Composers on American Music,* iv–v.

17. Henry Cowell to Dane Rudhyar, undated letter in Dane Rudhyar Papers, Stanford University.

18. The history of the New Music Society and the related entrepreneurial activities described below is thoroughly detailed in Mead, *Henry Cowell's New Music.*

19. Mead, *Henry Cowell's New Music,* 77.

20. Sidney Cowell, interview, typescript 1:16.

21. Henry Cowell, "Charles Ives," in *American Composers on American Music,* 145.

22. Mead, *Henry Cowell's New Music,* 199.

23. This and the previous quotation are from the first announcement of the New Music Quarterly Recordings series, reprinted in Mead, *Henry Cowell's New Music,* 259.

24. Mead, *Henry Cowell's New Music,* 271.

25. On these matters and all else discussed here about the Composers Collective, I rely on Dunaway "Charles Seeger and Carl Sands"; also Dunaway's "Unsung Songs of Protest: The Composers Collective of New York," *New York Folklore* 5 (Summer 1979): 1–19; Barbara A. Zuck, *A History of Musical Americanism* (Ann Arbor: UMI Research Press, 1980), 111–35; and the Marc Blitzstein Papers, State Historical Society of Wisconsin, Madison.

26. This information and the "quotation" from Cowell come from Dunaway, "Charles Seeger and Carl Sands," 161.

27. "Undated Notes on the Work of the Composers Collective of New York," Blitzstein Papers.

28. Sidney Cowell, interview, typescript 2:23, 25.

29. Henry Cowell, "Kept Music," *Panorama* 2 (December 1934), 6.

30. "~'Useful' Music," *New Masses* 17 (29 October 1935): 26–27.

31. For the history and chronology of the New School I have relied chiefly on <http://www.newschool.edu/intro/history/index.htm>, accessed 24 November 2001.

32. The detailed catalog description of this and all other New School courses taught by Cowell and cited herein are transcribed in Edward R. Carwithen, "Henry Cowell: Composer and Educator" (Ph.D. diss., University of Florida, 1991), 49–71. The quotation from Carwithen in the following paragraph is also from this source, 47–48.

33. Henry Cowell to Charles Ives, 16 May 1933, Yale University Library.

34. The sexual orientation of these composers is discussed briefly in Eric A. Gordon, *Mark the Music: The Life and Work of Marc Blitzstein* (New York: St. Martin's, 1989), 132, 175. Lou Harrison suggests how societal attitudes toward such composers may have differed from one coast to the other. Speaking of his own young manhood, about the time Cowell was arrested, Harrison says: "At that time, San Francisco was really fairly relaxed already about being gay. I never had any trouble with it at all. None of my friends did either. The first time I encountered that feeling of tightness and constraint, or uptightness, was in New York" (Winston Leyland, ed., *Gay Sunshine Interviews; Volume I* [San Francisco: Gay Sunshine Press, 1978], 166).

35. The information on Cowell's sexual history in this and later paragraphs comes from Cowell, "Some Autobiographical Notes" (the quotation is from this source); Olive Cowell, interview, 16; and "Proceedings on Sentence." A letter from Cowell to John Varian, 30 March 1929 (Varian Papers), gives the return address as "Pension Schmolke, Nuernberger St. 65, Berlin."

36. This is documented and discussed in "Proceedings on Sentence."

37. "Proceedings on Sentence"; also Cowell, "Some Autobiographical Notes." Some letters from Schmolke are in the Cowell Collection.

38. The quotation and details of the arrest appear in "Morals Charges Jail Noted S.F. Composer," *San Francisco Examiner,* 23 May 1936. Louis Dematteis, the only surviving source witness for this article, sent me a copy of the article and confirmed that it "correctly sets forth the events and circumstances leading to Cowell's arrest as I remember them" (Dematteis to author, 23 November 1988). During the ensuing years, Dematteis's notes made at the time were discarded along with the case file at the destrict attorney's office, for reasons of space. The "Summary History" of the crime, prepared for the California State Board of Prison Directors (filed on 11 July 1936, in County Clerk File), states that "these facts [concerning his relationships with the young men] were admitted by the defendant at the time of his arrest and he further stated that he was unable to prevent such occurrences." Cowell's appeals attorney, John Douglas Short, confirms in a letter to Adolf Meyer, 12 August 1938, that Cowell indeed had confessed to Francis Robinson, as the *Examiner* had reported (Meyer Papers). See also Cowell, "Some Autobiographical Notes." For more on Cowell's arrest and incarceration, see Michael Hicks, "The Imprisonment of Henry Cowell," *Journal of the American Musicological Society* 44 (Spring 1991): 92–119

39. The two quotations are from Manion, *Writings about Henry Cowell,* 164, 166.

40. ["Music"], *London Musical Standard,* 3 July 1926.

41. Henley, "Music," 10.

42. As reported in "Henry Cowell Returns," *Musical West,* May 1933, 2.

43. Cowell, "The Impasse of Modern Music," 677.

44. "Cowell Concert Is Revelation of Genius," *Palo Alto Times,* 8 November 1920.

45. See, for example, the article on Cowell by Raymond Dannenbaum entitled "Elbow Music!" *Emanu-el and the Jewish Journal,* 8 July 1932; also, the biographical note to Cowell, "Kept Music," refers to Cowell as "the inventor of 'tone clusters,' a method of increasing the sonority and expressiveness of the pianoforte by playing with the elbows as well as with the fingers and hands."

46. Russell Varian to Parents, 12 November 1920, Varian Papers, refers to Cowell's "elbo music" [*sic*]; Redfern Mason, "Persinger in Music Honors Elias Hecht," *San Francisco Examiner,* 20 October 1927, notes that Cowell's method of playing "has been called his 'elbow technique'"; Cowell's neighbor Angela Kiefer recalled that Cowell "can play the piano with his feet or his elbows if he wants to" (quoted in Moore, "'Youngsters over 50' Gather to Exchange Talk"). Charles Seeger, as late as 1974, referred to Cowell's early cluster works as "elbow pieces" (Seeger, interview by Mead, 31).

47. Todd, "The Boy Who Heard the 'Music of the Spheres,'" 7.

48. Quoted in Jay S. Harrison, "Cowell: Peck's Bad Boy of Music," *New York Herald Tribune,* 22 November 1953.

49. Reminiscence of Jules Eichorn, signed and dated October 1976, typescript in Menlo Park Historical Society.

50. Slonimsky, *Perfect Pitch,* 20.

51. Henry Cowell to Harry Cowell, 5 January 1924, Cowell Collection.

52. This story is told in Goss, *Modern Music-Makers,* 270.

53. Samaroff, "Henry Cowell's String Piano."

54. "Slonimsky Conducts Chamber Concert," *Boston Globe,* 12 March 1929, 8.

55. The quotations are from Henry Cowell, *New Musical Resources* (New York: Knopf, 1930), x, xiii.

56. As recounted by Sidney Cowell in a letter to me and Steven Johnson, 18 May 1989.

57. Henry Cowell to Dorothy Varian, 28 April 1962, Varian Papers.

58. See "Henry Cowell: Activities and Achievements," July 1932, typescript in Henry E. Huntington Library, San Marino, California; Olive Thompson Cowell, comp., "Henry Cowell: A Record of His Activities," June 1934, typescript in Stanford University Libraries.

59. Henry Cowell to Amy (a.k.a. "Peter") Holman Seward, 18 September 1932, photocopy in my possession.

60. Henry Cowell to Charles Ives, 17 November 1931, quoted in Mead, *Henry Cowell's New Music,* 178.

61. Sidney Cowell, interview, typescript 1:18–19.

62. Henry Cowell, "Music," *The Americana Annual: An Encyclopedia of Current Events,* ed. A. H. McDannald (New York: Americana Corp., 1934), 390. See also the statements attributed to Cowell in Marjory M. Fisher, "Henry Cowell Gives Lecture and Musicale," *San Francisco News,* 1 June 1932.

63. Henry Cowell to John Becker, 25 April 1935, John Becker Papers, Music Division, New York Public Library.

64. Helen Hope Page to Percy Grainger, 14 June 1938, Percy Grainger Papers, microfilm in Music Division, Library of Congress.

65. See "Morals Charges"; also, "Ban on Bail Faced by Cowell," *San Francisco Call-Bulletin,* 23 May 1936; Henry Cowell, "Insurance against Return," typescript in Meyer Papers.

66. This document is in the Cowell Collection.

67. Some details of the legal proceedings appear in "Music Genius Denies Morals Charge Guilt," *San Francisco Call-Bulletin,* 3 June 1936; "Cowell Enters Not Guilty Plea," *San Francisco Chronicle,* 4 June 1936; "Prof. Cowell Held for Trial after Plea of 'Not Guilty,'" *San Francisco Examiner,* 4 June 1936; "Cowell Enters Plea of Guilty," *San Francisco Examiner,* 23 June 1936; Cowell to Nicolas Slonimsky, 29 June 1936, quoted in *Perfect Pitch,* 162.

Although the late Duncan Oneal, Cowell's attorney, steadfastly refused to discuss the case with scholars, the prosecuting attorney writes that Oneal "ably represented" Cowell (Dematteis to author, 23 November 1988). Louis Oneal, in a letter to author, 21 November 1988, cites attorney-client privilege as his father's reason for refusing to discuss the case and for his own unwillingness to furnish whatever documentation still exists on the case.

68. "Proceedings on Sentence," 25.

69. Ibid., 38–39.

70. Bacon to Percy Grainger, 21 April 1938, Percy Grainger Papers, Library of Congress. Cowell comments on Ruggles's disaffection in a letter to Becker, 28 May 1937, Becker Papers.

71. Quoted in Jan Swafford, *Charles Ives: A Life with Music* (New York: Norton, 1996), 405. The lines drawn in the closing modifiers are in the original.

72. Among these were Slonimsky, Wallingford Riegger, and Carlos Chavez. Cowell mentions Riegger's loyalty in his letter to Becker, 28 May 1937. Chavez, in a letter to Gerald Strang, 10 July 1936, remarks, "I am very sorry about all this although I do not really know what is all about" [*sic*]; in a letter to the San Quentin Board of Prison Terms and Paroles, 1 February 1937, Chavez writes, "Because of the fact that I live in Mexico City, I cannot estimate the cause for [Cowell's] imprisonment" (both letters in Carlos Chavez Papers, Archivo General de la Nacion de Mexico, Mexico City). Some of Cowell's stalwart friends misrepresented the case when trying to rouse support for him. Helen Hope Page, for example, in her letter of 14 June 1938 to Percy Grainger, writes that Cowell's homosexual intimacy was "not over a long period. It was just once." Gerald Strang also exaggerated when he wrote to Carlos Chavez to "discount" ninety percent of what was in the newspapers about Cowell (2 July 1936, Chavez Papers).

73. This is the story advanced by Slonimsky, *Perfect Pitch*, 161–67. When I wrote to Slonimsky on this matter, he responded that "I never tried to investigate the events leading to [Cowell's] imprisonment. . . . I had no idea that there was any definite complaint on the part of the alleged victim" (Nicolas Slonimsky to Michael Hicks, 28 December 1988).

74. Schoenberg to Olive Cowell, 1 May 1937, carbon of typescript in the Arnold Schoenberg Papers, Arnold Schoenberg Institute, University of Southern California (typography normalized for this quotation).

75. Kenyon J. Scudder, *Prisoners Are People* (Garden City, N.Y.: Doubleday, 1952), 17. On the daily routine and inmate restrictions at San Quentin in the period just preceding and during Cowell's incarceration see Leo L. Stanley, *Twenty Years at San Quentin* (n.p.: 1933); Kenneth Lamott, *Chronicles of San Quentin: The Biography of a Prison* (New York: David McKay, 1961), 201–47; Gerald Breckenridge, "Biggest Big House," *Saturday Evening Post* 214 (8 Nov. 1941): 20–21, 95–98; Basil Woon, *San Francisco and the Golden Empire* (New York: Harrison Smith and Robert Haas, 1935), 227–28; and the regulations for inmate correspondence, Form SQ 5M 4-37, copy in Grainger Papers.

76. These and other disadvantages are mentioned in Olive Cowell to Slonimsky, 13 July 1936, excerpted in *Perfect Pitch*, 162–63; and Henry Cowell's letters to Ernst Bacon, 29 September 1938, Ernst Bacon Papers, Department of Special Collections and University Archives, Stanford University; to Carlos Chavez, 26 November 1936; to Quincy Porter, 5 October 1938, Quincy Porter Papers, Music Library, Yale University; to Carl Ruggles, 8 July 1939, Carl Ruggles Papers, Music Library, Yale University.

77. Cowell to Becker, 5 August 1936, Becker Papers; see also Cowell to Grainger, 13 June 1937, Grainger Papers, on his work schedule.

78. The quotation comes from Henry Cowell to Nicolas Slonimsky, 16 July 1936, photocopy in my possession.

79. Lists of those who recommended Cowell are in the Meyer Papers. As far as I have been able to determine, the original letters of recommendation were discarded in the parole board's routine elimination of old files.

80. Lewis M. Terman and Catherine Cox Miles, *Sex and Personality: Studies in Masculinity and Femininity* (New York: McGraw-Hill, 1936), 319–20.

81. John Hendricks was a convicted killer whom a subsequent warden described as "a walking encyclopedia of music" (Clinton T. Duffy, *The San Quentin Story*, as told to Dean Jennings [Garden City, N.Y.: Doubleday, 1950], 235). Cowell speaks of Hendricks in his letter to Slonimsky, 14 August 1936, excerpted in *Perfect Pitch*, 163–64.

82. On Cowell's prison work during this period, see especially his letters to Slonimsky, 14 December 1937 and 26 February 1938 (photocopies in my possession); to Bacon, 8 April 1938, Bacon Papers; to Becker, 31 January, 22 June, and 3 October 1938, Becker Papers; and to Grainger, 10 March 1938, Grainger Papers. Assorted programs of San Quentin band concerts also appear in the Grainger Papers.

83. The book is amply surveyed in Godwin, "Music of Henry Cowell," 114–32, to which this description (including the quotations from Cowell's manuscript) is largely indebted. See also Gann, "Subversive Prophet," 202–9.

84. See the comments of David Nicholls in his review of Charles Seeger, *Studies in Musicology II: 1929–1979*, ed. Ann M. Pescatello (Berkeley: University of California Press, 1994), appearing in *Music and Letters* 77 (February 1996), 141–42.

85. Duffy, *San Quentin Story*, 234–35.

86. Cowell to Bacon, 31 March 1939, Bacon Papers.

87. He had actually begun this new stylistic direction with a piece written in Redwood City Jail, in which he served time between his arrest and sentencing: see David Nicholls, "Henry Cowell's *United Quartet*," *American Music* 13 (Summer 1995): 195–217.

88. "Reminiscences of Henry Cowell," as quoted in Johnson, "'Worlds of Ideas,'" 64.

89. For a discussion of elastic form, see Johnson, "'Worlds of Ideas,'" 63–67.

90. This estimate is based on Norman M. Stone, "Prison Recreation Today," *Recreation* 35 (October 1941): 451–54.

91. These statistics are derived from Cowell's letters to Slonimsky, 16 June 1939, excerpted in *Perfect Pitch*, 166; and to Carl Ruggles, 8 July 1939.

92. Cowell to Becker, 3 October 1938.

93. Pereira played the San Quentin premieres of works by Cowell and others. He was not a convicted murderer, as Lichtenwanger asserts (*Music of Henry Cowell*, 163). His pardon file, which details his judicial history, is in the California State Archives, Sacramento.

94. Cowell to Grainger, 19 September 1939, Grainger Papers.

95. The parole did entail some delays and political struggles. The machinations are discussed in Ernst Wolff to Adolf Meyer, 17 October 1939 and 17 April 1940, Meyer

Papers; and Olive Cowell to Percy Grainger, 29 August, 17 November, and 24 December 1939, Grainger Papers.

96. These details are drawn from the "List of Activities" from January–April 1941, in the Grainger Papers. His parole restrictions are outlined in his letters to Fabien Sevitzky, 9 October 1940, Fabien Sevitzky Papers, Music Division, Library of Congress; and to Carlos Chavez, 26 November 1936, Chavez Papers.

97. For a look at how the pardon story has been treated by other scholars, see Hicks, "Imprisonment of Henry Cowell," 94–95, 97, 111, 115–16.

98. For the information in this paragraph I have relied on Cowell's letters to Grainger, 31 December 1940, 29 May and 7 and 25 June 1941 (all in Grainger Papers); also to Ernst Bacon, 24 June 1941, Bacon Papers. In a telephone conversation with the author, 25 June 1990, Mark Sullivan independently confirmed that the principal motive behind Cowell's pardon was that "Henry couldn't leave the country" without it. Political background to these events may be found in James Desmond, *Nelson Rockefeller: A Political Biography* (New York: Macmillan, 1964), 87–96.

99. San Quentin Prison Board Minutes, 3 July 1941, California State Archives, Sacramento.

100. Sidney Cowell, "Charles Seeger," 306. The bulk of the information in this paragraph comes from a Library of Congress internet site, <http://memory.loc.gov/ammem/afcchtml/cowsonek.html>, accessed 24 November 2001.

101. Henry Cowell to Harmony Ives, 15 September 1941, Charles Ives Papers, Music Library, Yale University.

102. Cowell called his authorization to "make use of the name of the Union for our office" a "major victory" (Cowell to Richard Goldman, 22 October 1941, Richard Franko Goldman Papers, Music Division, Library of Congress).

103. This is discussed in a typescript summary of Cowell's employment, Pardon File.

104. Robert F. Burke, *Olson's New Deal for California* (Berkeley: University of California Press, 1953), 220. See also Olson's comments on the critics of parole in his *State Papers and Public Addresses* (Sacramento: State Printing Office, 1942) 356–57.

105. This quotation is from Cowell's application for pardon, 12 November 1942, excerpted in Pardon File.

106. Sidney Cowell to Culbert Olson, 1 December 1942, Pardon File.

107. Stanley Mosk to Paul Yarwood, 1 December 1942, Pardon File.

108. Advisory Pardon Board to Culbert Olson, 14 December 1942, Pardon File.

109. The official pardon document, which includes the quotation from Seeger's letter, is dated 28 December 1942 (Pardon File).

110. In a letter to Ernst Bacon, 29 September 1938, Cowell comments that he had always "tried over" piano works and revised them accordingly. Not being able to do so in prison, he explains, made composing for piano far more difficult. See also Cowell to Quincy Porter, 5 October 1938, in which the composer laments having had no opportunity to try out a recent work on *any* instrument.

111. Henry Cowell to Marc Blitzstein, 6 March 1939, Blitzstein Papers.

112. Quoted in Gann, "Subversive Prophet," 206.

113. Sidney Cowell to Charles and Harmony Ives, 29 July 1942, Ives Papers.

114. As quoted in Michael Tilson Thomas, notes to *The Complete Music of Carl Ruggles,* CBS Masterworks, M2 34591.

115. The quote and similar ones may be found in Solomon, "Charles Ives," 466–67.

116. As quoted in Catherine Parsons Smith, "On Feminism and American Art Music," paper delivered at the annual meeting of the American Musicological Society, 29 October 1989 (Austin, Texas), 7–8.

117. Slonimsky, "Henry Cowell," 59.

118. Dannenbaum, "Elbow Music!"

119. Cowell and Cowell, *Charles Ives and His Music,* 9.

120. Henry Cowell, "In Time of Bitter War," *Modern Music* 19 (January–February 1942): 83.

121. During this period, for example, Copland entered his most celebrated period, with ballets such as *Billy the Kid* (1939) and *Rodeo* (1942) as well as isolated works such as the *Fanfare for the Common Man* and *A Lincoln Portrait* (both 1942). At the same time, Stravinsky's newer works, such as the Symphony in C, reached the zenith of neo-classicism.

122. Quoted in "Cowell—Tone Cluster to Symphony," *Dartmouth Summer News,* 18 August 1964.

123. Olive Cowell, interview, 31. See also her letter to Grainger, 20 February 1940, Grainger Papers: "He has matured so much as a person. All the fine qualities that are in him have blossomed, so that the experience has not materially harmed in the slightest—but the cost in strain, in adjustment, in loss of achievement, etc.[,] that can not be reckoned. But I feel he has grown all that is possible to grow under the circumstances."

124. Seeger, interview by Mead, 21–22. In the full quotation Seeger refers specifically to Cowell's eschewing of political radicalism after prison; I have adapted his quotation as one of general principle.

125. See Robert Craft, ed., *Stravinsky: Selected Correspondence, Vol. I* (New York: Knopf, 1982), 360–61 n. 75.

126. David Nicholls, "Henry Cowell: A Call for Restitution," *Institute for Studies in American Music Newsletter* 24 (Fall 1994): 2.

127. Seeger, interview by Mead, 13.

128. This list is taken from Carwithen, "Henry Cowell: Composer and Educator," 116–17.

129. All of this information is taken from Harry's obituary, *Palo Alto Times,* 21 January 1954.

130. Quoted in Olive Cowell to Anna Strunsky Walling, 30 January 1954.

131. All of the information contained in this paragraph comes from Cowell's FBI file, which I obtained in 1989 through the Freedom of Information Act.

132. Quoted in Gardner Read, "American Composers on American Music," *Journal of Music Theory* 6 (1962): 308.

Index

MICHAEL HICKS is a professor of music at Brigham Young University, a composer, and the author of *Mormonism and Music: A History; Sixties Rock: Garage, Psychedelic, and Other Satisfactions;* and many articles about twentieth-century music and musicians.

Music in American Life

Transforming Tradition: Folk Music Revivals Examined   *Edited by Neil V. Rosenberg*

The Crooked Stovepipe: Athapaskan Fiddle Music and Square Dancing in Northeast Alaska and Northwest Canada   *Craig Mishler*

Traveling the High Way Home: Ralph Stanley and the World of Traditional Bluegrass Music   *John Wright*

Carl Ruggles: Composer, Painter, and Storyteller   *Marilyn Ziffrin*

Never without a Song: The Years and Songs of Jennie Devlin, 1865–1952   *Katharine D. Newman*

The Hank Snow Story   *Hank Snow, with Jack Ownbey and Bob Burris*

Milton Brown and the Founding of Western Swing   *Cary Ginell, with special assistance from Roy Lee Brown*

Santiago de Murcia's "Códice Saldívar No. 4": A Treasury of Secular Guitar Music from Baroque Mexico   *Craig H. Russell*

The Sound of the Dove: Singing in Appalachian Primitive Baptist Churches   *Beverly Bush Patterson*

Heartland Excursions: Ethnomusicological Reflections on Schools of Music   *Bruno Nettl*

Doowop: The Chicago Scene   *Robert Pruter*

Blue Rhythms: Six Lives in Rhythm and Blues   *Chip Deffaa*

Shoshone Ghost Dance Religion: Poetry Songs and Great Basin Context   *Judith Vander*

Go Cat Go! Rockabilly Music and Its Makers   *Craig Morrison*

'Twas Only an Irishman's Dream: The Image of Ireland and the Irish in American Popular Song Lyrics, 1800–1920   *William H. A. Williams*

Democracy at the Opera: Music, Theater, and Culture in New York City, 1815–60   *Karen Ahlquist*

Fred Waring and the Pennsylvanians   *Virginia Waring*

Woody, Cisco, and Me: Seamen Three in the Merchant Marine   *Jim Longhi*

Behind the Burnt Cork Mask: Early Blackface Minstrelsy and Antebellum American Popular Culture   *William J. Mahar*

Going to Cincinnati: A History of the Blues in the Queen City   *Steven C. Tracy*

Pistol Packin' Mama: Aunt Molly Jackson and the Politics of Folksong   *Shelly Romalis*

Sixties Rock: Garage, Psychedelic, and Other Satisfactions   *Michael Hicks*

The Late Great Johnny Ace and the Transition from R&B to Rock 'n' Roll   *James M. Salem*

Tito Puente and the Making of Latin Music   *Steven Loza*

Juilliard: A History   *Andrea Olmstead*

Understanding Charles Seeger, Pioneer in American Musicology   *Edited by Bell Yung and Helen Rees*

The University of Illinois Press
is a founding member of the
Association of American University Presses.

Composed in 10.5/13 Minion
with Minion display
by Jim Proefrock
at the University of Illinois Press
Designed by Dennis Roberts
Manufactured by Thomson-Shore, Inc.

University of Illinois Press
1325 South Oak Street
Champaign, IL 61820-6903
www.press.uillinois.edu